Alissa,
Please join me in the fight for justice.
God Bless,
Ken Wyniemko

DELIBERATE INJUSTICE
The Wrongful Conviction of Ken Wyniemko

Netflix
"The Innocence Files"
Episode #9
Million Dollar Man

DELIBERATE INJUSTICE
THE WRONGFUL CONVICTION OF KEN WYNIEMKO

Published and Printed by ZGServe, LLC

Grand Rapids, MI

United States of America

All rights reserved

Copyright © Deliberate Injustice, LLC

Any reproduction of any of the contents of this book in any form without the proper permission is strictly prohibited.

Cover design by Scot Robert Henige

ISBN: 978-1-939909-40-4

First Printing 2017

This book is available at www.deliberateinjusticethebook.com

From The Author

Kenny Wyniemko and I have been friends for over fifty years starting with our days as freshmen at St. Ladislaus High School in Hamtramck, Michigan.

The two of us were raised in white middle-class homes with hard-working dads and stay-at-home moms. Our fathers served in World War II before spending their careers in one of large Big Three automotive factories in Detroit. We grew up in devout Catholic homes and attended Catholic grade and high schools.

Our classmates were never part of the extreme social discontent of the 1960s and 1970s. We had absolute faith in the American judicial system and in law enforcement back then. And we certainly felt the same as we progressed into middle age.

What happened to Kenny in 1994 is something we never dreamed could happen to anyone in this great country, let alone to a friend or a classmate. Here was an ordinary Joe who the system conspired to convict of a heinous crime that he had nothing to do with. He had never been arrested for anything, let alone a savage rape. This inexperience with the system would prove to play a large part in his undoing.

Upon learning of Kenny's release from prison in 2003, I read the review of his wrongful conviction on the Thomas M. Cooley Law School website. As more and more facts came to light in my conversations with Kenny, his story both infuriated me and gave me reason to pause. Kenny wasn't the first wrongfully convicted individual in our great country and he surely would not be the last.

In our first face-to-face after his exoneration, Kenny and I enjoyed a meal at one of our favorite eateries, Loui's Pizza, on Dequindre Road in the city of Hazel Park, Michigan. We spoke about his recent experiences and how grateful he was to have this second chance at a normal life. After he described the events leading up to his conviction,

I thought for a moment then asked him, "You mean that if the people behind your railroading had the forethought to destroy the forensic evidence used in your exoneration, you would never have been released and you would have spent decades behind bars?"

A wry smile came over him and he gently shook his head. "Never thought of that."

The realization of the effort necessary to write *Deliberate Injustice* was overwhelming. I had never reviewed a case transcript, witness statement, deposition, or judge's decision. My legal education was limited to watching a couple hundred *Law & Order* episodes and movies like *A Few Good Men*. Kenny wanted his story written from a layperson's perspective. He certainly got his wish.

As part of the preparation for writing *Deliberate* Injustice, I read several books about wrongful convictions. One of those books was *Picking Cotton* by Jennifer Thompson-Cannino. It is unique in that the book is narrated by the victim and the exoneree.

In *Picking Cotton*, after the wrongly convicted man was released, the victim contacted him to personally apologize for her misidentification of him. Despite discouragement from the friends and family of both parties, they decided to meet. They became extremely close friends. Today, they travel together to speaking events, relating their personal experience and the shortcomings of today's system.

There was a scene in the book that was very impactful to me. The two of them were relaxing on the back porch after dinner, silently enjoying each other's company as only close friends can.

The victim turned to the exoneree and said, "I'm glad I picked you."

The exoneree paused for a second and replied, "Me, too."

It was a profound and inspiring moment in the book.

I thought about Kenny's life before, during, and after his incarceration. In 1994, he was going nowhere, accomplishing little. Today, his life has purpose. It is amazing how a man can be sentenced to 40 to 60 years, spend close to nine years in prison, and end up where Kenny is today, inspiring others and fighting for justice.

Kenny and I sat down to reflect when we were wrapping up the writing of *Deliberate Injustice*. We spent a lot of time together interviewing, planning, and editing. He was heavily involved with the process from beginning to end. After all, I was writing Kenny's story the way Kenny wanted it told.

I brought up that particular scene from Picking *Cotton* and decided to ask him about it.

"Do you ever wonder what it would be like if you were never convicted and incarcerated? Was your conviction a blessing in disguise?"

Kenny replied, "I think about that all the time. I definitely believe I came out of prison a better man than when I went in. And I have come to realize that this whole ordeal was God's plan. He will never give you a cross you cannot bear. Things happen for a reason."

Kenny's story is a tale of triumph in the face of most extreme adversity. To have turned his life around after going through that nightmare is truly a testament to his faith and resolve. When Kenny asked me to write his story, I was both flattered and terrified. How could I accurately describe the experiences and the transformation of such a remarkable man?

I am honored to write this book about an absolutely amazing friend.

Bob Henige

Introduction

Freedom is defined as *"the quality or state of being free: such as a: the absence of necessity, coercion, or constraint in choice or action . . . "*
—Webster Online Dictionary.

Freedom is a right of every citizen of the United States, a right we rarely contemplate. Imagine that right being taken away. Imagine being publicly accused of a horrific rape. Imagine being convicted and sentenced to 40-60 years of incarceration. Imagine facing your family and all your friends as a convicted felon.
Imagine all of this while knowing that you are innocent.

This is the story of Ken Wyniemko, a regular guy whom the judicial system not only failed, but illegally conspired to convict. His nightmare is the result of the circumvention of the laws and practices that are designed to prevent this very injustice from happening: the conviction and incarceration of an innocent man. Kenny's case, and that of hundreds of others, has placed in question one longstanding, gold standard of proof: eyewitness testimony.
The National Registry of Exonerations lists the primary contributing factors in wrongful convictions as mistaken witness identification, perjury or false accusation, false confession, false or misleading forensic evidence, and official misconduct. Other major contributors to wrongful convictions include the use of informants and snitches and inadequate defense. Kenny's case encompasses all of the above, except for the false confession.

Former **Judge Patrick T. Cahill** received his undergraduate degree from the University of Detroit in 1970 and his Juris Doctor (Law Degree) from Wayne State University in 1973. After more than 16 years as a general practice trial lawyer, he was elected to the bench in 1990. He served as judge of the 31st District Court in Hamtramck, Michigan from January 1, 1991 until his retirement on October 19, 2001. I relied on Judge Cahill for advice on many legal issues throughout my research for this book.

Here is his take on Kenny's case:

Kenny's case, when taken as a whole, is one of the most egregious miscarriages of justice I have ever seen. The whole system failed Kenneth Wyniemko.

While Kenny's arrest and conviction was a tragedy for the American Justice System, his life story is one of celebration. It is celebrated in his unshakable faith and in his belief that his relentless efforts would be rewarded and that he would be released. It is celebrated in the countless friends he has made and the profound impact he has had on so many lives since his exoneration, especially those of his fellow exonerees.

Kenny has become a dedicated spokesperson for the Innocence Project. He is passionate in his work, his own horrific experience driving him every minute of the day. Whether the venue is the Michigan State Legislature, Harvard School of Law, or an impromptu conversation with an interested party, Kenny's zeal for the cause of the wrongfully convicted continues to inspire.

The Interviews

Individuals from all walks of life were more than happy to assist in the writing of *Deliberate Injustice* by agreeing to being interviewed. Excerpts from these interviews are interspersed throughout the book.

Some of these individuals, despite the adversarial nature of their initial relationship with Kenny, have become close friends with him and remain so to this day.

Bill Proctor

Mr. Proctor was the investigative reporter covering Kenny's release in 2003. He has become a passionate supporter of righting wrongful convictions. He has founded Proving Innocence, a non-profit organization that investigates wrongful convictions in the Detroit area. Mr. Proctor has become one of Kenny's closest friends. Kenny and Mr. Proctor have appeared together in numerous venues related to wrongful convictions.

Carl Marlinga

Mr. Marlinga was the Macomb County Prosecutor during Kenny's trial in 1994. After Kenny's release in 2003, he retired as a prosecutor after serving 20 years in that position and became a defense attorney. In 2010, Mr. Marlinga worked pro bono alongside the University of Michigan's Innocence Clinic in obtaining the release of Julie Baumer, wrongfully convicted in 2005. In 2013, Mr. Marlinga was elected to the Macomb County Probate Court in Macomb County, Michigan. Mr. Marlinga has become an ardent supporter of righting wrongful convictions and has appeared with Kenny in support of this cause on several occasions. He has remained close friends with Kenny to this day.

Gail Pamukov

Ms. Pamukov was the lead attorney for Kenny's DNA appeal that resulted in his exoneration. She and Kenny have remained very close friends and often speak together on the causes of wrongful convictions.

Jerry Innes
Mr. Innes was a juror in Kenny's 1994 trial. His interview provided very incredible insight to the jury deliberations that convicted Kenny.

Kathy Swedlow
Ms. Swedlow was the attorney for the Innocence Project of Lansing, Michigan, during Kenny's DNA appeal. She has appeared in many venues with Kenny in support of righting wrongful convictions.

Marty Hacias
Mr. Hacias was a life-long friend who became one of Kenny's first supporters while he was incarcerated. He assisted Kenny in his mission to gain support from Kim Shine, the *Detroit Free Press* reporter who broke Kenny's case.

Norm Fell
Mr. Fell was the founder of the Michigan Innocence Project. Under his direction, the Innocence Project successfully obtained Kenny's release with a DNA test of the forensics evidence.

Scott Nobles
Mr. Nobles was the Deputy Warden at the Ryan Correctional Facility in Detroit, Michigan, throughout Kenny's incarceration there. Mr. Nobles became convinced of Kenny's innocence and assisted him in every way possible. They have remained friends.

Stephanie Chang
Ms. Chang was the sponsor of the Michigan Wrongful Conviction Compensation Act (2016) in the State House. She has appeared with Kenny in various venues for the wrongfully convicted.

Stephen Bieda
Mr. Bieda was the sponsor of the Michigan Wrongful Conviction Compensation Act (2016) in the State Senate. He and Kenny had worked vigorously for its passage for close to 12 years.

Thomas Howlett
Mr. Howlett was one of the primary attorneys who worked on Kenny's successful civil suit. He is the chief operations officer for the prestigious The Googasian Firm, P. C., one of the top civil law firms in the country. Mr. Howlett and Kenny have continued their friendship.

Testimonials

Ken's poignant story, so graphically illustrated in this book, sends the message that we cannot assume our criminal justice system delivers justice. It only provides the opportunity for justice. The price of that opportunity is constant vigilance and the willingness to pursue the ideals upon which our legal system is based. That is what Ken is doing with this book and his life.

— Professor Emeritus Norman Fell
*Founder of the Innocence Project at
Cooley Law School in Lansing, Michigan*

This book provides a valuable blow-by-blow account of how a wrongful conviction occurs and how, if he or she is very lucky, the wrongfully convicted person may get exonerated. By telling Ken Wyniemko's story in clear and unvarnished language, Ken and his co-author, Bob Henige, have made an important contribution to the growing literature of books documenting wrongful convictions and their aftermath.

— David A. Moran
Director, Innocence Clinic, University of Michigan Law School

We are proud at the Googasian Firm to have represented Kenny in the civil aspect of this tragic and avoidable case of justice gone wrong. The book, "Deliberate Injustice - The Wrongful Conviction of Ken Wyniemko" is an accurate history of this injustice and Ken's ultimate triumph. It is a must read for those interested in the justice system in America.

— George Googasian
The Googasian Law Firm, Bloomfield Hills, Michigan

Here author Bob Henige tells the story of a man sent to prison for a crime he did not commit. What sets this fine book apart is not only how Ken Wyniemko gained his freedom, but how he then struggled to help others, also wrongly convicted, to regain justice and their freedom. A moving narrative, skillfully told, of what was indeed "Deliberate Injustice." An important book. A must read.

— Arthur Woodford
Detroit Historian and Author, Harsens Island, Michigan

To The Reader

Please note that some of the names of some of Kenny's inmates have been changed.

References to source material are noted in the back of the book after the Appendixes.

Table of Contents

From The Author i

Introduction iv

Testimonials ix

To The Reader xi

Part I – Kenny's Journey 1

    Chapter 1 — The Crimes 2

    Chapter 2 — Arrested and Charged 3

    Chapter 3 — Trial and Conviction 27

    Chapter 4 — Incarceration 88

    Chapter 5 — Jailhouse Appeals 118

    Chapter 6 — Kim and Gail and The Innocence Project 130

    Chapter 7 — Freedom 153

    Chapter 8 — Acclimation to Society 178

    Chapter 9 — Lawsuit and Settlement 186

    Chapter 10 — System Failure 215

    Chapter 11 — Vindication 226

    Chapter 12 — A Juror's Regret 243

    Chapter 13 — Spokesperson 248

Part II – Quality Time 271

    Chapter 14 — The Prosecutor and the Warden 272

Chapter 15 — One More Time 277

Chapter 16 — Final Thoughts from the Author 282

Acknowledgements 284

Appendix A — 2003 DNA Test Results 285

Appendix B — Glenn McCormick's Declaration 287

Appendix C — The Innocence Network 291

Appendix D — The History of the Civil Lawsuit 306

References 311

Part I – Kenny's Journey

Chapter 1 — The Crimes

In the early morning hours of Saturday, April 30, 1994, a tall and overweight white man broke into a woman's apartment in Clinton Township, Michigan, and savagely raped her over a three-hour period. The victim endured every imaginable indignity. She was bound to the bedposts. She was blindfolded. She was raped vaginally and anally, and forced to perform oral sex. She feared for her life, unsure she was going to survive the horrific ordeal.

In July, 1994, the Clinton Township Police Department, acting on an anonymous phone call from two months previous, considered the possibility that the perpetrator of the rape was Kenny Wyniemko. Kenny was much smaller in stature and had none of the other physical characteristics of the assailant as described by the victim.

On July 15, 1994, Kenny was arrested and charged.

On November 2, 1994, the victim sat in a Macomb County, Michigan, courtroom and identified her attacker. She testified it was Ken Wyniemko.

On November 9, 1994, Kenny was convicted of 17 felony counts, including 15 counts of Criminal Sexual Conduct in the First Degree.

On December 15, 1994, he was sentenced to 40 to 60 years. It was a death sentence for a 43-year-old.

Make no mistake. There were two crimes committed.

An innocent woman was savagely violated in a most inhumane manner.

And the Clinton Township Police Department conspired to convict an innocent man. That innocent man was Kenny Wyniemko.

Chapter 2 — Arrested and Charged

"I was told that I would be placed in a lineup related to this B&E and rape. I couldn't believe it. I told the detectives, 'I don't know what you are talking about. I don't know who this lady is. You're making a terrible mistake.'" — Kenny Wyniemko

"You know what, Wyniemko? I am going to start calling you the million dollar man. By the time I am done fucking with you, it will cost you a million dollars to get your ass out of prison." — Clinton Township Police Department Detective Sergeant Thomas Ostin, July 15, 1994

Thursday, July 14, 1994, started as a normal day for Kenny. It would quickly become a day like no other, the start of a process in which he would not be a free man for the better part of nine years. He was tackled and handcuffed, then placed in a lineup. The next day he was arrested at gunpoint and charged with rape in the first degree. He was labeled a monster, a rapist, someone society should be protected from.

On Saturday, April 30, 1994, at 6:23 am, Clinton Township Police Officer Chris Wallington received a dispatch call regarding a rape. He responded immediately. Arriving at the scene, he found a distraught woman clothed in only a bath robe. She had fled her home to seek refuge at her neighbor's. The victim was identified as Diane Klug.

After a brief interview and run-through of the crime scene, Ms. Klug was escorted by Medstar Emergency Medical Service paramedics to St. Joseph's Hospital-West in Clinton Township, Michigan. An evidence kit was produced and transported to the Clinton Township

Police Department. Detective Bart M. Marlatt was assigned as the primary detective on the case.

Later that morning, Ms. Klug arrived at police facilities for a detailed interview. The taped interview was conducted by Officer Frank P. Woloszyk. She also produced a written statement.

Ms. Klug described her assailant as a white man, six-foot-three inches tall, about 220-230 pounds, with a large beer belly and a deep cleft chin. She also indicated that he was a smoker, a fact corroborated by the cigarette butts recovered at the crime scene. She detailed a three-hour ordeal of total humiliation and degradation. The brutality of the rape made the case Priority 1.

A composite drawing of the perpetrator was produced with the assistance of the victim despite the fact she repeatedly stated that she was blindfolded throughout the attack and that she never got a good look at her attacker's entire face. There was one occasion when she was able to peak under her blindfold and observe her attacker with his mask pulled up to his nose revealing his mouth and chin.

When it was completed, Ms. Klug questioned its accuracy and had issues with the lower part of the face. Regardless, the composite was placed in several local newspapers. Numerous tips came in. One anonymous male caller indicated the composite looked like a man named Ken Wyniemko, the counter-man at Kingswood Bowling Lanes. Two months later, the investigation became focused solely on Kenny despite the fact he did not remotely resemble Ms. Klug's physical description of her attacker. Kenny was five-foot-eleven and about 180 pounds. He didn't have a cleft chin or a beer belly and he did not smoke.

It was early July, 1994, two months since the attack on Diane Klug. The investigation was going nowhere.

In a conversation between Clinton Township Police Department Detectives Sergeant Thomas Ostin and Bart Marlatt, the name of Ken Wyniemko came up. Detective Ostin was investigating an embezzlement charge at Kingswood in which Kenny was implicated.

Detective Marlatt was examining a stalking charge from Cathy Whitcher, Kenny's ex-girlfriend. And, now, the two-month old anonymous call identifying Kenny as a possible suspect in the April 30th rape was being considered.

From that point forward, the investigation was headed by the veteran Detective Sergeant Ostin, replacing the less-experienced Detective Marlatt. They focused exclusively on Kenny. Calls on the composite were ignored. Phone tips from all sources, including other police agencies, were discounted. Leads were disregarded. No other theories of the crime were entertained.

According to police documents, Lieutenant Al Ernst, supervisor of the investigating officers, informed Detective Ostin that he had additional information about the case but would not disclose it since it would not further a conviction of Kenny. Withholding information because it would not further a conviction of a single suspect is an example of the blinders worn by the investigating officers.

Kenny related an incident that occurred a few months before his arrest.

> *I was working Family Night at Kingswood Bowling Alley. We received several complaints regarding one of the bowlers drinking beer from his bowling bag and being abusive to the kids. After I saw him take bottles of beer out of one of his bowling bags, I approached him. I told him that the beer was illegal and that he was bothering the customers and that he needed to leave. He informed me he was an officer with the Clinton Township Police Department, the same city as Kingswood. I told him that he still had to leave. It became confrontational and, eventually, physical, when I had him removed.*
>
> *Not more than an hour later, two uniformed Clinton officers came to Kingswood. They had that air that I was in the wrong and spent a half hour hassling me and asking*

questions. When they left, they said something that I will never forget, especially now, with all that happened. They said, "We'll be seeing you, Mr. Wyniemko."

I don't know if that had anything to do with what they did to me, but it sure makes sense now.

The incident was never mentioned in any of the documentation discovered in the investigation for this book.

The Embezzlement Charge
If Kenny didn't have enough to worry about during his arrest, he had to deal with a bogus embezzlement charge. Arduino Polisena, the manager at Kingswood, accused Kenny of stealing the night's take at the bowling alley. He recalled the embezzlement charge.

I remember speaking with Ostin about that embezzlement charge. It turned out that Art (Polisena) took the money. It was about $1,400. In fact, he was later fired for taking the end-of-the-season money from a Vegas Night bowling league.

Ironically, the Vegas Night bowling league was the same weekly league that Ms. Klug and her husband bowled in at Kingswood Lanes.

What is further disturbing is that the pending embezzlement charge was taken into account during the pre-sentence report after Kenny was convicted.

The Arrest

On July 14, 1994, Kenny was arrested on a stalking charge that had been filed by his ex-girlfriend, Cathy Whitcher. Their split had been quite contentious and Ms. Whitcher harbored a lot of animosity. The arrest was a sham. The investigating officers had a more serious charge in mind.

This is Kenny's account of his arrest.

> *It was July 14, 1994, about 8:30 in the morning. I answered a knock at the door and there was a young lady standing on my porch. I asked her if I could help her.*
>
> *She said, "Is your name Kenny?"*
>
> *I replied, "Yes, it is. What can I do for you?"*
>
> *She immediately stepped to the side and four plainclothes police officers barged in, tackled me, and threw me down on the floor. They handcuffed me behind my back and told me they were taking me to Macomb County Jail. They escorted me to the back seat of a squad car and drove me there. They told me I was being arrested on a stalking charge. I was in complete shock. I had no idea this was coming.*

Kenny was transported to the Macomb County Jail and led to a small room with a wooden table, several chairs, a tape recorder, and a large two-way mirror. He was seated in a rigid wooden chair facing the mirror on the back wall. Two white detectives entered and sat in two comfortable leather office chairs on the opposite side of the table. Both officers seemed relaxed as they introduced themselves as Detective Thomas Ostin and Detective Bart Marlatt. Kenny was nervous as hell.

It was clear to Kenny that Detective Ostin was the officer in charge. He was middle-aged and more experienced. Detective Marlatt was younger. Detective Ostin controlled the interview while

Detective Marlatt mostly observed, taking Detective Ostin's lead when necessary.

> When I got down there, I was interviewed by a couple detectives. They had a tape recorder running throughout. On several occasions, Ostin left the table and went to a door next to the large mirror on the wall behind them to confer with what I thought was a lady detective. I found out later it was Linda Davis, the (Macomb County) Prosecutor. They asked me a ton of questions about all sorts of stuff. Eventually, the detectives told me that I was to be placed in a lineup for this B&E, Armed Robbery, and rape of Diane Klug.
>
> I told them that I did not recognize the name and that I did not know the woman. I said, "I don't know what you are talking about. I don't know who this lady is. You're making a terrible mistake."
>
> They refused to listen.
>
> I told them, "I don't know that much about the law, but I do know that I am entitled to call an attorney."
>
> The lead detective, a Detective Ostin, told me he was not going to allow me to call an attorney at this point. However, he has one who will be in the viewing room and I will be able to speak to him after the lineup is over.
>
> I repeated, "I know I have the right to counsel. I want to make a phone call."
>
> He replied in a threatening voice, "One way or another, Wyniemko, your ass is going in that room for the lineup."
>
> I didn't know enough about the law to refuse. They put me in the lineup room with five other guys. Four of them had mustaches and I didn't. In fact, I had never had a mustache in my life. We were asked to recite a sentence that the victim claimed the attacker had made to her during the rape. The sentence was, "What time does your husband get home?"

When the lineup was finished, one of the officers opened up the door and I walked up to a detective and asked him, "Can I please speak to the attorney that the lead detective told me that would be in the viewing room?"

He chuckled and told me, "I'm sorry. He already left the building."

I said, "How could that be? You just opened the door five seconds ago and I was told that I would be able to speak with him."

During that conversation, Detective Ostin came up to us and I asked him, "Can I please speak to the attorney who you told me would be available when we talked?"

He said, "He did leave the building. He is already gone."

I said, "Then I want to call an attorney because I don't know what the hell is going on here."

Then he said, "Mr. Wyniemko, don't worry. Everything is okay. You can go home."

The Lineup

On July 14, 1994, at approximately 2:14 pm, Kenny and five fillers (non-suspects in a police lineup) were marched into a brightly lit sterile room with a large mirror along the wall. All were similar in height and build. Four of the other men had mustaches. Kenny noted the absurdity but assumed he had nothing to worry about. He knew he hadn't had anything to do with any rape.

Richard Reynolds was the attending public attorney on call, assigned to ensure the lineup was properly conducted. It was his duty to object to anything improper during this procedure.

Initially, Ms. Klug was unable to identify a suspect and left the viewing room. She returned after conversing with Clinton Township Detective John Berger and Linda Hocking, a victim advocate for Macomb County.

When Ms. Klug returned, she requested a voice sample from each person in the lineup. She indicated that the voice samples were of no help.

She then identified Kenny as her assailant.

The Showup Identification Record is a form that documents the lineup process. It contains descriptions of the individuals who stood in the lineup, and the events and the results of the process. The requested voice recognition was noted. There was no indication any of the fillers had mustaches and that Kenny did not. Nor was it noted that the victim left and returned to the viewing room before she identified Kenny.

Mr. Reynolds did not lodge an objection to the witness temporarily leaving the viewing room and conferring with representatives from the prosecutor's office and the police department. And he did not object to a lineup where four out of the five fillers had a physical characteristic (mustache) that most assuredly eliminated them from being identified by the victim.

Mr. Reynolds should have gone on record by objecting to all of the inconsistencies. The officer in charge should have noted any objection from Mr. Reynolds on Kenny's lineup sheet. None of this was done.

Kenny's arrest on the stalking charge was a ruse to get him in a lineup for the attack on Diane Klug. He was released because the proper documents were not available. A search warrant was subsequently obtained and it was executed later that day. The arrest warrant would be executed the following day.

This is an excerpt of Detective Marlatt's testimony at the Probable Cause Hearing on the warrant.

> *We were able to get him arrested on an unrelated stalking charge and my victim came in and positively identified him in a physical line-up.*

Showup Identification Record that omits mentioning that the lineup stand-ins had mustaches and that the victim left the viewing room before identifying Kenny.

Kenny left Macomb County Jail and headed home. Thinking he was over the ordeal, he was surprised to see a police car parked in front of his home.

> *After the lineup was over and I was released, I called my dad, who was 76 years old at the time, and asked him to come to the Macomb County Jail to pick me up. When I get back to my home, there was an unmarked cop car sitting in front. I wanted to go inside my home and take a shower because, at this point, I had been at the county jail for four or five hours and I could smell the stink on me. As my dad and I started to go inside, a detective got out of his car, came up to me, and asked me where I thought I was going. I told him I was going inside my home and taking a shower because I felt filthy.*
>
> *He said, "I'm sorry, Mr. Wyniemko. You are not allowed to go inside your home because they are waiting for a search warrant."*
>
> *I said, "I own this place. I've done nothing wrong and you're welcome to come inside with me because I have nothing to hide. I'm going inside."*
>
> *When I went to go and put my key in the door, he pulled his gun out and pointed it at my head and said, "Step away from the door."*
>
> *I kept saying I hadn't done anything wrong.*
>
> *At that point, my dad, who was a diabetic, started shaking and crying. He was pulling on my arm and said, "Come on. You can come to my place and take a shower." He was really upset.*
>
> *So, we went to my parents' house and I took a shower.*

When Kenny returned to his home later that evening, he discovered it had been demolished, ransacked in a search conducted by the Clinton Township Police Department.

> *I returned a few hours later. The police just destroyed everything inside. They even went as far as to take all my pickles, mustard, and ketchup that I had in my refrigerator, and threw everything on the floor of my kitchen. They broke the glass containers and there was a huge mess. I couldn't understand why they had to trash my place like that during the search.*
>
> *My dad started bending over to help and I said, "Dad, go home. I'll stay up and try to get everything back in shape."*
>
> *He went home and I stayed up most of the night cleaning up.*

Early the next day, Kenny went to the store to replace the destroyed items. When he returned home, he was surrounded and held at gunpoint. Kenny was handcuffed and arrested and charged with multiple felonies stemming from the assault of April 30th. His nightmare had begun.

> *I got up early the next morning since I had to work at the bowling alley that night. I went to the bank and to Meijer's to pick up some groceries to restock some of the stuff the cops had ruined the night before. When I came back home, I pulled in my driveway and got out of my car. I am holding this bag of groceries when a cop car pulled in behind me and blocked my car in my driveway.*
>
> *Several detectives rushed out of their cars with their guns drawn. Ostin walked right up to me and told me, "Wyniemko, drop that bag and put your hands on top of the car."*

I look at him and said, "What are you talking about? I haven't done anything wrong. Why are you bothering me?"

Suddenly several other marked police cars pulled up on my lawn and on my neighbors' lawn. They had me horseshoed in. Then all the uniform officers got out of the cars and surrounded me.

Ostin told me, "Mr. Wyniemko, I just want to tell you one more time. Drop that bag and put your hands on top of the car."

I looked around and there were about 10 guns pointing at me. I put the bag on the driveway and put my hands on the top of the roof of my car. Ostin put the handcuffs on me with my hands behind my back. He told me that I was identified in the lineup the day before and that I am now under arrest for 15 counts of CSC (Criminal Sexual Conduct), one count of B&E (Breaking and Entering), and one count of Armed Robbery.

I told them, "Look, I'm not the smartest guy in the world but I'm not stupid. Number one, if someone had identified me at the lineup, they are wrong. And, number two, if someone **had** identified me, you guys would have never allowed me to leave the building. You would have arrested me right on the spot to make me a suspect."

Ostin then made that statement that will always be in the back of my mind. He said, "You know what, Wyniemko? I am going to start calling you the million dollar man."

I said, "You want to tell me what that's supposed to mean."

These are his exact words. He said, "By the time I am done fucking with you, it will cost you a million dollars to get your ass out of prison."

That's how cocky this officer was. And he admitted saying that in his deposition in 2004, during the civil action suit against the Clinton Township Police Department and Clinton Township.

> *I was arrested and taken back to the Macomb County Jail.*

On the following day, Kenny was arraigned and held without bail.

> *When I was being led out of court after the arraignment, my dad was pleading with the detectives, "Why are you doing this to my son? He didn't do this."*
>
> *Ostin got right up in my dad's face and screamed, "How do you know, old man? Were you there?"*
>
> *I got real upset and told him to step away. We got into a shouting match. He threatened to have the cuffs removed to see what a big man I was. I told him, "If they do, then they could arrest me for something that I actually did do."*
>
> *That prick can yell at me all he wants. When he started on my dad, I lost it.*

Kenny and Detective Ostin were separated and Kenny was led back to his cell.

The whirlwind experience of the arrest, lineup, and arraignment was over. Kenny was in jail. He was arrested for rape. His life was turned upside down.

> *After the arraignment, I was given green prison clothes. I was able to use the phone to speak with friends and my family, my dad and mom, and my brothers. Only Tommy, my oldest brother, and my dad came to visit while I was waiting for the preliminary examination. Tommy was very supportive at this time and even put his palm up to the glass to show he cared about me. I kinda lose it now because of what happened between us later.*

> *A couple of months later, after the preliminary examination, Tommy and my other brother, Jimmy, came to visit. Tommy had been drinking and we had words. He told me I had fucked up my life and to leave our parents alone before I screw up their lives, too. He even threatened to change their phone number if I called again. I told him, "You better just leave right now and don't come back."*
>
> *Our relationship was never really the same after that. He passed away about a year after I was freed.*

It would be four weeks before Kenny set foot outside of Macomb County Jail. And that was in a prison suit for his appearance in court for his preliminary examination.

Preliminary Examination

Kenny's preliminary examination was on Thursday, August 11, 1994. Judge William H. Cannon presided. The attending prosecutor was Macomb County Assistant Prosecutor, Linda Davis. Public Defender, Laurence Peppler was defense counsel.

> *The prelim was the first time I appeared in public in prison clothes. It was embarrassing.*
>
> *My dad and brother, Tommy, were there for support. I hadn't had that falling out with Tommy yet. That came right after.*
>
> *I just kept shaking my head in disbelief at what was happening to me. I turned to look at my dad and I could tell he was so upset. This whole ordeal was really taking a toll on him. I felt so bad for him.*

The complaint listed charges of one count of Breaking and Entering, one count of Armed Robbery, and five counts of Criminal Sexual Conduct (CSC) in the First Degree. All charges were felonies.

In the state of Michigan, sexually related charges are defined as Criminal Sexual Conduct. There are four degrees of CSC, with CSC in the First Degree being the most serious.

Ms. Davis called two witnesses: Diane Klug, the victim, and Glenn McCormick, a jailhouse snitch.

Ms. Klug testified in detail about her three-hour rape. She also described her interactions with the police afterward and claimed that $2,500 in cash was missing.

Mr. McCormick testified that he had served time in Macomb County Jail with Kenny while he was awaiting trial. Mr. McCormick claimed that Kenny had constantly talked about his case, giving details of the crime and admitting his guilt.

In his cross-examination of Ms. Klug, Mr. Peppler established the fact she thought the police composite of her assailant was 60-65% accurate, that she smelled smoke on the breath of her assailant, and that she had stated on numerous occasions that her assailant was over six feet tall and weighed about 230 pounds. Ms. Klug also testified she had never seen Kenny before the attack.

In cross-examination, Mr. McCormick acknowledged that several felony charges against him were in the process of being dropped in exchange for his testimony.

Judge Cannon noted that the defendant had originally been charged with 15 counts of CSC in the first degree and inquired as to why these additional charges were not included in the complaint before the court. Ms. Davis agreed to amend the complaint to include the additional charges. Judge Cannon bound Kenny over for trial.

When I went to court for my preliminary examination, I was nervous as hell. You have to look at this from my point of view. I had never been in a courtroom like that. They brought me into Judge Cannon's courtroom and I sat down at the defense table next to Peppler. I'm looking around. I can remember my dad was there. And so was my brother, Tommy. There was a woman sitting at the prosecution's table. I looked over at Peppler and I asked him, "Is that Linda Davis, the prosecutor?"

He turned and looked at me and said, "What'd you say?"

I asked him, "Is that Linda Davis, you know, the prosecutor sitting by the table?"

He said, "What? You're kidding me, right?"

I said, "No, I'm not kidding. I don't know who that is. That's why I'm asking you."

He asked, "Kenny, you don't know who that woman is?"

I said again, "No I don't."

He told me, "That's Diane Klug, the victim, you know."

I said, "What are you talking about?"

On Tuesday, August 23, 1994, Kenny was officially arraigned on 17 felony charges. The charges included one count of Breaking and Entering, one count of Armed Robbery, and 15 counts of Criminal Sexual Conduct in the first degree. The Armed Robbery charges were the result of Ms. Klug alleging that approximately $2,500 cash was stolen during the attack. His trial date was set for October 25, 1994.

Kenny related a story about an incident that happened in Macomb County Jail while he was awaiting trial.

I was sleeping in my cell when I was woke up by the guards very early in the morning. I was led into a small office. Ostin

> *and, I believe, Detective Marlatt were there. Ostin put a large cup of black coffee in front of me and told me I was here for a polygraph test.*
>
> *I told him I know of no such arrangement. Ostin told me that he was given the okay from Peppler. I was real leery about this and asked if I could speak with Peppler.*
>
> *Ostin called Peppler at home and woke him up.*
>
> *I picked up the phone and asked Peppler what was going on with this polygraph test. He was just as confused as I was. I told him the story about how they had woke me up early, gave me a large cup of coffee, and told me it was time for my polygraph.*
>
> *"What!" Peppler yelled. "Tell them to go fuck themselves and do not take that test."*
>
> *And he slammed down the phone.*
>
> *I laughed and hung up.*
>
> *Ostin was watching me. He asked, "Well?"*
>
> *I told him, "Peppler told you to go fuck yourself and to bring me back to my cell."*
>
> *They didn't say much and the guards walked me back to my cell.*

In interviews, several law enforcement officers and Judge Patrick T. Cahill severely criticized this tactic. One law enforcement officer said that if a polygraph was obtained under those circumstances, the case could have been successfully appealed.

Judge Cahill was very clear in his assessment of Detective Ostin's actions.

> *Absolutely unacceptable and improper and grounds for a new trial if admitted. Ostin tried to trample on the constitutional rights of Ken Wyniemko in blatant violation*

of the 5th and 6th Amendments. This is bizarre and unsettling police misbehavior.

Defense Counsel

Kenny's initial court-appointed attorney was Laurence Peppler. For the first three-and-a-half months of his incarceration, he never felt comfortable with Mr. Peppler. Kenny was looking for a lifeline, someone who believed what he knew — that he was innocent. Instead, he found his lawyer disinterested and mostly unavailable. In their first meeting, Mr. Peppler told Kenny that the prosecution had a strong case, a statement that scared the hell out of Kenny. Kenny said that Mr. Peppler rarely returned calls and they met face-to-face only briefly on a couple of occasions. They never sat down and talked about the case, never strategized on Kenny's defense, never reviewed the prosecution's witness list to establish a line of questioning, and never put together any semblance of a plan to keep Kenny out of jail.

As his trial date approached, Kenny felt alone and had little faith in Mr. Peppler.

Well, the first lawyer I had was a court appointed attorney by the name of Laurence Peppler. I had a problem from the first time we met. It was bad enough I was being held for something I didn't do. I was nervous as hell. This guy came to see me and his eyes were constantly blinking. He would never look me straight in the eye. It just seemed to me that it was a sign he was really nervous or lying. When someone doesn't want to look you in the eye, especially in a situation like that, something's up.

But he kept telling me, "Don't worry, Kenny, everything's going to be okay."

He gave me the phone number to his office. But every time I called him, he wouldn't take my call. I was scared. I didn't know what to do. I had never been in this type of situation before. The waiting and doing nothing was so hard.

I was constantly rethinking how I could be in this position, how I could have been identified.

Like I said, Peppler and I just didn't connect. I did not feel he believed in me or he was doing much of anything. The big thing is he never called me back. Then I found out that his brother was a Clinton Township cop. Since Clinton Township cops arrested me, I didn't want to take any chances. I wrote a note to the judge asking for a replacement.

It was a few weeks before the trial date when Kenny discovered what he considered the glaring conflict of interest for Mr. Peppler. On Tuesday, October 25, 1994, in a hearing before the Judge Michael D. Schwartz, Kenny stated his concerns that Mr. Peppler would not provide an adequate defense. Mr. Peppler requested to be removed as Kenny's defense attorney and Judge Schwartz granted the request.

The trial was rescheduled to start on Tuesday, November 1, 1994. When Kenny protested that he did not think that was sufficient time for his new attorney to prepare an adequate defense, Judge Schwartz made it clear that he would not tolerate any delays.

Here is an excerpt from the court transcript.

THE COURT: What do you want the Court to do? Are you ready to try the case yourself?

MR. WYNIEMKO: No, sir, I'm not. I'd like to have a different attorney.

THE COURT: Well, I'm not in the habit of letting you select attorneys, especially at public expense.

MR. WYNIEMKO: I can appreciate that, sir.

THE COURT: What I'm going to do is I'll have Mr. Mellon appoint another attorney by blind draw, and this is the last attorney you'll have. . . . I don't appoint third attorneys. Do you understand what I'm saying?

MR. WYNIEMKO: Yes, I do, sir.

THE COURT: Otherwise, you try the case yourself, and I'll have the attorney sit next to you.

MR. WYNIEMKO: I'm not qualified to defend myself, sir.

THE COURT: Well, I'm not qualified to give up attorneys at public expense. I'll appoint another attorney on your behalf.

MR. WYNIEMKO: Okay.

THE COURT: And that's who you're going with, male or female, that's what it is. The Court was ready to go ahead with this matter this afternoon. I'm going to put it off one week. Next Tuesday we go to trial.

MR. WYNIEMKO: I don't know if that will give my attorney enough time to review all the, all the facts, Your Honor.

THE COURT: Well, you'd better start talking fast, because that's when we go to trial, on Tuesday. Monday afternoon, if there are any motions, we'll take all motions Monday afternoon. You (Mr. Peppler) cooperate with the other attorney.

MR. PEPPLER: Yes, I certainly will.

THE COURT: Give all the information. The other attorney will have to spend a lot of time with the defendant in this matter. No question about it. But that's when we're going to trial. I'm not going to have any defendant or attorney put these things off over and over again. You're entitled to speedy trial, and I'm going to give you a speedy trial.

MR. WYNIEMKO: I'm aware of that, sir.

THE COURT: Anything else, Ms. Davis?

MS. DAVIS: The only thing I'd like to note for the record, and I know the Court is indulging us for this already, the People are asserting our right to a speedy trial. We prepared a witness, the victim of this particular case. She is an absolute basket case over this matter. She has right to a speedy trial, and we are asserting it.

MR. PEPPLER: I would only indicate on behalf of Mr. Wyniemko, that Mr. Wyniemko is incarcerated. He represents no threat to the victim at this point in time whatsoever, and perhaps time would heal her and enable her to better testify at trial.

MS. DAVIS: Your Honor, she has indicated to me that she wants this matter behind her; that she lives with this daily. She wants this matter behind her.

THE COURT: She has as many rights as the defendant does. There's no question in my mind. And even though it may not be etched in stone, but take it from me, we'll go Tuesday.

Kenny recalled the hearing.

> *Judge Schwartz told me that this is my last attorney I would be given and if I didn't like it, then that was just too bad. He told me that the trial **will** start on Tuesday and I can defend myself for all he cared.*
>
> *I wasted close to four months with Peppler and now I was going to trial with an attorney who had a weekend to prepare. One weekend to prepare for a case like this? With my life hanging on it? Hell, you can't prepare for a DUI in a single weekend, let alone a case like mine. I couldn't believe what was happening. I didn't know what to do.*

Mr. Peppler's replacement was Public Defender, Albert Markowski. He was assigned on Friday, October 28, 1994. Mr. Markowski was given the unenviable task of preparing for a capital case with 17 felony charges over a single weekend.

At his first opportunity, Mr. Markowski should have stated for the record that he would not be able to give Mr. Wyniemko an adequate defense given the short time he had to prepare for the case. He would proceed as he was ordered and defend Mr. Wyniemko to the best of his ability, but he did not feel that the weekend was, in any way, sufficient lead time for a major case such as this. Mr. Markowski chose to not enter a formal, on-the-record objection. Kenny would suffer the consequences.

Mr. Markowski spoke with Kenny for about 20 minutes on the following day, Saturday, October 29, 1994. He told Kenny that everything would be okay. It was the *only* time they met outside the court room. Once again, the accused man and his defense attorney never sat down to plot strategy or to go over Kenny's testimony. Kenny was deeply concerned and very afraid. Imagine his thoughts as the judicial process relentlessly dragged him towards the trial for his life.

First day of the trial. Even though court proceedings didn't start 'til 9:00, and they never start on time, they woke me up about 5:00 in the morning to take a shower and to go downstairs to the bullpen to put on street clothes. You can sit there for two-and-a-half hours. It's a room with no chairs. There are cement blocks that you sit on, raised about two-and-a-half feet off the floor. Like a bench seat made out of cement. There is one toilet sitting in the open in the corner. If anyone has to go, there is no privacy. It looks like it was built to hold 15 guys, but they usually crammed in about 25.

Finally, we were allowed to leave for court. They handcuffed six guys and chained us together with leg shackles and waist belly chains. It's like a walking chain gang. That's what it was like. They stuffed us into the van and we go over to the courthouse.

They took us to the bullpen of the courthouse where our chains and handcuffs were removed. I waited until my name was called. I was handcuffed again and led in a secure elevator to a bathroom across the hallway from the courtroom where the handcuffs were removed. The bathroom had two stalls enclosed with diamond-shaped mesh fencing. You can barely see in or out. Each stall had a toilet. They put three people in each stall and you have to stand up and wait. Geez, you're standing there for a half hour to an hour until you are called for court.

The handcuffs go back on and you are led into the courtroom. It's not nice.

That's what the county jail is. That's what prison is. They always try to degrade you, embarrass you. They try to break you down. That's part of the job. But it didn't work with me, thankfully. They had the wrong guy.

Kenny remained in cuffs while he sat at the defense table until just before the judge and jury entered the courtroom.

> *You can't imagine the shame and embarrassment when everyone is watching you escorted by two cops into court in handcuffs. I remember sitting like that in front of my family, friends, and everyone else there. It hurt that my dad had to see me that way every day of the trial.*
>
> *I was scared. Every day I was wondering what I was doing there, still trying to figure out why the police arrested me. Then I was nervous about going to court 'cause I'd never been in court before. Even though I knew I was innocent, I didn't know what the police had in mind or how bad this was going to be. But I found out later.*
>
> *I remember they brought me into the courtroom for the first day of trial. I got to the defense table and Markowski came in and sat down at the table. I was still handcuffed. He told me not to worry about anything, that everything will be okay, which was a bunch of shit.*
>
> *He came to see me in county jail on Saturday and I talked to him for maybe 20 minutes. Part of that conversation was him telling me that he was second in his class at Orchard Lake St Mary's. I could care less about that. You're on trial for your life, really life in prison for me because I was 43 years old, and this guy is telling me how good he was in high school. That was the only time we sat down and talked outside of the courtroom.*

This is not even close to Judge Schwartz's directive during the hearing in which Kenny requested a new lawyer to replace Mr. Peppler.

> *The other attorney will have to spend a lot of time with the defendant in this matter.*

Chapter 3 — Trial and Conviction

"I couldn't understand how something like this could happen in our system. He (Judge Schwartz) said I failed to show remorse. My response to him was, 'Your honor, I feel terrible for what happened to this woman. But I can't show remorse for something I didn't do or have any knowledge of.'" — Kenny Wyniemko

Case Number 94-2001-fc
The People of the State of Michigan

vs.

Kenneth Wyniemko (Defendant)

Before the Honorable Michael D. Schwartz, (P-20134) Judge
Mount Clemens, Michigan, Circuit Court, Macomb County

Prosecuting Attorney – Linda Davis
Defense Attorney – Albert Markowski

The trial lasted seven days.
- Day 1 — Monday, October 31, 1994: Several motions and Wade Hearing.
- Day 2 — Tuesday, November 1, 1994: Witness lists exchanged. Jury selected.
- Day 3 — Wednesday, November 2, 1994: Prosecution presents its case.
- Day 4 — Thursday, November 3, 1994: Prosecution presents its case.
- Day 5 — Friday, November 4, 1994: Prosecution presents its case.

- Day 6 — Monday, November 7, 1994: Defense presents its case. Prosecution and defense present final arguments. Final jury instructions.
- Day 7 — Wednesday, November 9, 1994: Jury verdict.
- Thursday, December 15, 1994: Sentencing Hearing

DAY 1: MONDAY, OCTOBER 31, 1994

Court was convened at 3:49 pm.

The first day of the trial was spent hearing several motions.

Defense Counsel, Albert Markowski, requested a "*Wade Hearing to show this Court that there in fact may have been some impropriety*" in the lineup. (A Wade Hearing is a pre-trial process that determines the validity of a lineup.)

Assistant Prosecuting Attorney, Linda Davis, called several witnesses present at the lineup, including Richard Reynolds, stand-in counsel for the hearing, Diane Klug, the victim, and Clinton Township Police Detective, John Berger. They all denied witnessing or participating in anything improper.

Mr. Reynolds testified that he was provided a description of the assailant who matched Kenny, a far cry from the one given by Ms. Klug and the one used in the composite and throughout the investigation. Mr. Reynolds was also told that the victim never saw her assailant's face, that the attacker was masked. Mr. Reynolds testified that this was the reason he did not question why four lineup fill-ins had mustaches and Kenny did not.

Here is a disturbing conflict. The police depended on Ms. Klug's visual identification of her attacker's face yet they informed Mr. Reynolds that she never saw her attacker's face. It was a severely tainted lineup when four of five fillers had mustaches.

In addition, Mr. Reynolds was given a physical description that matched that of Kenny. The victim's description of her attacker at six-foot-three and 230 pounds was no longer used.

Mr. Markowski never addressed any of these inconsistencies during the Wade Hearing. It was just the beginning of Kenny's incompetent defense.

Here is an excerpt of Mr. Reynolds' testimony.

Q. Was there anything about any of the individuals that stood out to you just on physical observation of them alone?
A. I was given the general description in my notes, and I reviewed that. And the general description of the people in the lineup fit the general description of the defendant.

Q. Okay. And that was true for all of the individuals; is that correct?
A. White male, I think it is approximately 6 feet; the weight was approximately 180 to 190. I believe some of them had mustaches, but I didn't think — that didn't matter in this case because it was my understanding that the defendant — the alleged perpetrator had a mask on, and I think four other people had mustaches. It was not used as an identifying characteristic.

Judge Schwartz ruled against the defense and the identification was admitted. This lineup would come under severe criticism on numerous occasions in the future.

The last two motions were submitted by Ms. Davis.

Ms. Davis made a motion to call Linda Bradley to testify. She was the girlfriend of Wayne Burkhardt, a fellow prisoner of Kenny's. Ms.

Bradley was to testify that Kenny asked Burkhardt to instruct Ms. Bradley to provide an alibi for Kenny for the time of the attack.

The second motion was to allow two of Kenny's former girlfriends to testify.

Both motions were granted.

Ms. Davis then presented the list of charges against Kenny. Mr. Markowski argued against some of the charges to no avail. Kenny was charged with 19 felony counts: 17 charges of Criminal Sexual Conduct in the First Degree (CSC-1), one charge of Armed Robbery, and one charge of Breaking and Entering.

Court was adjourned at 5:00 pm.

DAY 2: TUESDAY, NOVEMBER 1, 1994

Court came in session at 10:45 am.

The first order of business was to finalize the charges. Two counts of CSC-1 were thrown out and a total of 17 felony counts were entered into court record: 15 counts of CSC-1, Armed Robbery, and Breaking and Entering.

The prosecution and the defense submitted their witness lists. The prosecution had 13 names. The defense had five, including Ms. Klug's husband.

The last item for the day was the selection of the jury.

Court was adjourned at 4:50 pm.

Mr. Markowski did not meet with Kenny that evening or the evening before. There was no strategizing. There was no prepping of Kenny in the event he had to testify and endure a cross-examination.

Kenny felt alone and helpless. The criminal justice system was steamrolling him to trial and not one word from his lawyer.

DAY 3: WEDNESDAY, NOVEMBER 2, 1994

The jury trial began at 10:40 am.

The pew-style benches in the gallery were heavily populated in anticipation of the first day of the trial of this most heinous crime. A three-foot wooden wall separated the gallery from the front of the court. The all-white jury of eight women and four men were seated at the front along the right wall in the jury box. Behind the judge's elevated bench, the United States and the Michigan state flags were on display.

Seated at the prosecution table on the right were Macomb County Assistant Prosecutor, Linda Davis, Denise Brainard (a law student assistant), and Clinton Township Police Detectives, Bart Marlatt and Thomas Ostin.

Seated at the defense table on the left were Kenny and his attorney, Albert Markowski.

Kenny viewed the courtroom, looking for a friendly face, someone who believed in his innocence. There was no more blind hope that the system would come to its senses and stop this colossal mix up.

> *I looked over the courtroom, the people in the gallery, the jury. It seemed like a lot of the victim's friends were there for her support, as it should have been.*

> *I could feel the stares. I felt like everyone was pointing their finger at me, saying, "There's the rapist. There's the monster."*
>
> *Throughout the trial, I remember one of the jurors sitting with his face in his hands and his elbows on his knees. Every time I looked his way, he was just staring at me. It was a stare of contempt, like he was going to do his best to hang me.*
>
> *My dad and my brother, Tommy, were there every day of the trial seated right behind me. Some friends came a couple times, but that was it.*
>
> *But I knew most everyone else there wanted me punished for what they thought I did to this poor woman.*

Judge Schwartz addressed the jury. He reviewed trial procedure and instructed the jury to not communicate with anyone involved in the trial and to not read or listen to case coverage in the media.

Opening Statements
Ms. Davis was very forceful and direct in her presentation. She meticulously described the three-hour rape, detailing each penetration and each Criminal Sexual Conduct act, outlining the reason for each First Degree Criminal Sexual Conduct charge. She presented Diane Klug as a broken individual due to the ordeal she endured at the hands of the defendant.

> *At the conclusion of the trial, after hearing Diane's testimony and seeing the evidence that the people have to present in this case, I am going to ask you to do your job and tell Kenneth Wyniemko that he is guilty of 15 counts of criminal sexual conduct against Diane Klug; that he is guilty of Breaking and Entering her home; and that he is guilty of Armed Robbery.*

Thank you.

Mr. Markowski began by asserting that it is the jury's duty to only convict his client if they are convinced beyond a reasonable doubt that Kenny is guilty of the charges. He asked the jury to keep an open mind as they hear the dreadful details of the attack, to deliberate the evidence, and to concentrate on the believability of the witnesses.

> *If you have that gut reaction that, geez, she failed to prove an essential element of any or all of those crimes. But then you think, my God, dear Lord, what happened to this poor woman, we heard all of this horrendous testimony, and it is horrendous. You're caught in a dilemma. You can't have that dilemma if you have a gut reaction he didn't do it. You can't say we're sorry, sorry for her; we're going to nail him anyway. You can't do that. That would be a breach of your sworn duty, that you swore that you will determine this case based on the believable testimony as it comes out during this trial. . . .*
>
> *All I can ask on behalf of my client, Mr. Wyniemko, is that you give him a fair shake. This is his one and only opportunity to appear in court before people of his peers. Give him a fair shake, keep an open mind.*

The prosecution's case began.

Clinton Township Police Officer Chris Wallington

Ms. Davis called her first witness, Officer Chris Wallington, the first officer at the scene of the attack. He described what he observed, what he did to preserve the evidence, and his efforts to interview the shaken victim. Officer Wallington followed the victim to St. Joseph's Hospital-West where she was examined and where a rape kit was produced. He then transported the kit to the Clinton Township Police Department where he turned it over to the detective in charge of the investigation, Detective Bart Marlatt. Officer Wallington detailed the crime scene investigation, including the presence of footprints inside and outside the home. Impression casts of several footprints were successfully preserved and submitted as evidence.

Here is an excerpt from Officer Wallington's testimony.

Q. What observation did you make regarding that bedroom?
A. Okay. The drapes were pulled closed. It was like blinds. And I could see footprints in that room on the carpeting. And I had asked Diane, you know, who else had been in the room, and if they wore shoes, because the room had looked like it had just recently been vacuumed. And there was only — there was several prints, but not — I could see clearly that it was like a boot or a shoe print, not just somebody's bare foot. . . .

Q. And did you find anything?
A. There was a footprint in the dirt behind the home of that spare bedroom that's directly across from the master bedroom. There was a footprint in the dirt that looked unusual to me at the time.

Q. I'm going to show you what's marked as People's Proposed Exhibit Number 16, and ask you if you can identify the picture?
A. That's the footprint I was referring to. It was behind the home under the window of the spare bedroom.

Several crime scene photos were submitted by the prosecution. There were no objections from the defense.

The fact that the footprints found at the crime scene were that of the assailant was never contested by the police. If the footprints had been a match to Kenny, the prosecution would certainly have presented that fact at trial. How that omission in the prosecution's case was not questioned by Mr. Markowski was another example of the incompetence of defense counsel.

Mr. Markowski's cross-examination was brief, less than two minutes. He verified that the officer considered the evidence and crime scene pictures as authentic and that the officer handed over all crime scene evidence to the lab tech. There were no questions regarding the footprints.

Diane Klug
The next prosecution witness was the victim, Diane Klug. Her testimony impressed on the jury the severity of the crime and its devastating effects.

Ms. Klug described the day's events leading up to her assault. Several facts were established. She and her husband bowled at the Kingswood Lanes Bowling Alley where Kenny worked. It was common knowledge at Kingswood that her husband was out of town on a golfing trip at the time of the attack. The husband's mother had cleaned the apartment earlier in the day before the attack.

Ms. Davis had Ms. Klug go into every detail of her attack, her thoughts during the attack, and her actions to survive it. She visibly struggled as she described her ordeal, every penetration of every orifice, every position, and every indignation.

She was tied up and blindfolded. She was fingered and fondled. She was raped anally. She was forced to perform oral sex and then ordered to wash the evidence down with a can of Pepsi. It was a morbid account of the dreadful experience Ms. Klug had to endure over a three-hour period.

Ms. Davis asked her to identify her attacker. Ms. Klug contradicted all previous statements, taped and written, by testifying that there was one time during the attack where she had seen her assailant's face.

> Q. You indicated that you had gotten glimpses of this individual during the course of the night. Is that correct?
> A. Yes.
>
> Q. Had you ever seen that individual before?
> A. No.
>
> Q. Did you have an occasion some months later to see that individual?
> A. Yes, at a line-up.
>
> Q. And were you able to recognize that individual as the individual that raped you on April 30, 1994?
> A. Yes, I was.
>
> Q. Is that individual in this courtroom today, Diane?
> A Yes, he is.
>
> Q. Where is he seated?
> A. At the defense table over there.
>
> Q. Okay. And you have to indicate what he's wearing.
> A. He's wearing a cardigan sweater, a white shirt, and glasses.
>
> MS. DAVIS: Your Honor, I would have the record reflect that she's identified the defendant.
>
> THE COURT: So noted for the record.

> *Q. Diane, is there any doubt in your mind that the individual that you described as being the man that did this to you that night is the man seated at this table?*
> *A. No, no doubt.*
>
> *Q. There's not any doubt at all in your mind?*
> *A. No.*
>
> *Q. Diane, what has this done to your life since this rape occurred?*

Ms. Klug described how the attack has continued to fill her life with constant fear, depression, and trips to a psychiatrist.

It was a powerful testimony.

Kenny was clueless as to how this woman could have identified him as the one who committed these terrible acts.

> *I could not grasp how this whole ordeal could come to this. She was pointing at me, calling me a rapist, in front of everyone. I just dropped my face in my hands and shook my head. I cannot describe the feeling and you can't imagine it.*
>
> *I couldn't turn around to look at my dad. He had to sit there and listen to this woman accuse his son of those horrific things.*
>
> *I was so thankful my mom wasn't in court to hear her testimony. My dad was real protective and told her it would be better if she didn't come and hear the things that everyone would be saying about me. As usual, my dad was 100% correct.*
>
> *It was bad enough my mom read in the paper or heard things on TV where Linda Davis called me a sexual pervert, a menace to society, a predator on the weak. Sitting in court would have destroyed her.*

Diane Klug's identification of Kenny was by far the most damaging evidence the prosecutor had. Yet, Mr. Markowski's cross-examination lasted only two minutes. He went over some of the details of her ordeal. He referenced her initial statement in which she told the police that she had never seen her attacker's face. There was very little effort to discredit her testimony.

Ms. Klug had repeatedly claimed that she never saw her attacker's face in taped and written witness statements and in conversations during the creation of the suspect composite. Now, the prosecutor wanted everyone to believe that Ms. Klug saw her attacker's face. Mr. Markowski never addressed these conflicting facts.

In addition, Mr. Markowski's cross-examination never cited the pronounced physical differences between Kenny and her attacker in all of her statements. There was no mention of the size differential, or the presence of the deep cleft chin, beer belly, or cigarette odor. Her attacker suddenly went from a six-foot, three-inch, 230 pound man, with a beer belly, deep cleft chin, who smoked, to a five-foot, eleven-inch man of medium build, with no beer belly, a normal chin, who never smoked.

The deep cleft chin on the assailant, as declared in every one of Ms. Klug's statements, and reiterated in her testimony, is as distinguishing a characteristic as a scar. It was completely ignored throughout the investigation and the trial. It certainly begged direct questioning from Mr. Markowski as to how she could explain its absence on Kenny.

Here are a couple questions Mr. Markowski could have used to drive home the inconsistency of the absence of a cleft chin on the defendant and the presence of the cleft chin on the victim's numerous physical descriptions of her assailant.
- There is one physical characteristic that you insisted your assailant had, and I quote from several of your earlier statements, "a deep cleft chin." Didn't it bother you that the

cleft chin was left out of the composite drawing created by the Clinton Township Police Department?
- And doesn't it bother you that the man accused of this crime does not have a cleft chin, a specific characteristic you insisted your assailant had?

Ms. Klug gave several statements and testified at trial that her rapist smelled like cigarette smoke. This made sense since cigarette butts were found at the crime scene and neither she nor her husband smoked. This was also in direct conflict with Kenny being identified as the assailant because he never smoked. Ms. Davis tried to smooth over that bothersome fact by insinuating that the source of the smoke could come from something other than a cigarette.

> *Q. You also indicated that you smelled what you believed to be cigarette smoke on Mr. Wyniemko or the defendant. Is that correct?*
> *A. Yes.*
>
> *Q. Could it have been cocaine smoke, marijuana smoke, cigar smoke or some other kind of smoke?*
>
> *MR. MARKOWSKI: Your Honor, if I may.*
>
> *THE COURT: Is there an objection?*
>
> *MR. MARKOWSKI: Yes, Your Honor... I believe the questions are leading.*
>
> *THE COURT: Objection sustained.*
>
> Ms. Davis continued.

Q. Could it have been some other kind of smoke?
A. It could have been.

There are two issues with this line of questioning.

First, the prosecution, at several times during the trial, indicated that the defendant had, in the past, used cocaine. She brought it up in her examination of Ms. Klug. She brought it up on several other occasions during the trial, including in her closing arguments. Defense should have argued that it was totally irrelevant, immaterial, and prejudicial to the extreme. These statements and this line of questioning had no probative value and should not have been allowed. In fact, the words "cocaine" and "coke" were associated with Kenny 16 times during the trial. But Mr. Markowski never objected.

Second, Ms. Davis should never have been allowed to insinuate the smoke was anything other than cigarette smoke. The cigarette butts recovered at the crime scene were submitted as evidence from the perpetrator. The butts were forensically tested in an effort to connect them to Kenny. Since Ms. Klug had previously testified that she considered the smell cigarette smoke, that she knew what cigarette smoke smelled like, and that neither she nor her husband smoked, it begs the question, "Where the hell did the cigarette butts come from if not the assailant?"

Here is a simple line of questioning that Mr. Markowski could have used to discredit the prosecution's allegation that the smoke Ms. Klug smelled on her assailant was anything by cigarette smoke.
- You testified that neither you nor your husband smoked. Correct?
- So, the cigarette butts found at the crime scene and submitted as forensic evidence could not belong to you or your husband. Correct?
- You have always contended prior to this trial that your attacker smelled like cigarette smoke. Correct?

- So, the prosecutor's claim that the smoke on the assailant could be anything but the cigarette smoke is ridiculous. Correct?

Another line of questioning that Mr. Markowski did not pursue was whether Ms. Klug had ever seen Kenny. According to the prosecutor, Kenny had noticed Ms. Klug at the bowling alley where he worked and where she frequented. Mr. Markowski never brought up the possibility that Ms. Klug could have seen Kenny and unconsciously recognized his face as her assailant in the identification process. The prosecution had it both ways.

Court was recessed at 3:45 pm and reconvened at 4:10 pm.

Ms. Davis continued to present her case by calling two minor witnesses — one was a friend of Kenny's who confirmed he used drugs years ago and the other was the Kingswood Bowling Lanes manager who verified Kenny was employed there.

Both testified that Kenny had won significant amounts of money at Hazel Park Raceway in the spring of 1994. The prosecution was trying to disprove Kenny's claim that the money he had told his friends he won in April was really the cash taken from the crime.

Mr. Markowski did not cross-examine either witness.

Clinton Township Police Lieutenant Al Ernst
The prosecution's next witness was Lieutenant Al Ernst, the commander of the Clinton Township Police Department Criminal Section and the supervisor of the detectives assigned to the investigation.

Lieutenant Ernst testified that he worked with Ms. Klug to create a composite picture of her assailant. The composite was presented in court, verified by Lieutenant Ernst, and entered into evidence. Lieutenant Ernst confirmed that Ms. Klug thought the sketch was about 60 percent accurate and that she had an issue with the chin.

Here is the first oddity of Lieutenant Ernst's testimony. In the composite description, there was no mention of Ms. Klug's dissatisfaction with the chin. In the remarks, Ernst indicated she had a problem with the eyes and lips. Very puzzling.

> *Remarks:*
> *Suspect had nylon over his head for most of the assault. Victim feels this composite is approx. 60% accurate. The lips and eyes may be different, but victim could not explain what changes to make.*

The composite also contained the original physical description from Ms. Klug — a description that did not remotely match that of Kenny.

> *Suspect: W/M 35 6' TO 6' 2", 220 TO 230, HEAVY BUILD, SLIGHTLY CHUNKY WITH A BEER BELLY, BROWN HAIR, THIN ON TOP, FAIR SKIN, WEARING A JEAN JACKET, AND DARKER COLOR JEANS, DARK SHOES, VOICE VERY LOW AND RASPY.*

Defense attorney Mr. Markowski never questioned this discrepancy in the composite and lodged no objection when it was submitted as evidence.

Lieutenant Ernst also testified that he received an anonymous call on May 11, 1994, stating the composite matched that of Ken Wyniemko, the counterman at Kingswood Lanes. Lieutenant Ernst testified that he relayed the information to Detective Marlatt. Here is an excerpt from his testimony.

Q. Did you have any further participation in the investigation of this case other than that composite drawing?
A. Other than overseeing the detectives who are assigned to me, who are doing the investigation, none, until I received a phone call on May 11th in reference to this case.

Q. And what was that phone call regarding?
A. It was a white male, sounded like an adult on the phone, stating that he had information concerning the case.

Q. And what information did he give you?
A. He said that the person involved was Ken Wyniemko who was the counterman at Kingswood Lanes and also at Rosebowl Lanes.

Q. And did he say where he got that information from?
A. No. He said — he said he got it from the Clinton Chronicle Paper, which published the composite. He said that's where he got it from.

Q. And what did you do with that information after you received it?
A. I wrote it down on one of our investigative forms and gave it to Detective Marlatt.

Ms. Davis concluded her direct examination.

Mr. Markowski's cross-examination was very brief, just over a minute. His only line of questioning concerned the creation of the composite, verifying that the composite sketch system used to create the composite included foils with cleft chins. Mr. Markowski never questioned Lieutenant Ernst why these foils were never used when Ms. Klug insisted her assailant had a "deep cleft chin."

TRIAL AND CONVICTION | 44

CLINTON TOWNSHIP POLICE DEPARTMENT

Incident: BREAKING AND ENTERING, AND CRIMINAL SEXUAL CONDUCT

Location: JOLGREN ST., WEST RIVER ESTATES

Date: 04/30/94

Time: 0500

Suspect: W/M 30-35, 6' to 6'2", 220 to 230, HEAVY BUILD, SLIGHTLY CHUNKY WITH A BEER BE BROWN HAIR, THIN ON TOP, FAIR SKIN, WEARING A JEAN JACKET, AND DARKER COLOR JEANS, DARK SHOES, VOICE VERY LOW AND RASPY.

Vehicle:

Weapons: UTILITY KNIFE

Accomplices:

Method: PRIED SIDE DOOR

Department: CLINTON TWP. P.D.

Complaint#: 94-17059

Identi-Kit Code:
A4, N32up2, C6,E20,L7 up 1, H11 down 2
Operator: Lt. A. Ernst

Remarks:
Suspect had a nylon over his head for most of the assault, victim feels this composite is approx 60% accurate. The lips and eyes may be different, but victim could not explain what changes to make.

Police suspect sketch and physical description

Q. If you have different mustaches, you have different chins; you have chins with clefts, chins without clefts?
A. That's correct.

Q. You have different hair, hairlines, and then you proceed based on the information you receive from the complaining witness to pull certain foils and then come up with what is perceived to be somewhere near a characterization of the individual?
A. That's correct.

Q. And this particular case, I believe, there is an indication that she was 60 or 65 percent accurate as far as the features?
A. That's correct.

That's it. Mr. Markowski's cross-examination stopped there. He did not pursue the fact that Ms. Klug, the only eyewitness to the crime and from whom Lieutenant Ernst built his composite, had an issue with the way the chin looked, insisting her assailant had a deep cleft chin. It is very puzzling how Lieutenant Ernst could flat out refuse to include the cleft chin in the composite when Ms. Klug insisted her assailant had one.

Questions never asked.
- Is the presence of a cleft chin considered a distinguishing characteristic when trying to apprehend a suspect?
- What percentage of the population would you estimate has a deep cleft chin?
- Why was the cleft chin omitted from the composite when Ms. Klug insisted her assailant had one?
- Did you try another foil with the cleft chin to see if the witness thought it to be more accurate?
- If not, then why not?

- Why did you testify today that Ms. Klug had an issue with the chin in the composite drawing and state on the composite drawing itself that she had an issue with the lips and eyes?

Clinton Township Detective Bart Marlatt
Detective Marlatt was the first detective at the crime scene and the original lead detective on the case. When Detective Thomas Ostin was named the primary detective, Detective Marlatt assisted in the investigation.

Detective Marlatt testified what he observed at the crime scene and his initial interview with Diane Klug. He further testified that he obtained the rape kit from Officer Wallington at the precinct.

He described the initial investigation, the canvassing of the neighborhood, etc. There were no leads and there was no revealing physical evidence from the scene. The first break in the case was the anonymous tip he received from Lieutenant Ernst.

The timing on when the anonymous tip was received by Lieutenant Ernst and when it was followed up on by Detective Marlatt was never addressed by Mr. Markowski. The tip was received on May 11th and the first indication of any follow-up was early July. That's a two month delay in addressing the tip.

In interviews, several law enforcement officers agreed that the tips should have been received, recorded, and addressed immediately to determine if they were credible. This is essential.

The Case Investigation Work Report on which Lieutenant Ernst manually wrote the tip was dated May 11th and signed.

5-11 1410
TIP ON C.S.C. & BE
CALLED REFUSED TO GIVE NAME
HE SAID HE SAW THE PICTURE IN THE CHRONICLE.
SAID IT LOOKS LIKE KEN WYNIEMKO COUNTER MAN

FROM KINGWOOD LANES M-97 & HALL AND AT ROSE BOWL LANES M-97 AND MARTIN.

The next entry was dated July 6, 1994. It was the first indication of any follow-up on the anonymous tip. It was related to an interview with Cathy Whitcher, Kenny's girlfriend at the time of the April 30, 1994, attack.

CHECK AT KINGSWOOD LANES ABOUT OTHER BOWLING ALLEY. CATHERINE SAYS IT MATCHES THE DESCRIPTION.

In another Case Investigation Work Report, it was noted that Detective Marlatt met with Ms. Klug on June 27, 1994, and informed her that there was no new information on this investigation. The entry was signed by Detective Marlatt himself.

INTERVIEW WITH DIANE KLUG. DISCUSSION ON WRITTEN REPORTS FROM C.S.C. NO NEW INFORMATION AT THIS TIME. STILL UNDER INVESTIGATION.

The next entry was also dated July 6, 1994, and it spoke of the same interview with Ms. Whitcher.

INTERVIEW W/CATHERINE WHITCHER SHOWED HER COMPOSITE SHE WAS STARTLED AS TO HOW MUCH THE COMPOSITE MATCHES HER EX-BOYFRIEND, KENNETH WYNIEMKO.

Catherine Whitcher, Kenny's former girlfriend, was initially contacted by Detective Marlatt on July 6, 1994. She was shown the composite and confirmed that it looked like Kenny. The first recorded interview with Ms. Whitcher occurred on July 9, 1994, at 11:15 am.

CLINTON TOWNSHIP POLICE DEPARTMENT
Press Release

May 2, 1994
Authority of: Chief of Police R. W. Smith
By: Deputy Chief of Police Donald O. Brook
94-17059

Clinton Township Police are asking the assistance of the public in identifying a suspect wanted in a Breaking and Entering and rape of a 28 year old Township resident.

The female resident had arrived home around 2:30 a.m. to her home in the Canal and Clinton River Road area when at approximately 5:00 a.m. she was awakened by a man in her bedroom. The man handcuffed the female and caused her to participate in several sex acts in different locations within the home.

In addition to the sex acts, the man stole money and jewelry from the home. The suspect then left the home at approximately 6:30 a.m. The victim was tied to the bed posts in her bedroom. She was able to free herself and went to a neighbor's home and called the police.

Police are looking for a white male 30 -35 years old, approximately 220 pounds with a "Beer Gut", short light brown hair, wearing a blue jean jacket, blue jeans and suede rubber soled black shoes.

Anyone with any information that can assist the Clinton Township Police are asked to call 791-2020

-30-

Police press release describing the crime and a description of the suspect.

The testimony of Lieutenant Ernst and Detective Marlatt regarding the anonymous tip identifying Kenny as a possible suspect was conflicted and misleading.

Consider the following statement from Lieutenant Ernst during his testimony.

I wrote it down on one of our investigative forms and gave it to Detective Marlatt.

Consider the following statements from Detective Marlatt during his testimony.

Q. How long did this case go without any real suspect that were involved in it?
A. Approximately a couple months, two months, I would say.

Q. And what was the first tip, if any, that you got that there was connection to, if any?
A. I received a tip from Lieutenant Ernst about a possible suspect that worked at Kingswood Lanes. And his name was Ken Wyniemko.

Q. And did you follow up on that, and did it lead you anywhere else?
A. I followed up on that, and through my investigation was able to develop — find a former girlfriend of his.

Notice that there is no direct reference as to when the tip was passed on and when the tip was received. Lieutenant Ernst certainly implied he received the tip and passed it on immediately. And Detective Marlatt certainly implied that he promptly acted on the tip when he received it. One of the statements has to be incorrect.

There are two possibilities regarding the delay in the following up of the anonymous phone tip on Kenny. Either Lieutenant Ernst sat on the tip for two months or Lieutenant Ernst passed the tip to Detective Marlatt in a timely fashion and Marlatt ignored the tip for two months.

Regardless, it was sloppy police work and Mr. Markowski failed to take advantage.

Mr. Markowski's cross-examination of Detective Marlatt was brief, again less than two minutes in duration. He established the fact that Detective Marlatt had received several anonymous tips that were ignored. He did not pursue the reasons why the police failed to pursue many of the numerous leads. He did not question the delay of two months before they pursued the tip on Kenny.

This is the type of police ineptness that, if brought to the jury's attention, could have shed doubt on two of the prosecution's witnesses. What kind of investigation was conducted when a tip that proved to be credible in the eyes of the police was ignored by them for two months?

How would Lieutenant Ernst explain the delay if he were recalled to the stand and had to answer the following hardline questions from Mr. Markowski?
- What is purpose of placing a composite of a suspect in the local newspapers?
- Did you pass the anonymous tip on Mr. Wyniemko to Detective Marlatt immediately?
- How can you explain the two-month delay in the follow-up?
- Is this department's standard procedure in the investigation of a high-profile case such as this horrific rape, to not instantly forward tips to the investigating officer or to not follow-up on leads immediately?

INCIDENT NO. 94-17059

249

CLINTON TOWNSHIP
POLICE DEPARTMENT

CASE INVESTIGATION
WORK REPORT

5-11 1410
Tip on C.S.C. case
Called Refused to give name
He said he saw the picture in the
Macomb Jt Chronicle, said it looks like
Ken Wynemko counter man from Kingwood Lanes
M-97 & Hall and at Rose Bowl Lanes M-57
and Martin

Dodge minivan wood panel on side. GKZ G2K
Damage on passenger side

Check at Kingswood Lanes about other
Bowling Alley
Catharine says it matches the
description. Police said to
Cathy Op looked

Police Report on the anonymous tip

What would Detective Marlatt say to the delay in the follow-up of the tip if Lieutenant Ernst did indeed pass it to Detective Marlatt in a timely period? Could Detective Marlatt explain the reason why he sat on it for two months? He alluded several times to the fact that they had no leads so they couldn't have been so busy with the investigation to not follow-up on this tip.

Here is another interesting fact regarding Detective Marlatt's testimony. Consider his following statement.

> *We didn't have physical evidence from the scene. We didn't have that much to go on to lead us to a suspect.*

Actually, there was a great deal of forensic evidence recovered at the crime scene, including the casts from the footprints. Mr. Markowski never questioned that statement either.

That was the last witness called that day.

Judge Schwartz reminded the jury to not read or listen to any coverage regarding the case.

Court was adjourned at 5:00 pm.

Kenny remembers the evening after he was identified by the victim in court.

> *I sat in my bunk in shock. I cried. All these lies. All these accusations. When I was identified, I saw the look on the jurors' faces. It was a look I will never forget. They thought*

me evil, someone who had to be destroyed. I just couldn't stop thinking about my parents and what this was doing to them.

DAY 4: THURSDAY, NOVEMBER 3, 1994

Court was reconvened at 1:55 pm.

Mr. Markowski submitted a motion to disallow the hearsay testimony of Linda Bradley, the girlfriend of Wayne Burkhardt, an inmate at the Macomb Correctional Facility when Kenny was imprisoned. Ms. Bradley would have testified that Kenny approached Mr. Burkhardt and asked that Burkhardt's girlfriend provide Kenny an alibi for the time of the attack. Judge Schwartz agreed and Kenny was spared the indignation of another lying witness.

Mr. Markowski also objected to the relevance of several pictures that the prosecution was going to submit into evidence. After a discussion, the pictures were not admitted.

The jury was seated and the first prosecution witness was called at 2:14 pm.

Steve Daybird

Steve Daybird, Hazel Park Raceway comptroller, took the stand. He verified that Kenny had won $1,127.50 on April 8, 1994. Daybird also verified that he had no record of Kenny signing for any winnings on April 29, 1994, or April 30, 1994.

Cathy Whitcher

The next witness was Kenny's former girlfriend, Cathy Whitcher.

Cathy and Kenny were living together in Kenny's home the night of the attack. They broke up soon after. Their relationship became so contentious that Cathy left messages on his phone, threatening to kill him and ruin his life. The tape went missing during the Clinton Township Police Department's search of Kenny's home.

Kenny had relayed information about the messages on the tapes to Mr. Markowski. The recordings could have been used to damage the credibility of Ms. Whitcher during cross-examination. If the police hid the fact they removed the answering machine tape from Kenny's home, the court could have interpreted this as failure to disclose exculpatory evidence. Mr. Markowski never brought it up.

Ms. Whitcher testified to Kenny's sexual proclivities. Ms. Davis's intent was to depict these sexual acts as similar to the acts committed in the rape. Ms. Whitcher's testimony was slanted to make Kenny out to be a bad guy. She testified that she was never comfortable with Kenny's sexual demands and she confirmed she filed a restraining order on Kenny shortly after their breakup. She could not provide Kenny an alibi because she was asleep during the time Ms. Klug was raped.

Mr. Markowski's cross-examination of Ms. Whitcher was designed to expose doubts on her recollection of the timetable of events on the night in question and to elicit testimony from Ms. Whitcher that any sex act with Kenny was consensual. It was ineffective.

Mr. Markowski never questioned Ms. Whitcher about the threats she left on Kenny's answering machine. He did not demonstrate to the jury the animosity felt by Ms. Whitcher towards the defendant.

Kenny sat in disbelief at what he was hearing.

> *I couldn't believe her testimony. She described our time together like it was hell and I forced her to . . . (Kenny's voice trailed off.) I just shook my head as I was listening to someone who I still cared about.*

It was like I was in the middle of a ring of people and I was getting sucker punched and blindsided back and forth. Everyone was lying and I couldn't do a damn thing about it. The victim identifies me. Cathy tears apart our relationship. And that lying bastard, McCormick, was up next.

One thing I didn't understand. I had told Markowski that Cathy had left threatening messages on my phone. I had told him that the cops had taken the tape from my home. He never brought this up in Cathy's cross or during the trial. It didn't make any sense to me.

Glenn McCormick

Mr. McCormick was the infamous jailhouse snitch. He testified Kenny confessed to committing the crime when the two of them were together in a cell at the Macomb County Jail.

Mr. McCormick admitted that he was getting a great deal for his testimony, the "deal of the century," as Ms. Davis put it. He was currently charged with several felonies: Unarmed Robbery, Assisting and Obstructing, and Habitual Fourth (criminal being charged with his fourth felony). His testimony was extremely self-serving, avoiding 30-50 years of incarceration. He was given the option to either testify accordingly or "he would never see the light of day." He received a one-year sentence with time served that hinged on his performance in court.

Mr. McCormick had details of the crime that he alleged were given him by Kenny. Kenny was bewildered as to how he got them because Kenny never knew them himself. Here is an excerpt of Mr. McCormick's testimony.

Q. Okay. And did it proceed from there, did you ask him questions, did he volunteer—
A. Yes, I did ask him questions. I asked him, oh, well, if you didn't do, why are you here then. Then I asked him were you in a line-up, he said, yes. And — but prior to this, he

told me that the assailant was wearing a mask. Now, when I asked him about the line-up, I said, were you picked out of the line-up? He said, yes. And I thought to myself, that was strange. Well, if this assailant was wearing a mask and how did you get picked out of a line-up which didn't make sense to me.

Q. Okay. And did he volunteer any information at that point to you?
A. Other than that, no, that he wasn't the person that did it. And it wasn't until prior a couple days later, until he kept talking about it to the point where I just got sick and tired of hearing what he had to say. And I asked him, I said, well, did you do this or what? And he said, yeah, but they ain't not got shit.

Q. He said yes but they didn't have shit?
A. Exactly.

Q. And did you talk to him about that comment? What did you mean by that?
A. Yes. I said, well, if they picked you out of a line-up and they don't have anything against you, and he said, well, I got rid of everything.

Q. And did he tell you what he got rid of?
A. Handcuffs and a pair of gloves, latex gloves. And that's basically it.

Q. Did he give you any other facts in relationship to the charges that were against him?
A. What do you mean?

Q. Did he tell you what he did to the person?

A. Oh, that he handcuffed her behind her back, that he had gagged her mouth with something or whatever, and that he had intercourse with the woman.

Q. Did he indicate i [sic] he just did one sexual act or —
A. No, he — more than one.

Mr. Markowski's cross-examination established the fact that Mr. McCormick had been convicted of a long list of felonies: three counts of Medicaid Fraud, Health Insurance Fraud, Attempted Uttering and Publishing, Breaking and Entering, and Receiving Stolen Property. Mr. McCormick once again admitted he was using his testimony as a means to avoid a lengthy prison sentence and that his reduced one-year sentence depended on his testimony in court.

Kenny had this to say about McCormick's fabricated story.

I could tell McCormick's testimony was rehearsed. Anyone could tell he was lying and just trying to save his ass from jail. It burned me to just sit there and hear his lies. And I couldn't understand how he could have all those details to the rape, stuff that I didn't even know. Who else could he have got them from but the people trying to put me away?

Drilling a lifelong convict in a cross-examination about his obvious self-serving testimony would not have alienated the jury. Mr. Markowski needed to demonstrate that this unsympathetic witness was someone who had no problems giving false testimony if he could avoid long term jail time.

Mr. Markowski never insisted that Mr. McCormick was a "lifetime liar," as evidenced by his crimes. The old "if you have lied all your life, how can we believe you now?" question would have served Kenny well.

There was no direct accusation of Mr. McCormick lying about Kenny like he had done all his life. "Kenny never admitted anything to you. Did he? In fact, he never spoke to you about the crime and never gave you details of the crime because he didn't do it. Isn't that right?"

Mr. McCormick's testimony concluded Day 4 of the trial.

Court was adjourned at 4:12 pm.

DAY 5: FRIDAY, NOVEMBER 4, 1994

Court was reconvened at 11:12 am.

David Woodford

David Woodford was a Michigan State Police crime lab scientist, specializing in forensic serology. He obtained blood and hair samples from Kenny and tested them against evidence collected from the crime scene and from the rape kit. Based on blood type and hair samples tests, there was absolutely no scientific proof that Kenny was at the scene. At no time during Mr. Woodford's testimony does the term "DNA" appear.

According to the prosecution, Kenny had been so careful in the three-hour rape, that he had successfully avoided leaving any forensic evidence. Since the blood type of the semen samples matched that of the husband's, the prosecution claimed that it had to be his. This assumption prevailed for the rest of the trial despite the fact the husband had been out of town for over a week prior to the rape and the bedroom (crime scene) had been cleaned by Ms. Klug's mother-in-law hours before the attack. These conflicts were never touched on by Mr. Markowski during the trial until his summation.

Here is an excerpt from Mr. Woodford's testimony regarding the tests he conducted on the forensic evidence.

Q. What other kind of analysis did you do in regard to this particular case?
A. I was also submitted a multi colored robe. I was also submitted some pair of panties, a silk belt, two pairs of panty hose, some piece of some nylon hose, bed sheets, hairs collected off the bed sheets, cigarette butts, two pillows and pillow cases, one nylon, part of a telephone, the base part. And that pretty much was it for that, that one instance when they brought in this evidence.

Q. And did you do any analysis on those items that you received?
A. Yes, I did.

Q. And what kind of analysis did you do?
A. I looked at the fitted sheet and I did find semen located on the fitted sheet. In fact, there was quite a bit of it. Also a pubic hair was found in a pair of panties. And I looked at a cigarette butt that indicated the presence of saliva. And then that was the extent of my preliminary examination of the evidence that originally came in.

Woodford indicated that he requested and received blood samples from potential suspects.

Q. Okay. And did you, after receiving those items, then do an analysis and comparisons?
A. Yes I did.

Q. And what are your findings?
A. I found out that Diane was blood A, excuse me, Diane was blood type O, Shawn (the victim's husband) was blood type

A, and Kenny was blood type O. . . . I went ahead and I checked out the semen stains. I'm finding blood type A, which means that these could not have originated from Ken Wyniemko because he's blood type O.

Q. And were you able to establish whether they originated from Shawn Klug?
A. Based on blood typing, it looks like they could have come from Shawn Klug.

Mr. Woodford testified that blood type tests on hair found at the crime scene and hair samples taken from Kenny were compared and there was no link to Kenny. Tests on the saliva from the cigarette were inconclusive.

Mr. Markowki's cross-examination was short, less than two minutes. He never questioned Mr. Woodford on the reason why there weren't any forensic tests conducted on the footprints found at the scene, especially since the Clinton Township Police Department believed from the beginning of the investigation that the footprints belonged to the assailant. At no time did he ask for the reasons why DNA testing was not conducted and what positive conclusions DNA testing could have offered.

DNA had been used to convict in the United States beginning in 1988, and to exonerate starting in 1989. In 1990, Virginia was the first state to make it mandatory that convicted felons provide a DNA sample. Other states followed. DNA was recognized in Michigan as an acceptable source of evidence since 1991, three years prior to Kenny's case.

While DNA was not as widely used in 1994 as it is today, it was available, especially for cases like Kenny's where there was so much forensic evidence present. Once the blood type tests ruled Kenny out, the prosecution and the police decided it wasn't necessary to perform any DNA testing.

A good lawyer is always hesitant to ask a question when he or she does not know the answer. One can assume that Mr. Markowski's lack of preparation was partly to blame for some of the shortcomings.

It made no sense as to why Mr. Markowski did not pursue the DNA angle. Since the blood type did not match Kenny, identification of the source of the forensic evidence could never have implicated him. The prosecution was allowed to continuously promote the headshaking theory that the source of all the tested evidence was the victim's husband. Mr. Markowski never challenged it. He did not demand a jury instruction stating that the lack of such evidence testing (DNA) should be taken against the prosecution and in favor of the defense.

A defense attorney had every right to demand DNA testing on any forensic evidence by the Michigan State Crime Lab or by an outside testing facility. There is no court record of Mr. Peppler or Mr. Markowski ever requesting such a test.

Here are two questions that could have been used to discredit the prosecution's sole forensic witness and shed a cloud of suspicion on the actions of the police in the investigation.
- Can you say for certain that the forensic evidence left at the scene is positively that of Mr. Klug as the prosecution is claiming?
- There were footprints at the scene, in the victim's bedroom and outside the spare bedroom window where it is accepted the perpetrator was lurking. In your expert opinion as a forensic scientist, wouldn't it make sense to have the footprints evidence analyzed and compared to the shoe size of the defendant? The tread marks of the shoes themselves? If not, why not?

Here are questions Mr. Markowski did not ask Mr. Woodford in an attempt to establish that DNA testing should have been pursued.
- Isn't DNA testing a more absolute method of ascertaining the source of the samples from the crime scene and rape kit as opposed to blood-type testing?
- Why did you not perform a DNA test on the forensic evidence from the crime scene and from the rape kit? Were you instructed to not run a DNA test? Who, specifically, instructed you to not run DNA test on the evidence?
- Did you avoid testing for DNA once the blood tests indicated the defendant was not the source of the forensic evidence?
- If the State of Michigan does not have the technology to run a DNA test with the forensic samples from this crime, is there another agency that uses a more sophisticated methodology that might be able to run a DNA test?

Clinton Township Police Department Detective Sergeant Thomas Ostin

Detective Ostin was the primary officer in charge. He testified that the investigation of Kenny started with the anonymous tip. He related the various interviews, lineup identification, residence search, and arrest. He also testified to the events leading up to Glenn McCormick becoming the jailhouse snitch, starting with a phone call from Wayne Burkhardt, another inmate from Macomb County Jail.

Detective Ostin described the search of Kenny's residence and the items collected. There was no mention of the confiscation of Kenny's answering machine tapes.

Detective Ostin stressed in his testimony that Kenny seemed very nervous and afraid at the booking after he was arrested.

In cross-examination, Mr. Markowski had Detective Ostin admit that anyone arrested for a serious crime such as rape would be nervous and afraid, whether he was guilty or innocent.

Mr. Markowski never questioned Detective Ostin how Ms. Klug could have identified Kenny as her assailant when Kenny did not remotely resemble descriptions she had made throughout the investigation. Mr. Markowski did not press Detective Ostin as to why the footprints were never analyzed and compared to Kenny's shoe size. He never asked him if any answering machine tapes were removed from Kenny's residence, why DNA analysis was not performed on the forensic evidence, and why numerous tips were never followed up on, including the tip on Kenny which sat in the police department office for over two months.

Questions never asked Detective Ostin, the officer in charge of the investigation.
- Casts were taken of several footprints at the crime scene in the bedroom and outside the spare bedroom window where the perpetrator lurked. Why weren't the footprints analyzed by the Forensics Department? Do you know the shoe size of the prints found at the scene in relation to the defendant's shoe size? Do you know if they match the tread marks of any of the defendant's shoes?
- Did you ever remove answering machine tapes from Mr. Wyniemko's residence when you executed a search warrant and not notify defense counsel?
- The prosecution is claiming the source of semen stains found at the crime scene was the victim's husband. That means the bed sheets had not been changed for over a week since her husband left, correct?
- Can you explain why the anonymous tip on Mr. Wyniemko sat for over two months before anyone in the investigation followed up on it?

The following questions would have been especially damaging if Mr. Markowski had established the importance of DNA testing when cross-examining Mr. Woodford, the forensic expert.

- The prosecution's expert forensic evidence witness testified that a DNA analysis is a more thorough and absolute form of testing for the source of the forensic evidence found at the crime scene and in the rape kit. Don't you agree?
- If that is true, why was DNA testing never conducted?
- If the Michigan State Crime Lab was unable to perform the test, why wouldn't the evidence have been sent out to a more sophisticated facility?
- Without conducting DNA testing, can you say for sure that semen samples came from the victim's husband and not an unidentified perpetrator?
- Is it a common practice for the Clinton Township Police Department to have DNA testing conducted in a case such as this?
- With a man's future on the line, are we supposed to just *assume* the source of the forensic samples? Especially when that alleged source was absent from the scene for over a week?
- Did the Clinton Township Police Department decide to not pursue DNA testing of the forensic evidence because the blood type did not match Mr. Wyniemko's blood type? Were they actually interested in finding out the truth or just in the conviction of Kenneth Wyniemko?
- Doesn't it seem that, with the police department's reluctance to use DNA testing, someone may think the police and prosecution are hiding something?

The prosecution rested after Detective Ostin's testimony.

Mr. Markowski moved for a Directed Verdict of Not Guilty at the close of the prosecution's case. His motion requested the removal of the count of Armed Robbery and several instances of the CSC charges. Judge Schwartz ruled against dismissing the charge of Armed Robbery, but he did vacate two counts of CSC.

Mr. Markowski received word of a death in the family and court was adjourned at 2:54 pm.

DAY 6: MONDAY, NOVEMBER 7, 1994

Court was reconvened at 1:40 pm.

Mr. Markowski presented his case. Kenny was the only defense witness called to testify.

Ken Wyniemko's Testimony
Before Kenny took the stand, Mr. Markowski and Judge Schwartz made it clear to the jury that Kenny did not have to testify and that defense counsel had recommended against him taking the stand. Kenny emphatically asserted that it was he who insisted on telling his side, in direct conflict with his defense counsel's advisement.

In Mr. Markowski's examination, Kenny went through, step-by-step, what he had done the night of the attack. Kenny emphasized the he had *never* smoked.

Kenny also testified that he had a large, deep scar on his knee and that there was no way Ms. Klug would not have seen it if he had been her assailant. It was astounding that this had never been brought up since Ms. Klug had seen her attacker without clothes from the waist down throughout the attack. Once again, Mr. Markowski dropped the ball by not establishing the presence of the scar during Ms. Klug's cross-examination. If Ms. Klug had seen her attacker in a state of undress, she could not have missed the scar on Kenny's knee. It was only through Kenny's insistence at testifying that this was ever mentioned.

Kenny's testimony did not refute the jailhouse snitch's accounts of Kenny's admission of guilt. It certainly had to be puzzling to the jury.

Kenny was asked about its omission.

> *I don't know why Markowski never brought up McCormick's testimony. But what am I going to do on the stand? Tell him to ask me about McCormick? Some of the things he did made absolutely no sense. And there were a lot of things that he should have done but didn't.*

During his testimony, Kenny emphatically denied having anything to do with the attack.

> *Q. Ken, you sat through this trial for several days now, and there's been some horrendous testimony. I'm going to ask you, did you at any time break into Diane Klug's home?*
> *A. Absolutely not.*
>
> *Q. Did you at any time sexually assault an individual by the name of Diane Klug?*
> *A. Absolutely not.*
>
> *Q. Did you at any time take money and/or rob an individual by the name of Diane Klug?*
> *A. Absolutely not.*
>
> *Q. When you were arrested and informed regarding these charges, how did you feel? What was going through you head?*
> *A. I was scared to death. I was literally scared to death. I was shaking in my shoes.*

Q. You heard the testimony of the Police Officer Ostin regarding his impression of you when you were at the police station and in your booking process, correct?
A. Yes, I have.

Q. At that time, what was going through your mind?
A. I thought that the charges, to me, it seemed like a bad dream. I thought the charges were absurd. That's just – I'm just not capable of doing anything like that.

Q. Did you inform Detective Ostin of your feelings?
A. Yes, I did, almost immediately.

Q. What's going through your mind right now?
A. Again, I'm — I'm scared. I'm scared because I've been accused of something that I did not do, and I know it could affect the rest of my life.

Q. Well, how has it affected your life so far?
A. It's just about ruined my life, if it hasn't ruined it already. Not only mine, the rest of my family. I don't know about my job.

Cross-Examination

Ms. Davis's cross-examination didn't rattle Kenny. He continued to deny any involvement in the crime and he had no idea why he had been identified. Ms. Davis tried to get Kenny to admit he knew Diane Klug, another fact he vehemently refuted.

Kenny insisted that any sexual act with Cathy, his former girlfriend, was consensual. Ms. Davis tried to discredit Kenny's testimony regarding Ms. Whitcher.

> *Q. And yet you also want that jury to believe that she talked to you long enough to tell you that she wanted to kill you and she was going to ruin your life?*
> *A. She did. She left – as a matter of fact, she left two messages on my machine, on my answering machine, saying that she was going to kill me.*
>
> *Q. And you have those tapes obviously with you?*
> *A. Sergeant Ostin took the tapes when he was in my house.*

Ms. Davis seemed taken off guard. Here was Kenny, under oath, accusing the Clinton Township Police Department of taking the tapes from his home, and not disclosing those tapes as evidence. Mr. Markowski did nothing. He didn't recall Ms. Whitcher to get her to admit leaving the threatening messages. He didn't question Detective Ostin about the missing tapes. Withholding exculpatory evidence can be grounds for an appeal and Mr. Markowski chose not to pursue it even when Kenny accused the investigating detective in sworn testimony before the court.

Ms. Davis closed with a spirited attack on Kenny and his motives for the rape.

> *Q. The truth of the matter is that you saw Diane Klug with her husband, and you thought she was beautiful, and the night you – because you were angry with Cathy Whitcher, you decided to get even, and you went to Diane's Klug's house. You knew Shawn Klug was gone because it was common knowledge in the bowling alley.*
> *A. I did not know.*
>
> *Q. You went to her house, sir, and then you broke in and you raped her over and over again, didn't you?*
> *A. No, I did not.*

Q. No, you did not.
A. That's correct, I did not.

Q. Can you explain why she picked you out as being the man that raped her?
A. I have no idea, ma'am.

Q. I have no idea.
A. No, I don't.

Q. Six individuals, she never seen you before in her life except the night you raped her, and she pointed to you and she said that man raped me. And you have no idea why?
A. No, I don't.

Q. It is because you did it, isn't it, Mr. Wyniemko?
A. I did not rape Diane Klug.

The prosecution hammered away relentlessly at Kenny in her cross-examination. Mr. Markowski never engaged in any aggressive questioning during any of his cross-examinations.

Even though Kenny and his attorney never went over Kenny's testimony and what questions could be asked in his cross-examination, when Kenny heard all the lies being told throughout the trial, he couldn't take it. He had to tell his side.

Markowski told me that I should not testify. He told me this a couple times when we took a break. I said, "What are you talking about?"

Especially after the first couple days of the trial where everybody that got on the stand, every witness, had lied, with the exception of the lab technician! That lab technician and the Comptroller from Hazel Park were the only ones who told the truth.

I told Markowski, "I'm not going to sit here and listen to these people lie about me and not get up and say what I have to say."

And he told me, he said, "Kenny, if you take the stand, Linda Davis will rip you a new asshole."

I said, "Al, how could she possibly rip me a new asshole when I didn't do anything? I'm not afraid of her. I'm not afraid of anybody. And I'm sure as hell not going to sit here and not take the stand in my defense."

He said, "I think you're making a mistake."

He was wrong. Linda Davis never intimidated me. And one reason I was glad I took the stand was there was the question that Ms. Davis asked me about Cathy's threatening messages she left on my phone.

When I told Linda Davis that Cathy had threatened to kill me, Davis started laughing and said, "I suppose, Mr. Wyniemko, that you can prove that?"

I said, "Yes I can."

She said, "How are you going to do that?"

I told her that Cathy left a message on my answering machine that if I didn't stop calling her mom to drop off her clothes that she was going to kill me.

She said, "Cathy left that on your machine, right?"

I said, "Yes she did."

Then Linda Davis got real arrogant and said, "I suppose you kept that tape, right?"

I said, "Yes. I did, but it is in possession of Detective Ostin, because he took it when he searched my house."

Then she dropped that line of questioning right away.

And Markowski never picked up on that. Some of this stuff is so ridiculous people are going to think we are making it up.

Mr. Markowski had several options at this point in regards to the answering machine tape. None of which he employed.
- Recall Ms. Whitcher and discredit her testimony like he should have in his original cross-examination.
- Recall Detective Ostin and have him explain why he took the tapes and did not declare exculpatory evidence.
- Make a motion for an adjournment so that the prosecution can produce the tapes so that they can be played in court.
- Make a motion to have the prosecution admit the contents of the tape, that Ms. Whitcher did indeed leave threatening calls to Kenny to the effect of, "I will kill you" and "I will ruin your life" on several occasions.
- Make a statement for the court record that the defendant's case was severely damaged when it did not have the tape available to discredit Ms. Whitcher.
- Make a motion for a specific jury instruction that the failure to produce the tape must be construed against the prosecution and for the defense.

When Kenny was finished with his testimony, the defense rested.

Closing arguments followed.

Closing Argument – Prosecutor Linda Davis

Ms. Davis's Closing Argument described the "elements" of the case. She went through each charge, graphically detailing each act once again, explaining to the jury why each one was legitimately related to the charges stemming from the attack. It was the third time the jury had heard Diane Klug's ordeal — blow by blow, violation by violation, indignity by indignity.

Ms. Davis concentrated on the testimony of Diane Klug, pointing out how hard it was for her to tell 14 strangers details of her horrific experience. She pointed out that it was no coincidence that Ms. Klug and her husband bowled at the same bowling alley where Mr.

Wyniemko worked, providing the link between Kenny and Diane. Then she concentrated on Ms. Klug's identification of Kenny.

> *Well, Diane tilted her head back and when he raised that mask on one occasion, Diane saw his face. She saw his face. . . .*

> *How do you know that it was Mr. Wyniemko that did it? Number one, you know pure and simple it was him because Diane Klug told you it was. She picked him out of a line up [sic] of six individuals. . . .*

> *People, there is no doubt; there is no doubt in Diane Klug's mind that this is the man that raped her. I asked her how sure are you that this man is the man that entered your home on April 30th. And Diane Klug said I am one hundred percent, one hundred percent sure that it is him.*

Ms. Davis covered the testimony of Cathy Whitcher, Kenny's former girlfriend. She claimed the details of sex acts with Mr. Wyniemko were similar to the acts forced on Ms. Klug by her attacker.

Ms. Davis reviewed the testimony of Glenn McCormick, the jailhouse snitch. She admitted his testimony is suspect and certainly self-serving. She claimed that here is a reason to believe him. Mr. McCormick had details to the crime that only the victim, the police, and the suspect were privy to.

> *He (McCormick) didn't tell some outlandish story. He had bits and pieces of — of what occurred. And who did he say gave him those bits and pieces, that man did, that man did.*

The prosecutor claimed that the money Kenny said he won at the racetrack was really the cash he took from the crime scene. Her insertion of Kenny's alleged use of cocaine was both prejudicial and irrelevant, just like it was throughout the trial.

> *And then low [sic] and behold, the night after this rape, he shows up for work the next day. And he's bragging about he's won money, twenty-five hundred dollars from a lottery to one person, race track to another person, and yet you've got absolute evidence that he never won from either one of those places during the relevant period of time. So, now he's got the money on top of all of the other evidence. He used an inhaler. We know he sniffs cocaine. Every single bit of possible evidence points to Mr. Wyniemko.*

Ms. Davis concluded her summation.

> *People, there is no doubt in this case that Diane Klug has told you her horrendous story about sexual abuse that occurred on April 30 in her home in Clinton Township in the County of Macomb. She has told you that she was violated in a way that no one, no one should ever have to repeat to 14 strangers. She told you a story of sexual abuse of violation of her home and of her body, and she told you that Kenneth Wyniemko is the man that violated her. She has no doubt and no doubt that when you go into that jury room and you review the evidence and review it carefully and then you will come back and you will tell this man that in our society that you cannot enter somebody's home and take away their life the way he took away Diane's. You tell him that he is guilty of B&E. You tell him that he is guilty of 15 counts of criminal sexual conduct in the first degree. You tell him that he is guilty of Armed Robbery, and then you go home and you feel very comfortable with that decision. Thank you.*

Closing Argument – Defense Attorney Albert Markowski

Mr. Markowski asked the jury to remember they had sworn to listen to the testimony and make a common sense decision on the verdict. He urged them to not act on emotion and entreated them to come up with a verdict based on the evidence and testimony presented. He reminded them that Kenny had steadfastly denied any involvement in the attack on Ms. Klug.

He then meticulously tried to take apart the prosecuting attorney's case. Here are excerpts of Mr. Markowski remarks regarding the victim's testimony.

- He questioned why there was no follow-up on numerous tips.
- He questioned why a positive piece of physical identification, Ms. Klug's description of her attacker having a cleft chin, was ignored and omitted from the composite of the suspect.
- He questioned the victim's eyewitness identification of Kenny after telling the officers that she could not help them and that she never saw the attacker's whole face.
- He pointed out that none of the physical evidence at the scene could be attributed to Kenny.
- He questioned why the footprints found at the scene were never forensically examined and compared to the shoe size of the defendant and attempted to match the soles of the defendant's shoes.
- He ridiculed the testimony of the jailhouse snitch as self-serving and that of a habitual liar.
- He dismissed the testimony of Ms. Whitcher as that of a jilted ex-lover.
- He lauded Kenny for taking the witness stand and declaring he is innocent.
- In conclusion, he pointed out that it is the prosecutor's duty to prove that Kenny was the assailant. He reiterated that none of the physical evidence matches that of Kenny's and concluded that the two main witness testimonies (that of the victim and the jailhouse snitch) are in question.

Here are excerpts of Mr. Markowski's remarks regarding Mr. McCormick's testimony.

All I can tell you is that what's in the record and the record is that Diane Klug by her own statements said she did not see the perpetrator because of the fact he had the mask on, she had nylons on, she had panties over her eyes.

Mr. Markowski labelled Ms. Klug's identification of Kenny as a mistake referencing her police statements that she never saw her attacker's face.

Here are excerpts of Mr. Markowski's remarks regarding the victim's testimony.

The testimony of Mr. McCormick, boy, here we have, ladies and gentlemen, a felon. He admitted it. He didn't hide it. Who got, Ms. Davis indicated, got the deal of the century to come in here to give you a story. . . . Ladies and gentlemen, he was facing life imprisonment or any number of years, life. He was a young man. What did he get for giving the story? One year. He's been through this before, ladies and gentlemen. Mr. McCormick can do a year lying on his back and wouldn't even think anything about it. All his past crimes were crimes that deal with honesty. Medicaid fraud. Writing bad checks. He's a liar. He was a liar with a purpose and a big purpose. . . . McCormick is facing life in prison. Boy, he'd do anything for a deal.

Mr. Markowski concluded his Closing Argument.

So, we have, outside of the testimony of Diane Klug, and you have to weigh her testimony however you want based on what was presented for you and her ability for identification. We have a building scenario where we don't have nothing, then all of a sudden we got a case that's built by a jilted girlfriend or a girlfriend that takes off and went back with her husband, ex-husband, and all the time she's living with Mr. Wyniemko. By a felon who's a liar and got a great deal. And they say believe us. Ken did it. You have too many unanswered questions, ladies and gentlemen of the jury. You should have too many unanswered questions at this time. Again, it is not my job. Those questions should have been addressed and/or answered by the People, by the government to you.

Ladies and gentlemen, I told you twice already that I do not envy your position. However, because of the numerous counts, if there is that doubt in your mind, and you determine it is a reasonable doubt, I'm going to tell you right out, you will not come out with a very popular decision of not guilty. But ladies and gentlemen, as I told you in the opening, that that's your duty, that's your obligation, you swore to do that. We're not here to win a popularity contest. If you feel in your heart that there's too many questions, Mr. Wyniemko did not do this thing, you have to come up with the unpopular decision, and that decision is not guilty. And I think based on all the testimony that has been presented here, that has to be your unanimous verdict on each and every one of the counts alleged in this Complaint. And I ask you, after you go into your deliberation room there, to weigh all the evidence, and I'm confident that you will come back a verdict of not guilty on each and every one of the counts alleged in the Complaint. And thank you for your time.

Mr. Markowski's Closing Argument addressed points that should have been used to discredit just about every one of the prosecution's witnesses during cross-examination. It wasn't enough to mention them in closing. It would have been more effective to hammer away with them throughout the trial and reinforce them in closing. It's puzzling this never happened, especially since his Closing Argument proved he thought of them.

Prosecution Rebuttal Argument
Ms. Davis refuted many of Mr. Markowski's claims. The evidence and testimony when taken as a whole indicates Kenny did indeed rape and torture Ms. Klug. She claimed that defense counsel was not arguing facts or law, instead trying to confuse the jury about the facts and testimony presented. Ms. Davis said there is no doubt Kenny is the rapist because Ms. Klug positively identified him as her attacker.

> *People, you heard a story that no one should have to come into this court room and tell you. Diane Klug trusted you with her security and her safety. She trusted you with a horrendous story of how she was violated in her home and in her body on repeated occasions. She told you a story that no human being should ever, ever have to tell. And she told you that Ken Wyniemko is the man that did that to her. You tell him that his flimsy excuse and his attempts to conceal evidence did not work. You tell him that you don't believe because he poured Pepsi down her mouth that there was no evidence left behind. You tell him he goofed up when he lifted that mask up and he showed Diane Klug his face. People, you tell this man that he's guilty of the crimes he's been charged with, and tell him that with conviction and with a feeling in your heart that will allow you to go home tonight and sleep well. Thank you.*

Judge Schwartz gave the jury members their final instructions and they were excused to start deliberations. It was 4:00 pm. When the jury could not come to a decision by 6:00 pm, they were called back to court and asked if they were close to a verdict.

Leonard Devine, jury foreperson, told the court that the jury needed another day of deliberations.

> MR. DEVINE: I'm not so sure we're that close, Your Honor. I think maybe come back Wednesday would be the best thing.

The jury was given instructions to not discuss the case with anyone and court was adjourned.

The Jury's State of Mind

Kenny's fate was now in the hands of the jury.

Did the prosecution prove its case? To find Kenny guilty, the jury had to believe Diane Klug correctly identified Kenny as her attacker. They didn't have to believe the jailhouse snitch. They had to believe a three-hour rape could occur with no physical evidence left at the scene and the prosecution's theory that the forensic evidence had to be that of the husband.

How do they justify the cigarette butt at the crime scene? Do they give the police a pass on never testing the footprints? How do they reconcile the marked differences between the attacker described in Ms. Klug's numerous statements and that of Kenny? It all came down to convicting Kenny primarily on the victim's identification.

Did Mr. Markowski raise enough reasonable doubt in his summation? Did the jury members have enough unanswered (and unasked) questions to acquit Kenny?

For a not guilty verdict, the jury had to question the lack of forensic evidence tied to Kenny. They had to consider the police investigation shoddy. They had to disbelieve the jailhouse snitch's testimony. They had to have an issue with the differences in the physical description of the assailant in Ms. Klug's numerous statements and that of Kenny. But, more importantly, they had to tell

Ms. Klug that she made a mistake in her identification. Rendering a not guilty decision would have been a most unpopular verdict.

DAY 7: WEDNESDAY, NOVEMBER 9, 1994

Court was reconvened on Wednesday, November 9, 1994, at 11:00 am.

The Jury Verdict

Judge Schwartz asked the jury foreman if a verdict had been reached. It had. Kenny was ordered to stand for its reading. The court clerk went over each charge and verdict.

> *THE CLERK: The People of the State of Michigan versus Kenneth Wyniemko. We, The Jury, make the following findings of fact.*
>
> *Count 1 Breaking and Entering Occupied Dwelling with Intent to commit a felony, guilty;*
>
> *Count 2 Criminal Sexual Conduct First Degree penile/vaginal, guilty;*
>
> *Count 3 Criminal Sexual Conduct First Degree Digital/Anal, guilty. . . .*

The jury verdict was guilty on all 17 felony counts, including the two CSC charges previously dismissed by Judge Schwartz, another strange occurrence at Kenny's trial. Each member of the jury was polled individually. They all affirmed the guilty verdict.

Judge Schwartz thanked the jury for their service and excused them. It was 11:10 am.

The next order of business was to set a sentencing date. Here is an excerpt from the trial transcript.

> THE COURT: *Madam Clerk, can you give us a date, please?*
>
> THE CLERK: *Friday, December the 16th, 1994, at 8:30 am.*
>
> THE COURT: *Friday, December the 16th, 1994, at 8:30. Please be here at 8:30 a.m.*

Kenny remembers the guilty verdict.

> *At that minute, it felt like somebody hit me in the stomach. All I could see was fog. It was just like there was nothing there. Just fog. It may sound stupid, but that's exactly what I felt. I said that this can't be. I am innocent.*
>
> *For a split second, I thought I was dead. Then I heard my dad screaming because he was sitting right behind me. He kept saying, "No! No! He didn't do it. My son didn't do it."*
>
> *And that kind of snapped me back to reality.*
>
> *He was crying and he kept shouting, "My son didn't do this. My son didn't do this."*
>
> *I tried to settle him down. I said, "Dad. It'll be okay. I'll be okay." I felt so bad for him.*
>
> *Judge Schwartz talked about sentencing for a few minutes. The he said, "This concludes this case."*
>
> *That was it.*
>
> *Four cops came behind me and told me to stand up. This was taking place right in front of my dad. They had me stand up, handcuffed my hands behind my back, and took me back to the restroom with the small stalls with the metal fencing that I told you about before. I sat there by myself for maybe 30 minutes. I was in total shock. Then they took me*

> *downstairs to the basement in the courthouse and into the van and back to County Jail.*
>
> *I kept thinking that I would wake up and it would just be a dream. But we all know that didn't happen. I kept going over the trial and all that stuff in my head and couldn't understand any of it.*

Court was adjourned at 11:20 am.

SENTENCING HEARING—THURSDAY, DECEMBER 15, 1994

The trial transcript clearly specified that the Sentencing Hearing was scheduled for Friday, December 16, 1994. To Kenny's bewilderment, he was summoned to court for the Sentencing Hearing on Thursday, December 15, 1994. He had no prior notification regarding the date change. He received no explanation from the court or from his attorney. As a result, his family was not available to testify in his behalf.

> *The sentencing was set for the 16th and they brought me to court on the 15th. I was shocked. I was never, ever told of the switch. I know it was set for the 16th because I talked to my Dad and my brother, Tommy. They were all going to be there. I would have immediately called my family and friends. They were all willing to testify on my behalf.*
>
> *I had no choice but to sit there. Markowski had no explanation for me. He was there. He had to get the word that the date was changed. But I got nothing from him. To this day, I have absolutely no idea how they could do this.*
>
> *I remember the victim sent a letter that the prosecutor read to the court.*
>
> *I told the judge, "I didn't do this, I am a good hearted person, I've given people the shirt off my back to help them out, but I'm not this guy."*

> *They took me back to Macomb County Jail where I had to wait for my transfer to Jackson. I couldn't help but feel my life had ended. Forty fucking years!*

Sentencing commenced on Thursday, December 15, 1994, at 10:30 am.

"People versus Wyniemko," barked the clerk.

Prosecutor Linda Davis opened the hearing by briefly outlining the charges and informing the court that Diane Klug would like to submit a written statement.

Mr. Markowski implored the court for leniency, claiming his client's innocence.

Ms. Davis outlined the violence of the crime and asked for the judge to exceed the sentencing guidelines.

> *This was a rape that had considerable amount of thought, and I would liken it to a first degree murder case where premeditation is what pushes a second degree murder to mandatory life sentence with no possibility of parole. Diane Klug has had her life taken away from her as a result of this rape. That premeditation is an aggravating factor, the fact that this man stalked her and prepared to rape her and put her through two and a half hours of absolute torture is reason enough for this Court to exceed the guidelines.*

Ms. Davis closed by reading a statement from Ms. Klug. She related her unending terror, her inability to have a normal life. She then turned her thoughts to Kenny.

> *I'm 28 years old, and I can't go out or stay home alone. I'm not secure and have no place I feel safe anymore. Kenneth Wyniemko took my life away from me. He turned it upside*

> down. He made us sell our home. He violated me, my home, and my life.
>
> Kenneth Wyniemko doesn't respect the rights of others. He is a very disturbed individual for doing what he did to me. He does not deserve to ever see the real world again. He deserves to be put into eternal hell like he has put me in. Kenneth Wyniemko has scared me and my family forever. That will never change. Don't allow him to scare anyone else, please.
>
> Signed, sincerely Diane Klug

Kenny spoke to the court briefly on his behalf. Here is the transcript of what he said.

> First of all, Your Honor, I'm — I feel terrible. I feel very, very bad for what happened to the victim in this case. That shouldn't happen to anyone. It really shouldn't. But I — I didn't do this. It's not me. And I feel bad not only for her but for any other lady that would be attacked like that. There's no — there's no reason for that. For anyone to do that. But, again, this — I didn't do it. I can — God forbid — I could drop dead right now and I wouldn't be afraid to look Almighty God eye to eye like I am to you, because I'm innocent of this charge. I — and by putting me away, Your Honor, it's not going to take a criminal off the street. It's going to — someone will be out there laughing. It wasn't me. I swear to God it wasn't me.

Before Judge Schwartz rendered his sentence, he referenced letters he received on behalf of Ms. Klug. Each of them told of her pain and misery and the suffering of her friends and family. He was especially moved at the long lasting effects the attack had on the victim.

> *Sad commentary when the victim has to go through this. Change of personality because of what happened to her because of this brutal rape. Here this victim was a sincere, nice individual, outgoing, and the defendant has changed all of this. Not caring what he did. The defendant was convicted of 17 counts. Jury came back with guilty on all 17 counts.*

Judge Schwartz then delivered his decision. The Judgment of Sentence stated that Kenneth Wyniemko was guilty of Breaking and Entering, Armed Robbery, and 15 counts of Criminal Sexual Conduct in the First Degree. For Breaking and Entering, the sentence was 10 to 15 years. For Armed Robbery, the sentence was 15 to 25 years. When it came to the 15 counts of Criminal Sexual Conduct, the judge threw the book at Kenny, sentencing him to 40 to 60 years. His sentences were to run concurrently. Judge Schwartz far exceeded Michigan's sentencing guidelines.

> *Criminal Sexual Conduct First Degree, it is the sentence of this Court that the defendant be committed to the custody of the Michigan Department of Corrections for a period of 40 to 60 years. No credit for time served. The Court has exceeded the guidelines in this matter. The guidelines are 120 to 300 months. For the following reasons: Number one, for the numerous times that the defendant raped the victim. Number two, for and on behalf of the safety of the community. Three, other incidence [sic] of stalking against women. Four, premeditation, preparation to rape the victim, what he did. It was a brutal rape . . . . Number five, the numerous times he raped her and tortured her. Number six, defendant's failure to admit culpability or remorse. And number seven, the seriousness of this offense. All these shall be concurred; that is, all these sentences shall be concurrent.*

When the judge imposed sentence, Kenny no longer was Ken Wyniemko. He didn't need his driver's license or his social security card. He would become prisoner A240889, a dangerous felon, a rapist, a ward of the Michigan Department of Corrections.

POST-TRIAL THOUGHTS

The prosecution's case was based on questionable victim identification, the self-serving testimony of a jailhouse snitch, and the testimony of a vengeful ex-girlfriend. Furthermore, when forensic test results eliminated Kenny from the crime scene, the prosecutor put a spin on the findings that defied logic. Yet, Kenny was convicted on all counts.

Defense Attorney

If Kenny was looking for a reason as to how he could possibly have been convicted and sentenced to 40-60 years in jail, he didn't need to look any further than his legal representation. From the outset, he was doomed to have the worst legal counsel possible.

Kenny's belief in Mr. Peppler's disinterest scared the hell out of him. Mr. Markowski had two weekend days to prepare. It was a recipe for failure, no matter how weak and contrived the prosecution's case. Mr. Markowski proceeded to trial even though he had options that would have prevented him from doing so. This contributed to, but was not solely responsible for, a grossly inadequate defense.

There was very little effort on the part of defense counsel to establish reasonable doubt.
- The victim identification had to be discredited.
- It had to be established that someone other than Kenny was the rapist.
- The missing answering machine tapes had to be pursued.
- The investigation had to be attacked.

None of the physical evidence could be connected to Kenny, yet there was never any mention of anyone else committing the crime during the trial. The footprints were never connected to Kenny. The cigarettes belonged to someone who smoked, not a non-smoker like Kenny. The blood tests proved Kenny was not the source of any forensic evidence. Individually, these anomalies create doubt as to Kenny's guilt. Collectively, they create serious doubt.

Mr. Markowski's cross-examinations lacked substance and bite. When cross-examining the prosecution witnesses, he was reluctant to ask the hard questions necessary to discredit them and ridicule the investigation, especially in regards to the mishandling of the forensic evidence.

Kenny spoke of his trial.

> *That's a standard problem in all the wrongful convictions. Markowski was nowhere near prepared. No way can anyone be prepared to defend a case with 15 counts of rape over a weekend. You couldn't prepare for a drunk driving ticket over the weekend, let alone a capital offense case like mine.*
>
> *Here's another thing. The original charge was five counts of CSC-1, one count of Armed Robbery, one count of Breaking and Entering.*
>
> *I said to Markowski, "Is somebody picking these numbers out of the fucking air? How can it go from 5 to 17 and now back down to 15 then back to 17?"*
>
> *He told me, "Well, Kenny, every time you stuck your finger in her…"*
>
> *I said, "Let me stop you right there. I didn't stick my finger in anybody. Don't you understand? I'm not the guy that did this."*

> He then said, "Okay. Let's move on, Kenny. Let's move on."
>
> How the hell do you think that made me feel, that my own lawyer believed me guilty of this terrible crime?

The Ill-Prepared Defendant

There are many who have heard or read about Kenny's story and have wondered how he could have allowed this to happen to him. But Kenny's story is very common for the wrongfully convicted. They are almost always novices to the system, ill-prepared for the overwhelming circumstances.

Trust is their major fault. Trust that their lawyer is competent. Trust that law enforcement officials and prosecuting attorneys treat them fairly. This trust results in the firm belief that they could never be convicted for a crime they did not commit. They don't see their conversations with the police and the prosecution as adversarial. They don't demand a lawyer. Instead, they cooperate because they see the very individuals that are trying to convict them as someone trying to help. Afterwards, they ask themselves, "How the hell could this happen when I am innocent?"

Kenny reflected on why he never hired an attorney.

> *I thought of hiring an attorney. But I knew next to nothing about the law at that time. And I had complete faith in our legal system, especially since I was innocent. Knowing what I know now and finding out how they actually conspired to convict me, I should have. Hell, it couldn't have been worse. It was the first time I was ever in that situation and I just didn't know any better.*

Chapter 4 — Incarceration

"You never feel safe in prison. You never know what's gonna happen. You don't know if you're going to be beat up or if you're gonna be stabbed. There are people in prison who'd kill you for a candy bar." — Kenny Wyniemko

Jackson State Prison – Jackson, Michigan

Jackson State Prison was a maximum security prison with ten-foot high cement walls and gun turrets at every turn. Until its closing in 2007, it was the largest walled prison in the world, peaking with 6,000 prisoners. It was a Security Level 4 facility that housed some very dangerous criminals.

In the Michigan Department of Corrections (MDOC) prison system, Security Level 1 is the lowest level of security. Level 6 is for maximum security inmates. Kenny entered Jackson as a Level 4.

It was a little over a month after Kenny's sentencing when he was transferred from the Macomb County Jail to Jackson. On December 27, 1994, Kenny Wyniemko stepped off the bus into Hell. Because of the horrific rape, Kenny was considered a dangerous offender. And Jackson State Prison was reserved for men like Kenny Wyniemko.

Kenny recalled that first day at Jackson.

> *I can remember the day I was shipped to Jackson. A guard came to my cell at Macomb County and said, "Wyniemko, let's go. Now! Time for you to go."*
>
> *They put me in a bullpen with like 20 other guys where we waited for hours. They were taking us to various prisons.*

I called my mom and told her, "Mom, you know I'm leaving." She broke down and started crying. I felt so bad for her.

Then my dad got on the phone and he's crying, too. I told him, "Just stay strong. I will protect myself. This will be okay. I'll figure this out."

When I hung up, I started to cry myself.

It was December 27, 1994. I will never forget it. Just two days after Christmas. I was transported to Jackson in a large van. There were six of us shackled together by ankle and waist chains. When we got in the van, we were shackled to the seats.

When I arrived at Jackson, we were led through this single metal door into Quarantine, or 7-Block. The guards directed us to a cell on the right where they took off our shackles and told us to strip. We just sat there naked. It was filthy and we were just sitting around there like that.

We were taken one at a time into another dirty room for our shower. The water was so cold. All the time these guards were screaming out orders and grinning at us. After I toweled dry, they sprayed me with this white disinfectant powder. Parading us around like that. Yelling at us at every turn. It's their way to break you down from the beginning.

We went to this counter where other inmates handed out our prison clothes. We were given three sets of blues, a pair of cheap vinyl shoes, three pair of underwear, three tee shirts, and three pair of socks. I was led into another room where they finally let me dress.

After a little while, we walked, one-by-one, down the hall to get our picture taken for our prison ID. This is where you get your prisoner number. My number was A240889. The 'A' meant I was a first time offender. After every conviction, the letter went up. There were guys with an 'F' meaning they were six-time offenders.

I was then taken to this big prison block. I was walking down this ramp and, man, I'm scared to death. The ramp opened to the cell block with five floors of one-man cells with iron bars all along the outer edges of the cell block. It was scary as hell.

I am walking to my cell with this female guard. She had my file, my court file, and she's going through it, which she shouldn't have. That's not supposed to be allowed. She's going through it and she says real loud, "15 counts of rape."

I said, "I didn't do it."

"Yeah. Yeah. That's what everybody says."

I said, "Well, I didn't."

Then they put me on the top floor — 41-4 was my first cell number.

I have never been so afraid or felt so degraded in my life. But that's how it is in jail. They try to break you down in every imaginable way.

The first night was the toughest. They locked my cell door and I just sat on my bunk and cried. In my mind, there was no way I could survive 40 years. I wanted to end it all so badly. I figured there was no reason for me to live. And I honestly thought of hanging myself. I remember tearing up my bedsheet into strips.

Some black guy across the hall that I couldn't see asked me, "What's the matter, man?"

I told him that I was here for a crime that I did not commit.

He laughed. "Everyone's innocent. Man, everybody says that."

There was a slight pause before he asked me, "Hey, man. You want a square?"

I said, "What's a square?"

"It's a cigarette, man." He laughed again. "You gots a lot to learn."

I was crying. I had thoughts of suicide. And I remember getting down on my knees and asking God to show me the way. A calm came over me. And I believe the good Lord touched my shoulder and told me, "Kenny, you're going to be just fine." My faith got me through the worst of times.

You never feel safe in prison. You never know what's gonna happen; if you're going to be beat up, if you're gonna be stabbed. There are people in prison who'd kill you for a candy bar.

This was about three weeks into my stay at Jackson. One day the cell door opened next to me and a guy by the name of John Braxton walked in. He had that same terrified look on his face as I did that first day. I told him, "Everything will be okay. Just give it time. Be careful and listen to what I tell you to do."

He made it out of Jackson and was released about a week before I was. When I got out, he sent me a note congratulating me. We were friends until he passed away a couple years ago.

Living in Quarantine allowed the prisoners to become acclimated to prison life before being transferred to the general population cell blocks or gen-pop.

Kenny had plenty of time to relive the events that sent him to prison, time to think about his grieving parents, time to think about his failed marriage. It hurt to realize that he left behind his eighteen-year-old son, Kenny, Jr., and that his son would have to deal with the publicity that his father was a convicted rapist. What an awful weight on a young man's shoulders. What does he believe?

Kenny would lie on his prison cell cot, stare at the discolored ceiling, and recall the injustice that put him there. A 40-year prison sentence can get overwhelming for a guilty man, let alone for someone innocent. Some don't care if they live or die. It is a maddening and depressing existence.

It was the job of the guards to break the spirit of each prisoner. Kenny was subjected to this every day.

> *In Quarantine, I remember they would allow us to take a shower only once a week. That's it.*
>
> *They would take one side of the cell block, one gallery at a time. They gave you a small bar of soap like you get in a hotel. We walked in our underwear with a towel. They would take us ten at a time. They would handcuff us to walk to the showers and then they'd handcuff us to a railing outside while we waited. Then they would let us go into the shower one at a time.*
>
> *And the guards would be controlling the showers. Believe this or not, there were times when we would be in there for maybe 30 seconds. My feet wouldn't even get wet and the fucking guard would shut the water off and yell, "Okay! Next! Let's go!" Other times it would be freezing cold or scalding hot.*
>
> *That's how they would fuck with you. All the time. That's what they did in Quarantine. The reason they do that, come to find out, is their first mission when they take someone into prison is to start to break you down right away.*
>
> *I can remember when they fed us. It was a joke. They had the tables on the base floor in the middle of the cell block. They'd bring the food with these small satellite kitchens in these stand-up boxes. Well, if you're locked up on the ground floor, that's not a big deal. But if you're up in*

the 4th Gallery, it's a long walk down to the eating area. You had to sit down with the person who was behind you. You couldn't walk around and look for a table to sit with a friend. By the time I got my tray and my food and sat down, I don't think I had more than 15 fuckin' minutes to eat before the guards would tell you to pack up and get back to your cell. 32 days of this shit. They let you know who was in charge.

During that period, you had to go for a series of tests. You had to go for a physical and to see a dentist. There was an IQ test where they had me draw pictures of women. To this day, I couldn't understand why they had us do that. Then, for my mental evaluation, I had to go and see three different psychologists and psychiatrists.

I could remember walking to take those psychological tests. We had to go to 6-Block for these tests, right next to 7-Block. The nickname for the top floor of 6-Block is Top 6. They had these cells that looked like rooms in a sanitarium. They stuck the people who had real problems there. All the cells had bars except for the ones in Top 6. Those cells had walls and a steel door with a small window where you can look in. And they had these little flap doors where they shoved the food through.

You could hear guys screaming when you walked by. There were times when I'd look through a window into the cells. They had guys chained up by their hands and their legs, lying on their fuckin' bunks. It was sad. I mean, you can't believe it. Some of the guys would stand in their cell naked and, I'm telling you the truth, sometimes they would take a shit in their hand and throw it at the window as we were walking by.

This means a lot to me. This shit I'm telling you about is true. I want this in the book so people can get a better understanding of exactly how they treat you when you first go in. On my dad's grave and as God as my witness, this is all completely true.

This is another thing they'd do to break you down in 7-Block. The front and back of the cells were bars. The back bars looked into these huge steam pipes.

The guards would start on the bottom floor and, with their billy-clubs, they would rattle the bars to our cells. From one cell to another on all four floors. Sometimes they would do this four or five times during the night. It just drove you nuts when you were trying to sleep. It was fucking hell. They must have done this a dozen times when I was in Quarantine.

In January of 1995, Kenny was transferred to Cell Block 12 (12-Block), part of gen pop. You exist in a four-by-ten foot cube with very little privacy. You are told when to wake up, when to eat, when to talk, and when to go to bed. You eventually get used to the routine. This is when you truly become "institutionalized."

Kenny had two objectives at Jackson: stay alive and gain his freedom. The first order of business was to figure out how to survive — how to avoid the beatings, the rapes, and the shanks in the halls, showers, and mess hall. It was simple. He had to make alliances.

In 12-Block, Kenny's cell was next to Tommy Rastall, Jackson's largest in-prison bookie. Tommy was incarcerated for several Breaking & Entering convictions. He would be in-and-out of prison for decades. At the writing of this book, his last conviction was a 6 to 30-year sentence for Unarmed Robbery in September of 2014.

Tommy's "associate" was John "Big Jack" Jackson. Big Jack was serving a life sentence for Armed Robbery and 15 to 25 years for multiple Criminal Sexual Conduct offenses. He had previously served nine years for Second Degree Murder.

Within a couple weeks after his transfer to gen-pop, Kenny met Tommy and Big Jack. They became friends immediately and remained so for the duration of his stay at Jackson.

> *I remember the first time I met Tommy. I was sitting in my cell, minding my own business, when this white guy walks by, stops, and does a double take, looking at me. He said, "You're a cop. I can tell."*
>
> *I said, "I am not a cop."*
>
> *"Well, you don't look like a criminal."*
>
> *I told him, "That's because I'm not. I'm innocent."*
>
> *We hit it off from the start. I was friends with Tommy and Big Jack from that day forward. It was the first of a lot of breaks that I got that kept me alive in there. Prison is such an ugly place, but someone was watching over me.*
>
> *Tommy was short, maybe only five-foot-seven, balding in front, with long hair and a thick mustache. You'd never know he was the biggest book in Jackson by looking at him. But he certainly was a big man there. Good friend to have. We got along great.*
>
> *Big Jack was this huge, broad-shouldered black guy. He was about six-foot-three and he took care of the enforcement side of Tommy's business. Scary dude.*

Kenny was also very lucky to have been befriended by Jimmy Jones. Jimmy took Kenny under his wing, schooling him in the ways of prison survival.

> *I met Jimmy Jones in Hobby Craft class and we took a liking to each other. Meeting him was a real blessing. He guided me through my stay more than anyone.*

Jimmy once told me, "One thing for sure is that you'll be tested. They always do. How you react will go along a long way in how you survive in this hell-hole."

The prisoners in Leather Craft made beautiful saddle bags for motorcycles and horse saddles. Jimmy made a lot of different stuff. He showed me how to make that heart and that cuckoo clock I have up on a wall in my family room.

When I first got out of Quarantine, I was offered a job as a clerk in the warden's office. I hesitated because everyone in that position had to wear their prison blues when they worked.

Jimmy said he'd talk to Dave Hawn, the director of the kitchen, and see if he'd accept me to work there. It was a great job. You could wear jeans or sweat pants, even shorts in the summer.

Jimmy's partner in the kitchen was this guy that was in for molesting little boys in his Boy Scout Troop. Jimmy couldn't stand the guy and, eventually, Jimmy got him booted from that job and it went to me. The kitchen clerk job was the best job at Jackson.

Kenny's first test came shortly after arriving in gen-pop. There was a black man standing along a fence in the Big Yard, the yard attached to Cell Block 11. Kenny was standing by himself along the fence in the yard to Cell Block 8. Separating the two yards was a walkway, about three feet wide, bordered by a ten-foot fence with barbed wire on top. The man in the Big Yard kept eying Kenny.

Kenny described the confrontation.

This black guy, who I never saw before, shouted to me, "Hey, what's your name?"

I just ignored him and started walking away. He followed me and continued to call out.

He yelled, "I said, hey, honky, what's your name?"

> *I told him, "Don't worry about my name."*
> *He said, "You a smart-ass honky, ain't you?"*
> *I continued to ignore him.*
> *He went on, "Guess I need to send some boys to holla' at you later."*
> *I asked him, "What is that supposed to mean?"*
> *He said, "You must be new if you don't know what I mean by holla' at you."*
> *I told him again, "I don't know what you are talking about."*
> *I kept walking and he kept following.*
> *This is the last thing he said just before I entered the building. "Just the same. We a coming."*
> *I got back to my cell and told Jimmy what happened.*
> *I asked him, "You know who that guy was?"*
> *Jimmy told me he was the second in command of a dangerous black gang called the Mo-bites.*
> *"Well, they'll be coming for you now. Watch yourself."*
> *I shook my head in disbelief.*

From the outset of his prison stay, Kenny attended Mass on a regular basis. Every Thursday, Kenny went to shower in preparation for church. It is routines like this that can make you predictable, a dangerous thing in prison. Less than a week after his conversation in the Big Yard, Kenny was confronted by the Mo-bites for the second time.

> *I was alone in the shower when a black guy came in from the left side, placed his towel on the towel rack, and stood to my left. Another black guy came in on the right, hung his towel, and stood to my right.*
> *The first guy said, "You must be new, boy."*
> *The second guy said, "Who are you? Where are you locked up?"*

> *I ignored them, but they both came closer to me saying stuff like, "You know you got a nice ass."*
>
> *"You can make us a lot of money."*
>
> *"No way, motherfuckers," I told them.*
>
> *I kicked the guy on the left in the groin, losing my flipper from my right foot. I was able to dodge a punch from the other guy and landed a punch to his stomach. He doubled over and I kneed him in the head, almost knocking him out. The guy on the left was starting to get up when I kicked off my left sandal and kicked him in the throat.*
>
> *The officer guarding the showers came in and saw the two moaning on the floor.*
>
> *"What the hell happened?" he asked me.*
>
> *I told him, "I have no idea. They just started to fight for no reason."*
>
> *He didn't believe me. "Aw, bullshit!"*
>
> *I finished showering and went back to my cell to get ready for church.*

It would not be the last time Kenny heard from the Mo-bites.

Kenny started working in the kitchen within a couple weeks after arriving in 12-Block. Jimmy introduced him to the workers, telling them that Kenny was a good hockey and softball player. A Hispanic gang called HASTA (Hispanic Americans Striving to Achieve) eventually recruited Kenny for their floor hockey and softball teams.

Kenny was excited for a variety of reasons. There was the opportunity to compete and to get some physical exercise. And there was another reason.

> *I was able to release a lot of frustrations slamming into the players in the floor hockey matches.*

HASTA members were ferocious combatants in sporting events. And they were fiercely loyal to HASTA, a gang feared by everyone in prison. Here is an irony of prison life. Most HASTA members attended weekly Mass and Rosary.

> *There were several gangs, primarily black like the Mo-bites and the Muslims. There were some white gangs like the White Supremacists. And there's a gang of Mexicans or Spanish Americans called HASTA. Some of these black gangs, they would bring drugs in and get guys that were weak and pimp them out. Sometimes they'd lend money. Each gang would have their "stores" to go to. Some of these gangs would kill you for the most ridiculous reason. I've seen it happen.*
>
> *I was really surprised to learn about HASTA. They had real good sports teams in softball, floor hockey, and basketball. I became good friends with two of the members, Paulie Ortizbay and Hernandez Bay.*
>
> *After I first got to Jackson, I was talking to Jimmy Jones. Jimmy was there for a while. He was plugged into everything. I was telling him about my experience playing for junior hockey teams and softball and he introduced me to Ortizbay. This Ortizbay, if you see him, I mean, I don't know how many life sentences he was doing for murder, but you could tell by just looking at him that he was a man you don't fuck with. He asked me if I wanted to play softball and floor hockey for him. I said, "Sure."*
>
> *The nice thing about the HASTA floor hockey team was we were the only team that had jerseys – actual Boston Bruins jerseys. I was thinking when I got mine, "How in the hell could they could afford these things?" HASTA had gangs nationwide and they got support from the outside. That's how.*

It was funny. The guys in HASTA — every Thursday we'd go to Mass together and every Saturday we'd go to church and say the Rosary.

The black gangs, like the Mo-bites, would never, ever fuck with HASTA. Because HASTA, they would kill you like that (snaps fingers), in a second. It was a good thing. Many good things happened to me in that bad situation. It was good that I was an athlete. And when I got tied in with these guys, if someone came at me, they would have to answer to them. So, it worked out well.

I can remember a couple of times when I was in the Big Yard, Cooper Field, where a fight would break out between a black gang and HASTA. I was scared to death seeing all the stuff going on. Blacks would be on one side and HASTA would be on the other. You would hear these chants real quiet. "Who's my brother? You're my brother." "Who's my brother? You're my brother." All these guys from HASTA were joining in, getting ready to go toe to toe with the black guys. At times, there were close to 100 guys involved. There was nowhere to hide.

These gang riots were the worst. With everything going on, there was more than one occasion where, when the dust settled, people ended up shanked, beaten with bats or clubs. Quite often, there was an innocent victim that someone had it out for. The riots scared me shitless. I mean, you had to be there and see it to believe it. I've seen guys sliced and diced, beaten with fuckin' bats.

You never knew when someone would come for you. I mean, I seen guys get it in Jackson all the time. There are five levels of stairways. Guys would go in the bulk heads in the stairway and it looked like someone performed an autopsy. It was nasty.

The yard is a place with opportunities to off someone. The guards patrolling the yard had no weapons. Quite often, a fellow gang member would cause a disturbance in one area as a distraction for the gang's real intent — to shank someone on the opposite end of the yard. When you went to the yard, you gathered with a group for protection. When trouble broke out, you had to be on the alert for anything or anyone.

It was the same for the guards in the yard. They were mostly defenseless and outnumbered. When trouble broke out, they did the same as us. They gathered as a group away from the trouble. If they were lucky, they could make their way to the one secured door where they could unlock it and get to safety.

There were guard towers all over the yard. When a fight broke out, there was one warning shot fired right away. The next shot was near where you were standing. After that, the guards shot to kill.

It's a whole other world behind the walls. People don't see what goes on. It's a totally different fuckin' world there.

Kenny also let it be known that he knew a couple fellow inmates by the name of Augustino (Augie) Conte and Ernesto (Ernie the Gurney) Marzetti. Both were serving life sentences for murder, one Mafia related. Good guys to know.

Kenny met them previously when he managed Gino's Falcon Show Bar, an entertainment facility, bar, and bowling alley on the east side of Detroit. Gino's had a weekly Wise Guys Night every Monday in the 1970s. It was filled with local "personalities." Kenny never thought that those associations would come in so handy in a place like Jackson State Prison.

I met Ernie and Augie in the Big Yard. They were housed in 6-Block. I knew they were at Jackson. They were fearless and they had quite a reputation, even for a place like Jackson. We talked about the old days at Gino's. Another blessing as it turned out.

Kenny was determined to gain his freedom and asked Jimmy how he could start. Jimmy told Kenny that his best bet was to get with Bill Ramsey, the top legal mind in Jackson.

Mr. Ramsey became Kenny's mentor. He taught Kenny the law and assisted in his appeals. Mr. Ramsey was so proficient in the law that several outside law offices hired him to write briefs for them. Kenny handed over everything he had on his case and Bill agreed that Kenny had reasons to appeal.

Once Kenny started to work on his freedom, he spent hours with Bill in the Law Library.

Jimmy introduced me to Bill Ramsey when we were in church. He was a paralegal, doing work for some outside attorneys. He was getting paid to write briefs for them.

I spent countless hours with him in the Law Library. Bill was the one who taught me the law and I owe him deeply. He was always available to help with research and when writing a motion. Striving to gain my freedom was my passion. I had purpose in my life. Pretty unusual for Jackson.

Besides Bill, there was Pepper Moore, Chuck Whalen, and a funny, personable guy called Felonious Floyd. Whalen was real busy with a lawsuit the prisoners had brought against Jackson. But he always answered any questions I had when he had free time.

Kenny's last run-in with the Mo-bites was in a floor hockey game a few weeks after the trouble in the shower. The Mo-bites ran a stable of guys for sex income. They were always looking for new prospects.

I was lining up for the opening faceoff in a floor hockey game against the Mo-bites. It was in the new gymnasium with indoor-outdoor carpeting on the floor.

The Mo-bites' forward started into me before the ball was dropped. Stuff like "New meat." And, "You'll be making a fine-ass bitch for us."

He put his left heel on the front of my right foot and I immediately stomped on his right foot. We started jostling and we got in each other's face. I slid my upper hand down the shaft of my stick and when they dropped the ball, I speared him in his nuts as hard as I could. He went down, yelling in pain.

The Mo-bites guy I first saw in the yard came running from the stands, yelling and screaming that he was going to kill me.

Big Jack stepped right in front of him and warned, "You had better think twice of messing with this guy, motherfucker."

That Mo-bites guy took one look at Big Jack and backed off. That was it. They never really bothered me again.

Between Big Jack, Tommy, Ernie, Augie, and HASTA, it was enough to stop the Mo-bites from hassling me. I steered clear of them and they did the same.

The floor hockey squad was fun. We had Michael (Stormy) on defense and Jay Allen in net. Allen was huge, about six-foot-nine. He was serving several sentences for Breaking & Entering and numerous drug convictions. Stormy was in for bank robbery. He was a big man, too. Over six-feet and built like a linebacker.

There was this game against the Mo-bites when Stormy lined up someone and nailed him from behind straight into the wall. They had to cart the guy out on a stretcher.

We lost Stormy a couple days later when he was sliced up in a stairwell. The lockdown whistle, which sounded like an air raid warning, went off. We found out later what happened. I'm not sure if he died or if he survived and was sent to another facility. But we never saw him again.

There was the Smiley Face in the big chow house. We used to call it the Big Top or Big House. It seats about 350-400 guys, about the size of a football field. The roof is about 25-feet high.

There's an L-shaped, eight-foot wall that runs from along the side of the Big House and turns and runs along the front. It separates the dining table area and the feeding lines.

Guys come in along the back wall, walking right under this huge Smiley Face, which was about 10-foot in diameter. They would pick up a tray and make their way through the feeding lines, on the outside of that eight-foot wall.

At the turn at the front wall was the feeding line for the special diet meals. Above the special diet line was a guard tower, about 30 feet long, high above the dining area. The guards were armed with shotguns and rifles.

The first time I walked in there was with my buddy, Jimmy Jones. I couldn't understand why there was this damn Smiley Face up there.

So, I asked him, "Jimmy, tell me something, what's up with that Smiley Face? Why is there a Smiley Face in prison?"

He started laughing, "You'll find out."

I said, "Just tell me."

"No, no, you'll find out – don't worry."

Our office in the kitchen was behind the serving line, away from the inmates. When we would have lunch, we would get our food from the diet line because the food was better. We ordered all the foods. It was one of my jobs to *prepare the food for the prisoners who required a special diet.*

This one day, Jimmy and I left our offices and we were walking behind the diet line to see Big Jack who was serving there. We were right below this guard tower. So, we're getting our food when a fight broke out among some of the inmates at the tables. I saw a couple of guys get stabbed. I think there were like five or six guys, and two of them died.

When the fight first broke out, I was holding my tray of food, standing next to Jimmy. I was scared to death. I didn't know what the hell to do. I never saw anything like that before. So, I'm holding my tray right below this guard shack and I hear, "Boom!" This fuckin' shotgun goes off. I look at that Smiley Face and it exploded into a thousand pieces. And, after that, when that face blew up, another face automatically comes up right behind it. When I heard that first gunshot, I was so scared, I almost shit my pants. I dropped my tray and all the food fell onto the floor. I tried crawling under the food counter. I didn't know what the hell was going on. Jimmy Jones and Big Jack were still standing, laughing at me.

I said, "Man, why don't you guys get down?"

They said, "Don't worry Kenny. Nothing's going to happen to us in here."

The riot squad was called and they came in and broke up the fight. I was still shaking when Jimmy told me to get another tray of food and go back to the office to eat.

I said, "Jimmy, I can't eat. I don't have an appetite anymore."

I found out what the Smiley Face was for. When a fight breaks out, one guard shoots his shotgun into the Smiley Face with buck shot. They blow up the first one. That's meant to get everybody's attention. Then, after that, after a new Smiley Face comes forward, the next shot is to shoot to kill.

Inmates didn't have to be involved in gangs, drugs, or any type of violence for harm to come to them. In prison, the strong prey on the weak, regardless of the reason. Any poor soul could have their life snatched away just because they existed.

> *There was this slight, middle-aged white guy by the name of Brian Saylor. I felt sorry for him. He had no friends, no family, and absolutely no money. He'd search the grounds for cigarette butts, even picking them out of the water and the mud, drying them off to smoke. I would occasionally slip him a pack. I never saw him bother anyone. He kept as low a profile as possible.*
>
> *They found him face down in the yard, dead. It bothered me for a while.*
>
> *His killer was sliced up and found dead a couple days later.*
>
> *Stuff like that always served as a reminder to me of where I was. You can never let your guard down. No matter if I was associated with HASTA. No matter if I knew guys like Ernie and Augie. If someone decided that ridding the world of Ken Wyniemko was worth the blowback, they'd get me somehow.*
>
> *There isn't a day that goes by that you do not fear for your life in prison.*

In 1997, Jackson State Prison was re-organized to house the inmates according to their job types. Kenny was transferred to Cell Block 11 (11-Block), right next to Jimmy's cell, and across from Big Jack's. Tommy Rastall was transferred to 6-Block with Augie and Ernie.

11-Block was a real blessing for Kenny. The prisoners who worked in the Law Library were transferred there, too.

Kenny was fortunate in many ways during his stay in Jackson. He was able to ally himself with loyal and dangerous friends. And he had the good fortune to be able to tap into knowledgeable legal minds.

Ryan Correctional Facility – Detroit, Michigan

In 1998, as a result of good behavior, Kenny was transferred to the Ryan Correction Facility, a Level 1 and 2 prison, medium to low security.

Ryan was located on the east side of Detroit on Ryan Road, about a half mile north of McNichols Avenue, or what the locals call Six Mile. The prison grounds stretch eastward and are bordered on the east end by Mound Road. There are two similar prison buildings, one just off Ryan and one off Mound, with field gullies in between.

It was only three miles from the neighborhood in which Kenny grew up and much closer to where his friends and family lived. This made it much more convenient for them to visit.

One would think Kenny would have welcomed leaving Jackson for Ryan, a lower security level prison. But that was not the case.

> *I was scared and nervous because it was like starting a new prison term. You don't know who to trust. I was real lucky that Jimmy Jones was transferred at the same time. That set my mind at ease. The one benefit was that I was re-classified as a Level 2 prisoner from the Level 4 that I was in Jackson.*
>
> *When we got there, Jimmy ended up in the hole immediately. He was into hobby crafts a lot at Jackson. And he had all these tools to make statues, and a lot of different paints. All these things were legal at Jackson.*
>
> *They didn't allow that stuff at Ryan. It's normal procedure at Ryan to check all the things we brought. I had two footlockers, one with my clothes and one with my legal stuff in it. Jimmy had, I think, three footlockers. Half his stuff was all these tools that he brought with him. So, when they were going through Jimmy's shit, they came across*

some small molding knives. They got pissed and threw him in the hole for three days.

They put me in Building 200 and they put Jimmy, after he got out of the hole, in Building 500, 5B. There was no yard in Building 200. The building was for handicapped people. They were single man cells. A lot of the guys were in wheelchairs. I didn't like it.

One day I was playing racquetball and Deputy Warden Scott Nobles spotted me. He thought I was a cop or a plant.

I told him, "No, I'm not a cop."

We talked and he made plans to ship me over to Building 500. He turned out to be a good guy. We have remained friends to this day.

That is how I got back together with Jimmy. He ended up in a cell next to mine. In Ryan, we had cellmates. I was in a cell with a black guy. I can't think of his name. He stole some stamps from me and we set him up and had him thrown in the hole. Then I was in the cell with Arnie, of all people. This guy is fuckin' nuts. I knew him from the streets. He was like the head of a Chaldean gang in Detroit. I don't know how many people they murdered. His whole family, at one time or another, was convicted for all sorts of stuff like assault and murder.

There was this one incident when we were still in 5B. 5A & 5B are connected by a walkway. We're in unit 5B and some idiot inmate started setting fires in the waste baskets. That pissed the guards off. I remember the fire alarms would go off and we would have to go outside and wait in whatever weather. Then we were sent back to our cells and we were all put in lockdown.

One day the fire alarms were going off again and again, like every half hour. This time, I believe the guards set them off on purpose because every time these alarms would go off, everybody was locked down in our cells. Nobody could have gotten out of their cell to get to the alarms.

After the first time the alarm went off, they herded us into the yard. It was raining real hard that day and no one was happy standing out there. We were ordered back to our cells and we were once again put in lockdown. We got back inside our cells and, I don't know if Arnie and I took off our coats yet, the fire alarms go off again. The cops yelled, "Everybody out!"

They emptied both units back into the yard. Like I said, it was raining like hell. Everyone was getting pissed off because they knew the guards were setting this stuff off.

We're all standing out there and I remembered telling Arnie, "Man, this is not good." A group of inmates were starting to yell at the guards who were standing back in the cell block where it was warm and dry. The inmates started to pick up stones and throw them at the windows outside of 5B.

I told Arnie, "Let's get the fuck away from here. Let's go stand in a corner someplace. I don't want to get charged with anything."

So, that's what Arnie and I did. We went to the farthest part of the yard. We just stood there with our arms folded, looking at all these assholes throwing these rocks. I remember this one black guard nicknamed Olt. He came here from Africa, a real good guy. He came out the door from the unit into the yard and started yelling for everybody to come back inside. Well, after he tells everybody to get inside, he goes inside and slams the fuckin' door and it's locked.

Everybody is starting to go up to the door to get inside but they couldn't. More guys went back to picking up stones and throwing them at the building. The siren went off indicating the general count has just been sounded. When that happens, when that siren goes off, you have to stop what you're doing and go back to your unit, pronto.

So, the siren is going off at the same time the fire alarms inside the building are going off. Nobody knows what the fuck to do. We can't get inside the building because the doors are locked. And it continued to pour.

Then I saw Deputy Nobles and a couple of guards come out on the sidewalk on the outside of the fence. Nobles had this bullhorn. "Everybody return to your cells immediately. If anybody fails to comply, he will be charged with inciting a riot."

So, I'm thinking, "What the fuck!"

The one thing you do not want to do is to be charged with inciting a riot. Nobles said that five guys at a time are to line up along the fence leading up to this gate. The guards will take us around to the front of the building and bring us back inside through the front door. You're talking almost 200 people, 96 from each cell block.

By this time, a couple more guards came out and were videotaping everybody in the yard. I'm pissed off because it's bad enough that I was in there for something I didn't do. I don't want to get hit with inciting a riot ticket. That's the worst ticket one can possibly get. And, normally when somebody gets a ticket for something like that, they ship you up to a place like Standish, a Level 6, and nobody will see you for years.

After Nobles told everyone what to do, two columns of the Goon Squad came out in full riot gear. One group came right behind Nobles on the sidewalk and there's another column of maybe 20 guys coming on the opposite fence on the other side of the yard. They are dressed up in full battle gear, with fuckin' rifles out! I'm thinking, "Man, this ain't going to be good. I gotta get out of here ASAP."

All I wanted to do is get the fuck out of the yard and go back to my cell. So, Arnie and I jumped up to where we were in the second group of five to go out. They took us out and walked us to the front door. As soon as we get in the small vestibule, we had to strip down, and they strip-searched us before they let us back into our cell.

They eventually got everybody back to their cells but it took hours. I was watching the yard from my window when I got back in. The riot squad was out there and they were cuffing guys and taking them out. They had this big bus that was called Snowbird and they were just putting these guys on the bus. I knew they were going bye-bye, probably to a facility like Standish.

After everyone was back in their cells, they locked us down for couple days. They brought our food to the cells. We couldn't do anything but sit around. No shower. Nothing.

Then they brought some guys in from different prisons to fill up the spaces that were open.

They came up with this idea they were going to pick out who was causing trouble in the yard and move them from 5B over to 5A. They wanted to put everybody in the hole, but the hole at Ryan only held 16 people. So, they put Arnie and I over in 5A and locked us down like we were part of it.

We packed up everything. I will clarify this, okay. First of all, we did pack up all our stuff and take it with us. It was that way for a day or two. Then they came in with an order and took our TVs and other stuff. They took all our personal clothes. If you had any racquetball stuff, sports equipment, they took them. They left us with two pair of prison blues, two pair of underwear, two tee shirts and two pair of socks. That was it.

> We didn't go to the hole. But they locked us down, Arnie and I. Everybody in that unit was locked down with just two pair of clothes for 62 days! They were bringing our food in these stainless steel containers on wheels. They let the food sit there for an hour and cool off before then they would pass it out, one cell at a time.
>
> We had to put up with that shit for two whole months. We would get a shower once a week. It was pretty much like solitary confinement.
>
> Arnie and I were in cell 5A-25. I was in the upper bed, Arnie in the lower. The shower stall was two cells away from ours, about 15 feet away.
>
> Believe it or not, they handcuffed us just to walk 15 feet. That's how fucked up it was.
>
> Then, after those 62 days, we got our stuff back. They had put the stuff they took in a warehouse for storage. Other inmates were working there with a couple of street people who worked for MDOC (Michigan Department of Corrections). Guys said there was stuff missing out of their locker like clothes and other things. It was a big fucking joke. Ridiculous. That's just another example of how they screw with you.
>
> Those 62 days. Living like that. It was so fucked up. I will never forget it.

There were two items that Kenny cherished: his Rosary beads and the chain and cross he wore around his neck. The cross was a profession of his faith that he wore proudly every minute of his incarceration. It was his grandfather's and Kenny had worn it his whole life. His Rosary beads were of the upmost importance. He took great comfort in praying the Rosary several times a day.

An edict was issued that specified prisoners could only possess one religious article. Kenny faced a dilemma. Since he prayed the

Rosary three times a day, he sent the cross and chain to his parents for safekeeping.

> *There was this time when we were told that we could only keep one religious item. That's the kind of stuff they were always pulling. Anything to fuck with us. Since I prayed the Rosary several times a day, I mailed the cross and chain to my parents. It was originally my grandfather's.*
>
> *The Rosary sits next to my bed today. And I still have the cross and chain around the Blessed Mother statue outside my bedroom.*

> *Father Frank Skalski was always there for me in Ryan. I knew him from grade school at Queen of Heaven. Then he was transferred to St. Ladislaus when I went there for high school. He has been there for me through it all.*
>
> *He never saw me when I was in Jackson, but he visited me on a regular basis when I was transferred to Ryan. Some nuns who I knew from grade school, like Sister Bernetta, Sister Clarenda, and Francis Bernadone, and Sister Rose Angela from St. Lad's, wrote me regularly from the time I was in Jackson to the day I was released. I don't know how they heard about my conviction, but they did and they sent me letters all the time. You don't know what a joy it was for me to get them when I was locked up.*

Kenny discussed another incident at Ryan. It was in 2001, after Kim Shine of the *Detroit Free Press* and attorney Gail Pamukov of the Innocence Project had contacted him. He was sure that, with DNA testing, it was just a matter of time before he would get a new trial, or even be released. To say he was on his best behavior is an understatement. This event had the potential of Kenny being charged with a crime that could keep him in jail for a long time.

Arnie and Paulie and I were in the Level 2 cell block. 4D-37 was our cell number. We were in the corner cell. The corner cells were the best to have because they were a little bigger than the regular cells. Arnie was in another corner cell at the end of the hall. Arnie's cellmate was Ron Kramer, who we called Bubba.

From my cell, there were two cells, then a bathroom and a shower, then two more cells, then Arnie's cell.

Arnie had a store in his cell, selling stuff to inmates that you could buy from the commissary. Paulie and I did the same thing. Arnie was also taking a lot of bets. He always kept a lot of postage stamps on hand that he would get for lost bets. At that time, you could only have $75 total worth of stuff in your cell. If he would get too many stamps, he would approach other inmates that he was friends with, who didn't have a job or any money, and he would ask them to store his extra stamps in their cells. This stuff happens every day in prison. You're taking chances, but your odds of being caught are less by doing it that way.

Arnie was giving stamps to a guy named Phil Matt, a guy I used to play racquetball with at Ryan. I know Phil didn't have a job, no support from the outside. He's keeping all these stamps for Arnie, easily about $100 worth.

The funny thing is that Phil would come to see Paulie with stamp envelopes that he was holding for Arnie and buy items from Paulie's store. And that is a big no-no. You're just asking to get fucked up.

So, it came to a point when Arnie came up to Phil and told him that he wanted some of his stamps. Phil says he didn't have them and that somebody must have taken them. Whoa! Arnie was really pissed. I knew what was coming. Arnie was going to fuck this guy up — just a matter of when and where.

On this day I am talking about, Paulie got up early in the morning and went out to do four to five laps around the track to stay in shape.

I'm alone in my cell, drinking my cup of coffee, watching TV, waiting to go out to the yard for half time. Arnie was walking around in front of each cell with a big white bath towel over his shoulder. I could tell from knowing Arnie, just by the look on his face, that Phil's going to get fucked up. There was is no doubt in my mind.

Paulie was still in the yard when Phil came into my cell asking for a shot of coffee, which I had no problem with. I would buy coffee in the store and resell it. I would take these plastic gloves from the kitchen, cut the fingers off, pour the coffee grinds into the fingers, and tie them up. That was a shot of coffee.

I told Phil, "Just go down in my locker. You know where my stuff is at."

Phil took his own cup, filled it with hot water from the sink, and got the shot of coffee out of my locker. He gave me two stamps, the price for a shot of coffee, no doubt two stamps that belonged to Arnie. He put the cup on my desk, dumped the coffee into the cup, and started stirring it. He's sitting there sipping his coffee when he asked me what I am watching on TV.

Suddenly, before I could answer, Arnie came in like a flash. He went right up to Phil and took the towel off his shoulder. Under the towel was a leather belt with two padlocks on the belt. Arnie screamed, "You punk motherfucker," and he just started whacking Phil in the head. Phil went down on his knees, started to get up, but Arnie kept on hitting him over and over. Phil fell on top of Paulie's bunk, the bottom bunk, and he was bleeding badly. There was blood on the walls and on Paulie's blankets.

I kept yelling, "Arnie, man, get the fuck out of here. If guards happen to come around and you take off, and this is my cell, they're gonna charge me with attempted murder. And I don't need that shit now."

Arnie told me to go fuck myself and bolted out.

Two neighbors, Sanders Bay, who we called SB, and Daddio, walked in. SB said, "Kenny, are you alright?"

I told him, "Yeah, I'm okay. Go get some towels."

Phil's head was bleeding so much I didn't know if he had a fractured skull, if he was going to live or die or what. So, I wrapped his head in a bunch of towels. SB and Daddio took him back to his cell, right around the corner from ours.

When they returned, Daddio asked me, "Kenny, what can we do?"

"Go get some more towels and a bucket of water and some soap. I've got to try to get this blood off of the walls."

Then Frankie Weeheagan came by to see what the ruckus was all about. I told Frankie to get the bucket of water and I told SB to run out to the yard and tell Paulie he's gotta come back in because we have a big, fuckin' problem.

So, when the whistle blew for half time, Daddio went out and brought Paulie back. Paulie walked in the cell and screamed, "What the fuck did you do, Kenny?!"

I said, "I didn't do anything. I'm trying to clean this shit up."

He asked me what happened and I told him what Arnie did. He was fuming. "That motherfucker Arnie, did this?"

Daddio said, "Yeah, man."

So, with Arnie back in his cell, Paulie went to grab his shank out of his mattress. "I'm going to take care of this motherfucker."

I said, "Paulie, please don't get me involved in this any way. They are just looking for a reason to try to put something on me. I am waiting to go home."

I didn't want any fuckin' heat! So, I talked Paulie out of grabbing the knife, but I couldn't stop him from going down to see Arnie in his cell. I said, "Be smart. It's not the first time you killed somebody, you know."

He ended up going down to Arnie's cell and the door slammed shut. I remember Paulie yelled, "You motherfucker!"

Furniture was being tossed around and I could hear the body blows all the way back to my cell.

Paulie wasn't afraid of anything or anybody, even Arnie. He had some cuts on his face when he came back to the cell, but Arnie definitely got the worse of it.

The guards heard the ruckus and locked us down. Then they came in to do a head count. When they went to Phil's cell, he was bleeding so much they had to take him to the hospital. I think Phil must have told the guards what happened and gave up Arnie's name 'cuz right after that, the goon squad came in to take Arnie out. That was the last time I ever saw Arnie.

Phil was in the hospital for a couple weeks. When he came back, they put him in another building. 700 Building, I think. But it wasn't long after that when they shipped him out to another facility.

Stuff like this happened all the time. Guys get in beefs and someone gets beat up and, sometimes, even killed.

But this was a terrible time for me. The Innocence Project had taken my case and we were close to getting the results from the final DNA tests. Those DNA tests could prove me innocent. Getting another charge from this could have kept me in jail, regardless the test results.

I think about all this happening at that time and about how it could have screwed me up royally. Another time when the good Lord was looking out for me.

Chapter 5 — Jailhouse Appeals

"*I remember the day of my dad's funeral. I lay on the bunk in my cell and cried my eyes out, recalling him being at my side every day of my trial. He was sitting right behind me when the verdict came down. He was crying. I didn't have the opportunity to say good-bye to him and it was really painful.*" — Kenny Wyniemko

From the very beginning of his incarceration, Kenny was obsessed with gaining his freedom. Once he became comfortable in his surroundings, if one could associate "comfortable" with living in Jackson State Prison, he started to put his plan in action. This quest became *the* driving force in his life.

He repeatedly requested evidence from the Clinton Township Police Department. The evidence trickled in slowly, a fact that someone incarcerated has to live with when there is no assistance on the outside. It was very frustrating for a man serving time for a crime he did not commit.

Kenny submerged himself in the appeal process by reading law books and reviewing evidence from his case in the form of witness statements, police reports, and trial transcriptions.

To add insult to injury, Kenny received a letter from the Michigan Department of Corrections during his first appeal. The correspondence included a $6,250 bill for Mr. Markowski's "services." Kenny just shook his head and threw it in the trash.

Kenny's first appeal was with the Michigan Court of Appeals.

> *When you're convicted in court, the law entitles everyone to one appeal. It's called An Appeal of Right. If you can't afford an attorney, the local court, like Macomb County Court, will assign one for you. There are four or five different groups where the court can send your case to. It's the luck of the draw as to whether you get someone competent or not. One of the groups is called SADO, the State Appellate Defenders Office. Normally, that's the best. You're lucky if they accept your case. Deborah Keene was the first attorney from SADO who came to see me.*

Appeals History-State of Michigan Court of Appeals
On January 16, 1995, Deborah Winfrey Keene, Assistant Defender of the State Appellate Defender's Office (SADO), submitted a *Brief on Appeal with Oral Arguments Requested and Proof of Service* stating Kenny was appealing his conviction and requesting an oral argument before the Michigan Court of Appeals. Ms. Keene argued Kenny's conviction on two major points in the *Statement of Questions Presented* at the very beginning of her brief.

STATEMENT OF QUESTIONS PRESENTED

I. WAS DEFENDANT DENIED A FAIR TRIAL BY THE ADMISSION OF TESTIMONY OF HIS ESTRANGED EX-GIRLFRIEND ABOUT THEIR CONSENSUAL SEXUAL RELATIONS AND ALLEGATIONS OF STALKING BY DEFENDANT, BECAUSE THE PREJUDICIAL EFFECT OF THIS EVIDENCE SUBSTANTIALLY OUTWEIGHED ITS PROBATIVE VALUE?

II. WAS MR. WYNIEMKO DENIED HIS DUE PROCESS RIGHT TO A FAIR TRIAL BY THE REPEATED MISCONDUCT OF THE PROSECUTING ATTORNEY?

To say Kenny was displeased with Ms. Keene's work is an understatement.

> *I remember the first time I met Keene. I told her exactly what happened and she said, "Kenny, I'm a very good writer. I'll take care of this for you."*
>
> *Well, about two weeks later, she sent me her brief in the mail. I read it and I'm thinking, "What the fuck!?" It sounded like a prosecutor's writing. It actually was making me look bad.*
>
> *So, that's when I called my dad and told him, "Dad, this ain't going anywhere. We have to hire an outside attorney to have any chance with this appeal."*
>
> *An inmate by the name of Emil Mardenli recommended an attorney named Kenneth Karam. Emil was from Massachusetts. His dad owned a car dealership outside of Boston. We used to play Pinochle a lot together. I got him a job in the kitchen and he was going through his appeal and he had hired Karam. Emil was a good guy. I trusted him.*

Kenny's father procured the legal services of Attorney Kenneth H. Karam (Law Offices of Peralta, Johnston, & Karam) to assist in the appeals process. He wrote a $25,000 check in advance for the firm's services.

On May 15, 1996, the State of Michigan Court of Appeals approved Mr. Karam's request to replace Ms. Keene as Kenny's attorney.

On June 12, 1996, Mr. Karam filed a *Defendant*-Appellant's *Supplemental Brief on Appeal* with the Michigan Court of Appeals,

Docket 183157. The *Statement of Questions Presented* was the same with the addition of a third point.

> III. MR. WYNIEMKO WAS DENIED A FAIR TRIAL DUE TO INEFFECTIVE ASSISTANCE OF COUNSEL.

Mr. Karam introduced the concept of Unconscious Transference. Unconscious Transference is defined as "a memory error that occurs when an eyewitness to a crime misidentifies a familiar but innocent person from a police lineup."

It was Mr. Karam's view that Ms. Klug unconsciously recognized Kenny and mistakenly identified him as her assailant. Ms. Klug frequented Kingswood Bowling Alley where Kenny worked and, according to the Clinton Township Police Department, attended parties where Kenny was present. Once the identification was made at the lineup, the connection stood throughout the trial.

Here is an excerpt from Mr. Karam's appeal.

> *This explains why the complainant's description of her assailant changed after she saw Mr. Wyniemko. The complainant's original description of six foot to six foot two, 220 to 230 pounds, became five foot eleven around 200 pounds, which fit Mr. Wyniemko....*
>
> *This argument was not explored by Mr. Wyniemko's trial attorney nor touched on by Mr. Wyniemko's trial attorney nor was any explanation given by Mr. Wyniemko's trial attorney as to possibilities for an erroneous identification.*

Mr. Karam contended Mr. Markowski was negligent to have never mentioned the possibility that Ms. Klug had indeed seen Kenny prior to the lineup and, unconsciously, connected him to the rape.

Mr. Karam noted the importance of this omission since the primary reason for Kenny's conviction was the victim identification.

Attacking the identification would have been invaluable in obtaining a *new trial*

In addition, Mr. Karam severely criticized Mr. Markowski for not insisting that DNA testing be conducted on the forensic evidence. He noted the husband had been out of town and the theory he was the source of the forensic evidence was questionable at best.

Mr. Karam also noted that the prosecution never brought up the footprints, making it obvious they could not connect them to the defendant. The defense should have pursued finding the actual source of the forensic evidence and the footprints.

Mr. Karam's appeal must have been compelling. On December 17, 1996, the Michigan Court of Appeals granted an oral argument, a rare occurrence and a distinct advantage to the defendant in the appeals process. Kenny was elated.

The court date to hear arguments was set for January 15, 1997, at 11:30 am. Kenny's father and his brother, Tommy, were present, while Kenny awaited word in his cell. All of them were hopeful that this was the first step in gaining Kenny's freedom.

Then the system gave Kenny another gut shot. Mr. Karam got the time mixed up and failed to show for the hearing.

Mr. Karam and his firm filed numerous affidavits admitting their mistake and requesting their client not be punished for their oversight. Kenny would not be given that second chance. The Michigan Court of Appeals refused the request to schedule a second oral argument.

On May 2, 1997, the Michigan Court of Appeals denied the appeal for a rehearing on the grounds that there was no reversible error evident. Kenny and his friends and family were devastated

Kenny contacted Mr. Karam after the scheduling error. Here is Kenny's version.

> *I couldn't believe it. We had worked so hard and we felt that we got an unbelievable break when the Court of Appeals*

granted an oral argument. But that was shot to hell when Karam was a no-show.

*I called him immediately. He told me that he was at court at 1:30 pm and was surprised that no one was there. I told him the time was 11:30 am and that it was right on the court notice that **he** forwarded to me. He said he was sorry. I demanded my father's money back. He refused.*

I began to believe that there was this major conspiracy to keep me in jail for the whole term. I was very frustrated and angry.

Appeals History-Michigan Supreme Court

After the Michigan Court of Appeals rejection, Ms. Keene assisted Kenny and Mr. Ramsey by filing an appeal with the Michigan Supreme Court. On April 27, 1998, the Michigan Supreme Court sent notification that they refused to hear the appeal.

A few months later, Kenny was transferred to Ryan Correctional Facility. He shuddered at the thought that he would no longer have his mentor by his side.

Losing Ramsey's help and advice was a blow. I couldn't even imagine doing this without him.

We hired an attorney by the name of James Howarth for the U. S. District Court appeal. The reason I hired him was because he was recommended to me and I knew of him from the work he had done. He used to come a lot to Sinbad's Restaurant in downtown Detroit when I worked there. He was a high-powered attorney. He did work for some of the crime families around Detroit and for Jimmy Hoffa. High profile work.

Appeals History-United States District Court

On April 2, 1999, James C. Howarth filed a *Petition for Writ of Habeas Corpus* to the United States District Court, Eastern District of Michigan, Southern District. District Court Judge Patrick J. Duggan was the presiding judge.

> ISSUE PRESENTED:
>
> WAS PETITIONER DENIED EFFECTIVE ASSISTANCE OF COUNSEL, AS GUARANTEED BY THE SIXTH AND FOURTEENTH AMENDMENTS TO THE UNITED STATES CONSTITUTION?

Howarth's petition declared the defendant's constitutional rights had been violated on several counts. He focused on Kenny's ineffective counsel, from Peppler to Markowski to Karam. It was a scathing account of legal incompetence through the pre-trial, trial, and appeals process.

> *I thought Howarth's appeal was gonna work. He wrote an excellent brief. We had it assigned to a Judge Duggan, current Detroit Mayor Mike Duggan's dad. Judge Duggan's opinion came back and, if you read the whole opinion the way I was reading it, I thought, "Man, he's going to grant this!" But, in the end, I was denied. I really couldn't believe it.*

While awaiting the United States District Court's decision, Kenny was contacted by Kim Shine, *Detroit Free Press* Investigative Reporter. She was responding to his letters pleading for her assistance. Ms. Shine requested a meeting with Kenny to discuss his case. She promised nothing, but she was the first to give Kenny hope outside the scope of the appeal process.

On May 18, 2000, the United States District Court denied the petition on the basis that Kenny's constitutional rights were not violated. Here is the Conclusion from that order.

> *Conclusion*
> *Having carefully considered all of the issues raised by petitioner, this Court does not conclude that the state court adjudication of petitioner's claims resulted in a decision that was "contrary to, or involved an unreasonable application of, clearly established Federal law, as determined by the Supreme Court of the United States." 28 U.S.C. § 2254 (d) (1). Therefore, petitioner's petition for a writ of habeas corpus must be denied.*
>
> *An Order consistent with this Opinion shall issue forthwith.*

Kenny had one last chance in the legal process – the United States Court of Appeals. First, presiding Judge Duggan had to be convinced that an appeal was warranted.

When Kenny informed Mr. Howarth that he'd like to appeal the United States District Court decision, Howarth told him that it would be useless.

> *I called Howarth immediately because when you are denied in District Court, you only have 10 days to apply for a 'Certificate of Appealability' to file an appeal with the U. S. Court of Appeals. I told him, "Jim, we have 10 days and we need to get going on this."*
> *He told me, "Kenny, Duggan's not going grant the appeal. He's going to deny you again."*
> *I said, "Why would you say he won't grant it? Jimmy, please give it a try."*

> Then he told me, "Look, you've been studying the law all along. If you want to write it, you write it yourself!" Then he hung up the phone.
> I'm thinking, "You motherfucker! This is my life!"

After Howarth's blunt resignation, Kenny was left in the cold. That's when Bill Ramsey stepped back into his life.

> I was working as a clerk in the recreation department. I thought Ramsey was still at Jackson. I walked into Building 300 to go to work. There was a barber shop with a bleacher bench in the hallway where inmates sat to wait to get their hair cut. I passed the barber shop to get to work and I spotted Ramsey sitting there. I just stared at him and said, "What the fuck are you doing here?"
> He started laughing. "I came to see you."
> Let me tell you, it was a blessing because Bill's the one that taught me everything I know about the law. When I saw Ramsey there, I thought that it was just another indication that all was going to work out for me. He helped me on the appeal to the U. S. Court of Appeals to apply for the certificate.
> He got transferred when they were shutting Jackson down due to the lawsuit the inmates brought against the State about the conditions there. We kept in touch by letters. He never mentioned he was being transferred to Ryan. He wanted it to be a surprise. And a great surprise at that. I remember I was so happy to see him.

During the period Kenny and Ramsey worked to obtain the *Certificate of Appealability*, Kenny received the worst news of all. On May 28, 2000, his dad passed away. Kenny's staunchest supporter was gone. His dad had poured a great deal of his savings into Kenny's appeals. He was the one person who never wavered in his belief that his son was innocent.

Kenny's request to go home for his dad's funeral was denied. It was very depressing knowing that his dad passed without ever seeing his son released. Kenny wanted so much for his dad to see the day his son walked out of prison a free man.

> *I remember the day of my dad's funeral. I lay on the bunk in my cell and cried my eyes out, recalling him being at my side every day of my trial. He was sitting right behind me when the verdict came down. He was crying and yelling that his son was innocent.*

> *I was walking back from work at the gym when I was told by a guard to go to the counselor's office. As soon as I got into the doorway, the counselor, a guy by the name of Hernandez, told me my brother called and said that my dad died. No warning. He just blurted it out as if it was nothing.*
>
> *I was surprised because Fr. Frank had visited me the previous week and commented on how great he looked. I knew he had cancer, but I figured he still had a year or a year and a half to live. I had real hopes of getting out of jail in time to see him as a free man.*
>
> *I asked to use the phone to call my brother. My mom answered and she was crying. She asked me to come home as soon as I could. I told her that I would.*
>
> *The counselor interrupted the call and told me I had two minutes. I was pissed.*
>
> *I told him, "It's bad enough my dad died and I am sitting in this shithole for the last seven years for something I didn't do. I just find this out. My mom is crying. And you have the balls to tell me I have two minutes left. Don't ever tell me I have two minutes or ten minutes left."*
>
> *He started to move towards the panic button.*

I told him, "Do yourself a favor and stop. You'll never make it to that button."

I finished my conversation with my mom and told the counselor, "I was serious about that button if you think you're summoning the goon squad."

He called Deputy Nobles, the second in command at Ryan. I had no problems with that.

Deputy Nobles came to the office and called Hernandez to the side. He had a heated, one-sided conversation with the counselor. When it was over, Hernandez told me, "Don't worry. Sit in my office for as long as you want. Use the phone. Whatever you need."

I didn't have the opportunity to say good-bye to him and it was really painful. He knew, like I did, that I was incapable of doing what they said I did, that I was wrongly convicted. He couldn't understand why the system wasn't working. And I felt the same way. This whole ordeal, in my opinion, killed him. And he was a good man. He should never have suffered the way that he did. And neither should I have.

On June 2, 2000, Kenny filed a motion for a *Certificate of Appealability* to obtain permission to file a motion of appeal to the U. S. Court of Appeals. He also sent a personal letter to Judge Duggan, entreating him to grant his request.

When my dad passed away right after the U. S. District Court denial, I was in a total fog. My head was not on straight.

Ramsey was a tremendous blessing. He helped me file the motion for the certificate. We had to get it done in that ten day window. It was just like the old days back in Jackson. And we got the appeal granted by Judge Duggan without Howarth!

On June 7, 2000, Judge Duggan responded with an *Opinion and Order Granting Petitioner's Motion for Certificate of Appealability*. The firm of Ramsey & Wyniemko had won.

Appeals History-United States Court of Appeals
On July 31, 2000, they filed an *Appeal of the Order Denying Petitioner's Motion for Writ of Habeas Corpus* with the United States Court of Appeals for the Sixth Circuit Court.

On March 23, 2001, the United State Court of Appeals, in an unpublished opinion, affirmed the U. S. District Court ruling.

That was it. Kenny had run out of options. After over six years of legal battles, Kenny's only remaining hope was Kim Shine.

Chapter 6 — Kim and Gail and The Innocence Project

"*We would get updates in prison about laws passed by the Michigan Legislature. I remember reading the notice when Michigan made DNA testing mandatory. It was January 1st, 2001. MCLA 770.16. When I read that, I said, 'This is just what I need to prove my innocence.' I was right.*" — Kenny Wyniemko

http://www.legislature.mi.gov: 770.16 DNA testing; petition; filing; availability of biological material; court order; findings; costs; results; granting or denying request for new trial; notice of petition to victim; preservation of biological material identified.

With his legal appeals exhausted after the U. S. Court of Appeals denial in March of 2001, Kenny knew that *Detroit Free Press* Reporter Kim Shine and the Innocence Project, an organization dedicated to pursuing wrongful convictions through DNA evidence testing, represented his last chances at freedom.

Early in the summer of 2000, Kim had met with Kenny and promised to look into his case. With obstacles at every turn, she pressed on. She persisted despite protests and delay tactics from the Clinton Township Police Department.

Kim related her experience on a local TV show called *Legally Speaking*.

It's not uncommon to receive letters from prisoners. And, you know, usually, yes, everyone's innocent. I had to convince an editor who approached it with the same mindset.

> *I said, "Just let me look into these few things."*
> *So, finally, I got the police department to agree to it.*
> *The police department claimed that, "You know what? Other people have checked this out. They've all found it's, you know, it's a waste of time. Don't waste your time, Kim."*
> *I said, "You know I'd like to look for myself."*
> *There was some reason they didn't want me looking into it.*

The more resistance she got and the more she investigated, the more she was convinced of Ken's innocence.

> *I don't think he should be here. I really don't think he should be here.*

The Innocence Project decided to take Kenny's case in 2002. Kim turned over her findings and assisted in any way she could. Her contribution to Kenny's release was invaluable. Her personal interest in Kenny, the person, was a blessing during Kenny's DNA appeal and after his release.

Kenny recalled their first encounter.

> *I met Kim in 2000, before the Innocence Project came on board. She said she wanted to meet me in person. I already had her number at the Free Press where I could call her anytime. She asked if it was okay to come to Ryan so that we could talk. I told her it was fine with me. She just had to get clearance with the Department of Corrections. I assumed she wanted to meet me face to face to see if I was legit.*
>
> *They put us in a room by ourselves. In our first meeting, I asked her if it was my letters that got her here.*
>
> *She said, "Well, Ken, to be honest with you, they were."*

> She asked me who wrote the letters and who put all the evidence together. I told her that I did all that stuff. She said, "Well, after I read the whole thing, something didn't seem right. I could tell something just wasn't right."
>
> She promised me she was going to look into it.
>
> Kim talked about when she went to see the police. They kept telling her it's a waste of her time, that other people have checked my conviction out and there was nothing to find. Well, Kim told them, "I want to look for myself."
>
> Thank God she did.
>
> I think that was the first time anyone mentioned that something was not right with my conviction. I know the court system and the cops hate when their names are being brought up in the media for something like this. I can honestly say it was first time that I saw a light at the end of the tunnel that wasn't an oncoming train.

It had been a long and frustrating effort to get the Innocence Project involved.

On March 15, 1995, Kenny sent a handwritten letter to Barry Scheck, co-founder and director of the Innocence Project at the Benjamin N. Cardozo School of Law at Yeshiva University in New York City. Kenny professed his innocence, outlining the facts of his case and imploring assistance in a post-conviction DNA appeal. To Kenny's surprise, Mr. Scheck responded. In a letter dated August 14, 1995, Mr. Scheck explained the Innocence Project was overwhelmed with requests, but they would review Kenny's case, time permitting. Kenny sent them additional information about his case and awaited a reply.

Correspondence continued over the next several years. The answer was always the same. Due to an excessive case load, the Innocence Project at Cardozo did not believe they could assist with a post-conviction DNA appeal at this time.

Finally, in December, 2000, Kenny received welcome news in a letter from Michigan Public Defender F. Martin Tieber. Mr. Tieber notified Kenny that an Innocence Project branch would be opened in Michigan. He further wrote that he had received Kenny's file from Cardozo and that he would hold the file until the Michigan Innocence Project program started.

In May, 2001, the Thomas M. Cooley Law School in Lansing, Michigan, started an Innocence Project operation. Mr. Tieber immediately forwarded all the information about Kenny's case to Cooley.

On August 20, 2001, less than 6 months after the U. S. Court of Appeals denial, Kathy Swedlow, Deputy Director at Cooley, contacted Kenny, requesting a signed release and any documents pertinent to his case. Kenny was ecstatic.

Kathy recalled the events.

> *Kenny's case kind of drifted to the top because of the materials he provided and the things he said. Plus, Kim was actively writing about Ken's conviction and it pushed the public awareness. We became focused on his case pretty early on.*
>
> *At Cardozo, they couldn't handle the cases they received. They became involved in efforts to get other law schools in other states to establish Innocence Projects. When Cooley set up its Innocence Project, Cardozo forwarded the Michigan cases there.*

The Innocence Project assigned Attorney Gail Pamukov to work on Kenny's case. She examined the evidence from the Innocence Project, and from Kim Shine and Kenny. On November 21, 2002, Ms. Pamukov filed a *Defendants Motion for Release and Testing of Biological Evidence Pursuant to MCL 770.16*. The quest for Kenny's freedom had begun and Kenny couldn't have been happier.

> *After the U. S. Court of Appeals rejected our appeal, that was really the end of the appeal process. If it wasn't for Kim Shine and the Innocence Project, I would have been fucked.*
>
> *After the Innocence Project branch was opened at Cooley Law School in Lansing, it was a short time before they contacted me. I remember Kathy Swedlow and Donna McKneelen came with a couple students from the Project to meet me. I talked to them separate from Kim. But it wasn't very long before they were working together. Kim contributed a lot and they were constantly comparing notes.*

The time spent in jail during the Innocence Project's pursuance of DNA testing was a lifetime for Kenny. To have faith in the system was next to impossible. Kenny had no choice. The process took close to a year, from Kenny's first meeting with Ms. Pamukov in the summer of 2002, to her request for DNA testing on November 21, 2002, and, finally, to Kenny's release on June 17, 2003.

Ms. Pamukov recalled the process involved in the DNA appeal.

> *The Innocence Project called me. I think I spoke with Norm Fell, one of the co-directors at that time.*
>
> *He said "Look, we have a case in Macomb County. Would you take a look at it?"*
>
> *I made an appointment and went to Lansing and met with Kathy Swedlow and a student, Heidi Hagen. They gave me their file. Then I think I met with Ken shortly after that over the summertime.*

In 2002, when a prisoner has exhausted all appeals in appellate court, the evidence from his case can legally be discarded. The police could have destroyed all forensic evidence associated with Kenny's conviction and there would have never been a DNA appeal.

That is absolutely true. After all the appeals are exhausted, they don't have to keep the evidence.

Ms. Pamukov started the process of obtaining an order to test the DNA.

When you pick up a case like this, and someone has been convicted of multiple counts of rape and so on, you sit back and think, "Geez, what does that all mean?"

It took me a week to write the motion. I stood back and thought, "How does someone get convicted with this evidence? She's blindfolded. He's masked. The composite is only 60% accurate. The lineup was very shaky. How does this happen?"

And with no biological evidence linking Ken to the crime scene.

What Ms. Pamukov read about the lineup infuriated her. Four guys with mustaches. The victim leaving the viewing room before returning to identify Kenny.

That is really the thing that got my attention. That's where I went off the rails. I'm like, "What the hell?!"

I got the motion ready. I didn't want to file it until after the prosecutor's race was over in early November because I didn't want it to become a political issue where someone felt they **had** *to address the motion. I just wanted it to come in as a straight-up motion. So, I waited. I filed the motion and set it up for a hearing. Then I argued it in front Judge Servitto, who ordered all the testing. The prosecution would have stipulated that they agreed to the testing. But Lieutenant Ostin was there that day. He was adamant that everything was done properly and there was no need to go further. Ostin even went on the record and made those statements to* the judge. Judge Servitto said, "No, we are testing everything."

The order for testing was entered December 9, 2002. What the statute required at the time is that you had to go through a chain of evidence that required all of the evidence had to be reviewed and recorded before being shipped to Michigan State Police Crime Lab.

Everybody needed to keep a log so everyone knew what was being shipped to be tested. I want to say we did that in early January. I went to the Clinton Township Police Department. I recall that there were two huge Tupperware boxes full of stuff. We went through all the biological evidence and there was a ton — pantyhose, all kinds of swabs. I mean huge amounts of biological evidence.

After the DNA went to Lansing, I didn't hear anything so I started calling the State Police Crime Lab from time to time and they would say, "It's in process," or whatever.

In March or April, 2003, I got an indication that another sample had been taken up there, which I knew nothing about. It was being compared to the samples that they were already testing.

I was shocked. So, I filed a motion to pull all the testing out of the State Police Crime Lab. I didn't like what happened. I set that motion for a hearing.

I got a call from the prosecutor's office saying that I needed to put the motion off. There was some work being done with the file and to just sit tight.

In June, 2003, I got a call, maybe on the 10th, from Kim Shine from the Free Press and she said, "Gail, have you heard anything? I got rumblings that the testing came back."

I said, "I haven't heard a thing."

So, I contacted Carl Marlinga's office, the prosecutor's office, and left a message. Carl called me and said the tests came back and Ken is not the guy.

The History of Kenny's DNA Appeal (2002-2003)

November 21, 2002 — Ms. Pamukov filed a *Defendant's Motion for Release and Testing of Biological Evidence*, addressing separate memos to the Macomb County Circuit Court and to Carl Marlinga, Macomb County Prosecuting Attorney. In her motion, she requested that all biological evidence associated with Kenny's case be released for DNA testing and that the testing be paid for by the State of Michigan. She further requested that the DNA testing be performed by the Forensics Science Associates in Richmond, CA, by Dr. Edward R. Blake. Ms. Pamukov extolled the credentials of Dr. Blake, citing several instances where his work had been recognized by State Supreme Courts throughout the United States.

Here is the CONCLUSION of the motion.

V. CONCLUSION

Wyniemko has met the burden as set forth by the Legislature in MCL 770.16, regarding the release and testing of the biological evidence collected during the course of the investigation in this matter. Wyniemko therefore asks that the Court order the following:

1. *Release the biological evidence collected in this matter, specifically:*
   a. *Semen stained sheet;*
   b. *The lavender panties;*
   c. *The vaginal, oral, and rectal swabs and smears collected from the Complainant via the rape kit;*
   d. *The saliva stained cigarette butt;*
   e. *Hair found in the crotch of the lavender panties and hair collected off the bed sheets;*

  f. *Any other biological evidence that is available for testing, i.e., blood, Pepsi can, etc.*
2. *Wyniemko specifically requests that the semen contained within the bed sheets and the lavender panties be tested and compared to a sample from Wyniemko, as well as from the Complainant's husband, Shawn Klug. Wyniemko further requests that such comparative testing, i.e., between the semen stained sheets and the Complainant's husband, be done through an enhanced process.*
3. *Wyniemko requests that the materials itemized above, be subjected to STR DNA testing. If Wyniemko is excluded as a source of the DNA material, the DNA test results should be compared to DNA samples via the FBI (CODIS data bank) and Michigan State Police so the true perpetrator of this crime can be identified.*
4. *Finally, Wyniemko requests the STR DNA testing be performed by Dr. Edward Blake, of Forensic Science Associates, Richmond, California, at the expense of the State.*

December 9, 2002 — The appeal was heard by Judge Edward Servitto, Jr. Kenny was represented by attorney Gail Pamukov. Appearing for the State of Michigan was Assistant Prosecuting Attorney Donald Gillain.

 Mr. Gillain opened by introducing Clinton Township Police Department Lieutenant Thomas J. Ostin to speak to the court. Judge Servitto gave a preliminary peek at the direction of his ruling. Here is an excerpt from those proceedings.

> *GILLAIN: I would ask the Court to hear from him this morning relative to the evidence and how this was dealt*

with at the time of trial and pretrial because I think the Court may be enlightened as to some of the aspects of this.

OSTIN: Your Honor, I'm a little upset with this case because this was a very thorough case.

THE COURT: Personalities and personal opinion has absolutely no place in court.

Lieutenant Ostin argued vehemently against the testing. He testified that testing the DNA evidence would neither exonerate nor justify Kenny's conviction. He further testified that the victim had an affair earlier in the day of her attack and that the semen stained panties had no relevance on the case.

Ms. Pamukov notified the court that neither she nor her client had any knowledge of the affair partner.

Lieutenant Ostin countered that this information was exchanged at the trial with attorney Albert Markowski, Kenny's lawyer. (The fact that Mr. Markowski agreed to not pursue any line of questioning regarding the affair without notifying Kenny is something that will be explored later in this book.)

Judge Servitto was steadfast and said so during the hearing.

THE COURT: I want it all tested.

Judge Servitto considered the back-and-forth argument regarding the panties as irrelevant. He gave no credence to Lieutenant Ostin's opinions that the testing would be fruitless. He denied Ms. Pamukov's request that the testing be performed by an outside crime lab in California. Regarding the victim's affair earlier the day of the rape, DNA samples from the affair partner would be submitted and become part of the process. *All* of the evidence would be tested. No exceptions.

Macomb County Circuit Court Judge Edward Servitto, Jr., ordered all forensic evidence to be released to the Michigan State Police Crime Lab. The request for DNA testing was approved.

> THE COURT: *I read that the allegations here are incredible. The trial that took place involved the most heinous of all crimes that one could ever experience, but justice requires under the circumstances that there be a review of the evidence with the technology that is available today. There is no reason that we do not explore both for culpability and innocence, utilizing the technology that is available today. Under those circumstances we will have the evidence reviewed.*

January 24, 2003 — Ms. Pamukov addressed a memo to Charles Barna, Forensic Science Manager of the Michigan State Police Crime Lab. The memo stated that attached was "*an order requiring DNA testing in the matter of the People v Kenneth Wyniemko, case number 94-2001-FY.*"

April, 2003 — In a follow-up call with the Michigan State Police Crime Lab, Ms. Pamukov discovered additional DNA samples had been sent to the lab in March, unbeknownst to her. On April 16, 2003, she sent a strongly worded letter to Ms. Therese Tobin, Assistant Prosecuting Attorney of Macomb County, inquiring about the sample. Here are excerpts from that letter.

> *I am perplexed as to why the sample was sent, who the sample belongs to, and why I was not included in the loop regarding the obtaining of the sample. I have no preliminary test results at all.*

Could you please advise as to who submitted the "reference sample," who it belongs to, and why I was not included in the loop.

Ms. Pamukov was informed that Lieutenant Ostin had reacted to a request from the Crime Lab for a DNA sample from the victim's affair partner. Lieutenant Ostin had obtained the sample and submitted it under "John Doe." Ms. Pamukov was not notified.

May 22, 2003 — Ms. Pamukov submitted *Defendant's Motion for Release and Testing of Biological Evidence* to an outside lab for testing. She requested this matter be placed on Judge Servitto's docket for June 9, 2003. Ms. Pamukov waived the motion later when she received a call from Prosecutor Carl Marlinga informing her that the DNA tests were back and Kenny was not the perpetrator.

May 30, 2003 — Ms. Pamukov immediately submitted a request to review Kenny's case. The hearing was scheduled for June 11, 2003. Judge Servitto was again the presiding judge.

June 9, 2003 — The Laboratory Report from the *State of Michigan Department of State Police Forensic Science Division (Laboratory No. 21831-94 SUPP, Record No. 0300397)* excluded the presence of Kenny's DNA in all the forensic evidence collected at the crime scene.

Furthermore, the report indicated that on several occasions, the source of DNA did not come from the victim, the victim's husband, or the victim's sexual partner from earlier that day. An "unknown donor" was the source of the DNA found on the cigarette butt, from scrapings found under the victim's fingernail, and from the hip area of the nylons. The prosecution's trial theory that the DNA at the crime scene came from the husband didn't hold up.

The Innocence Project had proven their case.

Details of the DNA test results can be found in "Appendix *A – 2003 DNA Test Results.*"

While a DNA search of the FBI's CODIS (Combined DNA Index System) database did not yield a match with the "unknown donor," there was the possibility of a match in the future that could identify the real perpetrator of this horrendous crime. Make no mistake. There were individuals who considered Kenny's release just another example of a criminal getting off on a technicality. Others believed that if Kenny had not committed the crime, then he was guilty of some other one. Innocent people do not end up in jail. Finding the actual perpetrator would give Kenny full vindication, something he craved badly. A match on CODIS would accomplish that.

June 11, 2003 — Ms. Pamukov filed a *Motion to Modify and Obtain Relief from Judgment* in Macomb County Circuit Court. The motion outlined the history of the case and requested Kenny's release as a result of the DNA test findings. Here are excerpts from that motion.

> *Defendant is requesting immediate relief due to the DNA test results, which were published and made available to the undersigned counsel on June 11, 2003.*
>
> *At the time of trial in this matter, DNA testing was not performed. The results of the DNA testing in this case have clearly established that Defendant Kenneth Wyniemko is not the perpetrator of the acts complained of by the complainant.*

June 12, 2003 — On the day Kenny thought he was going to be released, another DNA test was ordered by Judge Servitto. It was called a buccal swab test where a sample was taken from the inside of

GAIL M. PAMUKOV
Attorney at Law
19900 East Ten Mile Road - Ste. 102
St. Clair Shores, Michigan 48080

Telephone: 586-777-3310   Fax: 586-777-3145

June 11, 2003

Clerk of the Court
Macomb County Circuit Court
40 North Main Street
Mt. Clemens, Michigan 48043

    Re: People v Wyniemko
           File no. 94-2001-FY

Dear Sir/Madam:

    Enclosed for filing please find Defendant's Motion to Modify and Obtain Relief From Judgment Pursuant to MCR 6.500 et seq.

    Thank you.

                                           Very truly yours,

                                           Gail M. Pamukov

GMP:jll
encs.
cc: Prosecutor's Office
       Kenneth Wyniemko
       Clerk - Judge Edward Servitto
       Norman Fell, Esq., and Kathy Swedlow, Esq.

Gail Pamukov Request for Ken's Release

Kenny's cheek. It was a huge disappointment for Kenny, but Ms. Pamukov assured him the request from Judge Servitto was legal and that the delay should be short.

June 16, 2003 — After the appeal for a second DNA test, Kenny frantically awaited word of the results. Had his freedom finally come? Had Ms. Pamukov and the Innocence Project provided sufficient proof of what Kenny had known – that Kenny was innocent of the 1994 rape of Diane Klug? On June 16, 2003, Kenny received word that the buccal swab DNA test came back the same. It was over. Kenny was going home.

Ms. Pamukov and Kenny related the final days of the DNA testing that led up to Kenny's release.

> GAIL PAMUKOV: *I drove to Ryan to tell Kenny the good news. I didn't know what to say. I'm driving and I was so excited. By the time I got there, I thought, "What do you tell somebody? 'Oh, this is just a big mistake. Sorry.'"*

> KENNY: *It was June 11, 2003. I was sitting in my cell about 7:00-7:30 in the evening when the guards came to get me. They told me I had to get up front to the Control Center immediately because one of my attorneys was there. My first thought was something had happened to my mom because it is very unusual to get an attorney to visit that late at night.*
>
> *My dad passed away when I was still in prison in 2000 and I had a hard time dealing with that. And I knew my mom wasn't feeling well. I thought that the only reason my attorney would be there was to give me bad news.*
>
> *I went to the Control Center and a guard sat me at a table in an interview room. Gail walked in and she had this look on her face. It looked like something was wrong and I started to get nervous. I came up to her and gave her a hug and said, "Gail, are you feeling okay?"*

And she said asked me, "Yeah. Why do you ask?"

I told her that she doesn't look as happy as she usually does. I asked her why she was here.

She replied, "Kenny, you better sit down. You need to take a seat."

When she told me that, I just knew she was going to tell me my mom passed away. So, I sat down at the table and Gail sat down directly across from me, staring at me.

I said, "Gail, please tell me what's, what's going on?"

She is looking at me and said, "Kenny, I don't know how to tell you this."

I said, "Gail, please don't tell me that something happened to my mom because I don't know if I can take it. I had a hard time losing my dad. When he passed away, I wasn't allowed to go to the funeral."

She interrupted me, telling me that my mom was fine, and that she spoke to her about an hour ago and she was really happy.

She told me that she had just received a call from Carl Marlinga, the Macomb County Prosecutor. Hard copy results of DNA test came in excluding me and proving beyond a shadow of a doubt that I could have not committed the rape. Carl wanted me released from prison the next day. She told me, "Kenny you are an innocent man. Carl wants you released tomorrow."

I spread my arms on the table and put my put my head in my arms and I started crying. I got up real quick and ran around the table and pulled Gail's chair out and I picked her up by her waist and I was swinging her around like in a circle. I said, "Gail, Gail, what happened? What happened?"

She was laughing and said, "Kenny, put me down and I will tell you exactly what happened."

And that's the way it went. Just like that. She told me that I am going to be released from prison as an innocent man. She brought the writ of *habeas corpus* with her to give to the warden. I'm going home tomorrow.

GAIL PAMUKOV: *I spoke with Ken and told him we had to figure out how we were going to proceed with this. I gave him a general outline of what I thought was going to happen. There was no provision for post-conviction monies or anything.*

I told him, "I need your shoe size, shirt size, pant size."

He told me he needed a pair of glasses.

I'm taking down a lot of nuts and bolts stuff for when he gets out, which was completely expected. What is the next part of this? Where does he live after all this time? I said, "Who do I call? Where will you go?"

The celebration and the excitement of it all were tempered by the fact that you have to start dealing with the realities of the next phase. I am trying to figure out how to make that happen.

KENNY: *I was so happy when I came back from the Control Center. I felt like I was walking on air. I got to my cell and everybody was in the yard at that time. All the inmates in my unit were there. I told George and Tony, "Man, I'm going home!"*

And they made a big cook up with all kinds of stuff. A cook up is a big thing in prison. We made Ramen noodles, Slim Jims, nachos, cheese, and onions. We stole the onions from the kitchen. We had a big, big dinner. All my good friends were there and I gave away everything. There were guys who I was locked up with who didn't have any street clothes, or a TV or radio. I gave all my stuff away — my TV, my radio, my typewriter. The only things I kept were some clothes and all my legal stuff. Everything else went to the guys who didn't have anything.

I did keep this green Ban-Lon shirt and pair of tan pants I wore during visiting hours. My prisoner number was stamped inside. In fact, I still have them in one of my dressers.

The next morning (clears throat) the cops came to get me and they said, "Come on, Kenny. Time to go back to court."

I was walking out of my unit, Building 4D, and it's about a 150-200 yard walk right down the middle of the compound. You had to walk down a sidewalk at the Ryan Center to get to the Control Center. It was a nice day, beautiful sunny day. As I'm walking down the center by myself, the inmates, who were in their buildings, had their screens open and their windows open. Everybody was yelling, "Kenny, Kenny," like a chant. It started quiet. Then it got louder and louder and louder. I tell you, by the time I hit that door at the Control Center, I was crying. I was crying my eyes out.

Doug Wallace, my boss at Ryan, came to see me. And Scott Nobles, the deputy warden, stopped by. They both gave me a hug and told me, "Kenny, we never believed that you were guilty."

There was this guy who I never got along with. His name was Reverend Joe Green, the prison chaplain. This guy was a fake, a phony, a supposed man of God.

He would come in just about every week and mess with me about wearing my cross and chain outside my shirt. This was before they told us we could only have one religious item. He would tell me every time he'd see me, "Man, Wyniemko, you can't show that cross like that. You have to put that under your shirt."

> *I asked him, "Why are you picking on me? What about these Muslims that are wearing their moon and a star? You don't say a thing to them, do you?"*
>
> *"That's my business, man. You do what I tell you to do."*
>
> *I'd say, "Yeah," and I'd walk away.*

> *Well, the night it got around Ryan that I was to be released, here was Reverend Green, wearing a silk suit and a full-length mink coat. He came up to me and stuck his hand out and said, "Congratulations. Congratulations. You are innocent."*
>
> *I told him, "Oh, now we're friends? Why don't you go fuck yourself!"*
>
> *He walked away.*
>
> *Come to find out, he was bringing drugs into the prison. After all that bullshit that he put me through. I can laugh about it now. Like I said before, what a phony.*

On June 12, 2003, Kenny entered the Macomb County courtroom with the intent of walking out a free man. But that would be derailed when presiding judge, Judge Edward Servitto, ordered the additional DNA test from a buccal swab from Kenny.

It was a disheartening moment. Instead of a straight shot to freedom, he was transported back to Macomb County Jail. How could he possibly trust a system that had caused him and his family so much grief?

> *On June 12th, they took me from county jail back to the court room. It was the same courtroom I got convicted in.*
>
> *I thought it was just a formality where Judge Servitto would sign the papers and I could go home. But it was a curve ball. Judge Servitto ordered another DNA test called a*

buccal swab where they take a swab from the inside of my cheek. I wasn't expecting that.

But, under the DNA statute, Judge Servitto had that right. I didn't know that at the time. I don't think Gail did either. I thought it was a done deal when Gail came to see me the day before and told me that Marlinga wanted me released the next day, which was the 12th.

I had family and friends waiting outside the courtroom to take me home. They came there for nothing. And there wasn't anything I could do about it.

We went into an empty jury room for the buccal swab. There was Gail, myself, Kathy Swedlow from Innocence Project, and Kim Shine from the Free Press. Plus about 12 to 14 cops.

Carl Marlinga came in for the buccal swab. He sat across the table from me. I felt sorry for him. He was in a tough position. I can't say anything bad about Carl. He was just doing his job. It wasn't his idea to take the buccal swab.

As I was sitting there, I took Gail aside and said, "Gail, you know we caught them lying. We caught them cheating. They are going to try and do something at the last minute to switch this swab if I give it."

I wanted her to go in front of Servitto with hopes that he would make sure everything would be on the up and up.

Kathy Swedlow told me, "Kenny, give the swab. Don't start any problems right now. You are so close to going home."

She said that she and Gail would go to the lab with it. They will go in the car with Marlinga and drive it up to the State Police crime lab to have it tested. So, it will never be out of their sight.

One of the officers took the swab. Marlinga was sitting across the table from me and I turned over to Gail and said, "Gail, I have something I want to say to Carl."

Gail said, "Kenny, don't start any shit."

> I said, "I'm not going to start any shit. But there was something I have been waiting nine years to say and I want to say this"
>
> She told me that if I start to go off track and say something wrong she was going to kick me.
>
> I said, "If you kick me, I am going to kick you back."
>
> I looked Carl straight in the eye and he looked me straight in the eye. I said, "Carl, you know I have maintained my innocence all along for all these years. I have been saying, 'You have the wrong guy. You got the wrong guy.' I was praying for several things every day for the past nine years. Number One: that the truth would come out. And, Number Two: I was praying for you that you would have the courage to stand up and say we made a mistake and I thank you for saying that."
>
> Tears welled up in his eyes and he broke down.

> They took the sample and put it in an envelope. Gail, Kathy, and Carl took off with the State Police. They took me back to the county jail to wait for the results. They didn't come back until the 16th, a day after my 43rd birthday. On June 17th, they took me back to court. That is when I was freed.

The days leading up the 17th were greatly anticipated, not only by Kenny, but by his friends and family, too. Helen Wyniemko, Kenny's mom, gave a TV interview during which she couldn't hide her exuberance. Her son was finally coming home to her.

> I said, "Oh, thank you, Jesus. Thank you, Jesus." Because we always, my husband and I, we always said, "He didn't do that. He didn't do that. I know it's going to be a valley of tears. He's going to be crying. I'm going to be crying."

Just before his release, Kenny called his mom's home to make sure his family had the specifics of the time and place of his release. What he got was something he did not expect. It was crushing news when his brother told him that his family would not be attending his release the next day.

> *I called my mom's house. Jimmy and Tommy, my brothers, were there. Tommy answered the phone. I couldn't believe what he was saying. He said that no one from the family, including our mom, was going to be at my release.*
>
> *I didn't see it coming at all. I thought my family would be extremely happy that I was found innocent and that I would be getting out of jail.*
>
> *I told him, "I have to be at court by 10 so can you pick up Mom and make sure she's there?"*
>
> *"Your mom doesn't want to come!"*
>
> *I said, "Tommy, I don't want to hear that shit."*
>
> *"Well, I don't want Mom to be there. Let's put it that way."*
>
> *I said, "Let me talk to Jimmy."*
>
> *"Jimmy agrees with me, Kenny. Don't bother Mom. She ain't coming. You have caused Mom and Dad enough pain."*
>
> *And he hung up the phone. I stood there with the receiver in my hand in disbelief. I could not understand what I just heard.*
>
> *You have to excuse me if I'm sniffling or tearing up. This is not an easy thing to talk about.*

Kenny paused for a moment to gain his composure.

> *I don't know what he could have been thinking. I know he had a drinking problem. But nothing explains what he did. Nothing.*

The cruelty with which Kenny's own brother spoke was hard to comprehend. It's impossible to imagine the hurt Kenny felt. As for his Mom, what could she have thought? She had to be crushed.

Ken, Gail Pamukov, and Barry Scheck

Chapter 7 — Freedom

"*Kim Shine and Gail Pamukov are my guardian angels. Without their efforts, I would have died in jail. I really believe that.*" — Kenny Wyniemko

"*Naturally, because it happened on my watch, it really disturbs me. I'm frustrated and angry that it happened. The mistake is not having something like this happen on your watch. The mistake would be to try and deny it and cover it up.*" — Carl J. Marlinga, Macomb County Prosecutor (1985-2004)

Waiting for the results of the buccal swab had been exasperating. All Kenny could think about was how he was going to be screwed in some manner by the very system that had framed him and sent him to close to nine years of hell.

> *On the 16th, Gail and Kathy (Swedlow) came to see me at the Macomb County Jail. They told me that everything was set. The final result of the buccal swab had come back. I was declared innocent.*
>
> *They told me I was due back in court the next day at 10:00 in the morning. I was going to be taken out of the jail in a van by myself and driven to the courthouse where I was to be released.*

Freedom! Finally! The buccal swab test came back negative. Kenny was finally going home. His release was set for Tuesday, June 17, 2003.

During the early morning hours of the day of his actual release, Kenny experienced one more reminder of what prison life was like.

> *It was the 17th — about 5:30 in the morning. I was in my cell. In Macomb County Jail, there are speakers hooked up to the intercom system in each cell. These speakers are connected to the Control Center. If a guard wants to get a hold of you without coming down to your cell, they just click the switch and talk.*
>
> *I'm half asleep and I hear a voice come over the intercom, "Wyniemko, get up and get in the shower. You got 20 minutes before you gotta go downstairs to the bullpen. The van's waiting for you."*
>
> *I yelled back into the speaker, "I am not due in court until ten."*
>
> *Then I hear another voice say, "What'd you say?"*
>
> *I said, "I'm not due in court till ten o'clock and I am not taking a shower right now."*
>
> *The officer then said, "Wyniemko, I am giving you a direct order! Get your ass in that shower!"*
>
> *I said, "I'm not takin a shower right now!"*
>
> *So, about five minutes later, the guard who was talking on the intercom and his partner came down to my cell. This may sound goofy, but these guys' names are Officer Green and Officer Brown. Those are their real names. They come in my cell wearing their riot gloves, you know, the red gloves.*
>
> *I can't remember which one of the two, Brown or Green, came up to me and said, "Wyniemko, get your ass in that shower and you have to get downstairs, because the van is ready and waiting for you."*
>
> *I said, "I told you I am not due in court 'til ten. My attorneys were here yesterday and they told me they were going to come and get me about half hour before then, using*

a separate van. So, about 8:30-9:00, that's when I will take a shower."

Then he got on his radio and asked for backup. And about six or eight more cops came in in riot gear! They had their masks on, their shields. This guard told me, "Wyniemko, you see what's back there?"

I said, "I don't see a thing. I mean, so what are you going to do? Are you gonna beat my ass?"

I heard one of the guards in riot gear yell, "Hey, you think you're going home. You say you're innocent. We know you are not innocent. You ain't going nowhere. You're going back to fucking prison."

I said, "Oh yeah. Why don't you go fuck yourself!"

The one guard who was shouting in the riot gear started walking towards me.

I said, "Well, come on. You want to fuck me up? Then fuck me up. It will look real good when I'm on TV about noon with bruises all over my face. So, go ahead, do what you want!"

The goon squad was told to get out. Green and Brown were standing there and one of them said, "You know what Wyniemko? I'd really like to beat your ass. I should beat your fuckin' rapist ass right now!"

I said, "You know what's between us? Air and opportunity, man. And you can go fuck yourself, too!"

And they walked out.

Later, about 8:15, I get the call over the PA system over the intercom, "Okay, Wyniemko, ready for your shower."

I just replied, "Yes, sir."

They came down and gave me a towel. I took a shower and then they led me downstairs in an elevator.

I'll never forget that. Never!

I was still dressed in my prison clothes when they took me down to the bullpen at Macomb County Jail. The Macomb County Jail van picked me up to take me to the courthouse. I was led downstairs to the holding cells. It wasn't long before I was led to a small bathroom just outside Judge (Edward) Servitto's courtroom. Gail and Kathy brought civilian clothes that I could change into after my appearance in court.

I was really excited.

Gail told me, "Kenny, this is your day. You're coming home today! A bunch of people are outside waiting. After, Greg and Terry (friends of Kenny) are having a big party. Jimmy Sardelli will be there, too." Jimmy was a good friend of mine.

It was messed up that my mom wasn't there. My brothers weren't there either. Tommy saw to that. I tried to block it out of mind. Once the proceedings started, I was too excited to think of anything else but walking out that courtroom a free man.

Ms. Pamukov recalled her conversation with Prosecutor Carl Marlinga regarding the next steps in this process.

Carl and I spoke. No one had used the post-conviction DNA test statute before. We were the first case to use it. And to get to the point where the DNA results came back and the defendant, now the convicted person, was not the guy. So, we had to figure out what the next steps were. The idea was we were going to writ (use of court order) Ken out from Ryan Regional. He was going to be brought over to Macomb County and then we were going to have a hearing on Friday.

It was June 17th. The Michigan State Crime Lab people came into court and explained what they did. At the end of the hearing, the judge found Ken was innocent and he was released.

> Marlinga said, "You know he was actually an innocent man."
>
> The judge was going to release him right from the courtroom, but he needed to be processed back out through the jail. He was released later that day, very close to his birthday. We had a birthday celebration.

Prosecutor Carl Marlinga filed a *Motion to Dismiss* before Judge Edward Servitto, requesting the release of prisoner Kenneth Wyniemko. Sarah Thibault, Forensic Biologist for the Michigan State Police, testified that DNA testing had eliminated Kenny from being at the crime scene. Furthermore, DNA test results identified the presence of an unknown donor.

Here are excerpts from Mr. Marlinga's motion.

> *The Michigan State Police Crime Laboratory has conducted the requested DNA tests. The test results exclude the defendant as a possible perpetrator of the crimes. Specifically, a cigarette butt found at the scene, semen stained pantyhose used as a gag, and scrapings of tissue found under the victim's fingernail show that an unknown person was the contributor of the DNA for each of these items. . . .*
>
> *This DNA does not match the DNA of the victim, the victim's husband, an affair partner of the victim with whom she had consensual sex, nor the defendant Wyniemko. . . .*
>
> *Upon the granting of defendant's motion for a new trial (which is also pending before the court) the undersigned prosecutor represents to this court that the remaining evidence in this case would not justify a retrial. The DNA evidence affirmatively proves beyond any doubt that a perpetrator other than the defendant committed these crimes. Defendant Kenneth Wyniemko is an innocent man.*

STATE OF MICHIGAN

MACOMB COUNTY CIRCUIT COURT

PEOPLE OF THE STATE OF MICHIGAN
PLAINTIFF

-vs-

File No. 94-2001FY
Hon. Edward A. Servitto

KENNETH WYNIEMKO
DEFENDANT
_____/

Carl J. Marlinga (P17102)
Macomb County Prosecuting Attorney
1 South Main
Mt. Clemens, MI 48043
(586) 469-5350

Gail M. Pamukov (P43929)
Attorney for Defendant
19900 East Ten Mile Road – Ste. 102
St. Clair Shores, MI 48080
(586) 777-3310

Norman Fell (P13360)
Kathy Swedlow (P64244)
Of Counsel for Defendant
Innocence Project – Thomas M. Cooley Law School
300 South Capital Avenue
Lansing, MI 48901
(517) 334-5764
_____/

MOTION TO DISMISS

Plaintiff, People of the State of Michigan, by the undersigned prosecuting attorney moves this court to dismiss all charges against defendant Kenneth Wyniemko in this case, and in support of this motion says:

1. A jury convicted defendant of breaking and entering, MCL 750.110, armed robbery, MCL 750.529, and fifteen counts of first-degree criminal sexual conduct, MCL 750.520b(1). The court sentenced defendant to ten to fifteen years

Prosecution Motion to Dismiss

Wherefore, plaintiff moves this court to grant the motion for new trial filed by the defendant, and to further grant this motion to dismiss.

Kenny walked into Judge Edward Servitto's court room as prisoner A240889, a ward of the State of Michigan Department of Corrections. When Judge Servitto dismissed the charges against him, he was finally a free man. The long, hard battle for his freedom had finally been realized.

There was cheering and high fives. A feeling of relief and of joy exuded throughout the gallery.

Kenny exchanged hugs, kisses, and tears with everyone who came to witness this glorious event.

He turned to his twenty-seven-old son, Kenny, Jr. It was a special hug between a father and son who now had a chance to reconnect for the first time in close to nine years.

That was special. Having my son in my life was something I dreamed of throughout my time in prison.

Ken Wyniemko became the second exoneree in the state of Michigan and the 129th nationwide. He would no longer be told what to do every minute of his day—when to rise in the morning, when to eat, when to exercise, when to bathe, and when to talk.

Kenny's feeling of elation was hard to describe. He was finally going home.

When I walked into the court room, it was surreal. I couldn't believe that this was all going to be behind me. There were so many people there for me.

I had the outside hope that Tommy had changed his mind. I shook my head when I realized my family wasn't there. But, when I saw Gail smiling, I pretty much forgot about it.

Gail talked about the motion for my release. The woman from the State Police Crime Lab testified that the DNA reports prove that I am innocent. Marlinga then said that he agreed that I was innocent and he would like to drop all charges and have me released. So, that's when I started to really get excited.

I can remember Carl when he was making his statement to Judge Servitto about the reliability of DNA evidence. He said people are going to have to realize DNA is the only piece of evidence that is 100% positive. It is unique to every person. But this number that Carl pointed out, when he made that point clear to Servitto, I never heard a number that big. Carl told Judge Servitto that the odds of me committing the crime were one in four quadrillion. And for anybody who does not know what a quadrillion is, it is a million billion. Carl said that number of people haven't even been born yet and never will be born.

After a few comments, Servitto said, "Mr. Wyniemko," then he slammed the gavel down, "You're free to go. Good luck."

Everybody started cheering in the courtroom. My son, Kenny, was there with Greg and Terry. Two of my childhood friends, Dusty and Marty, were there. Marty brought his wife, Kathy.

I hugged Gail first, then Kathy, then Kim. Gail broke down and started crying. And Kathy and Kim did, too. Then I turned around and saw Marty. My son, Kenny, was standing right behind him. I gave Kenny a hug and that's when I broke down. We just stood there with our arms wrapped around each other, both of us sobbing. Then I made the rounds and hugged and thanked everyone else.

It was very emotional.

I thought they were going to take me downstairs and I was going to change into the clothes that Gail bought. That's what everyone thought would happen. Everybody was waiting outside. The media was there.

That's when my ex-wife, Denise, pulled that shit about me owing back child support for the time I spend in jail. They led me straight to the bullpen and told me I was under arrest. I asked them, "For what?"

But they refused to answer me and just locked me up! Again!

I didn't know if they made a deal with someone in there who would be happy to beat the shit out of me. Who knows? I could have been brought up on an assault charge if a fight had broken out. I felt that they would have done anything to prevent me from being freed. All I know is that I was locked up and I didn't know what the hell was going on. There was no explanation from anybody. Until you actually walk out that door, you never totally believe they are really going to let you go.

I used a payphone to get a hold of Joanne, Gail's secretary. I said, "Joanne, where's Gail at?"

She said, "I thought she was with you."

I said, "They are still holding me. They put me back in the bullpen. I have no idea what is going on. Have her get me the hell out of here! Please!"

Joanne called Gail on her cell to tell her I wasn't coming out. Gail got a hold of Marlinga and asked him what the fuck what going on. Carl told her he'd find out and call her back on her cell. Carl called back and told her that there was a warrant out of Wayne County for back child support that Denise had filed, which turned out to be bogus. Carl called the courtroom and had me released immediately.

So, Gail and the Undersheriff came to get me out of the bullpen. The Undersheriff said, "Wyniemko, let's go. We have to go out right now."

With Ken's mom, Helen Wyniemko, Father Frank Skalski

The Day of Ken's Exoneration with Attorneys Gail Pamukov and Kathy Swedlow, and Detroit Free Press Writer Kim North-Shine

I remember these other guys were looking at me real funny when the Undersheriff came to get me out personally. They took me into the changing room so I could finally put normal clothes on. My release was over an hour and a half late.

I am in the process of changing my clothes when one of the guards came in and told me, "Come on, Wyniemko. Hurry up. Let's go now. You gotta get out of here."

So, I'm thinking, "What the fuck! First, they're doing anything to keep me in and now they're kicking me out."

I walked right through the double doors down this long corridor and Gail was standing right there. Gail and the Undersheriff. We started walking towards the front doors of the jail and it was, I don't know, maybe 150 feet. I kept asking Gail what took so long. She said, "Kenny, I don't want to upset you so let's just go. Okay?"

The Undersheriff told me, "Mr. Wyniemko, there is a bunch of media right out the front door. If you want, I can take you out the back door."

I said, "No way. I'm going out the front!"

I walked out and several camera lights went on. Flashbulbs were going off like crazy. Bill Proctor, from Channel 7 News, was the first person who shoved a microphone into my face. And Jeff Vaughn, who was at Channel 4 at the time, was there. They were both trying to get to me. I got Gail on one side and Kathy on the other side. Then Kim came by me. They were all trying to protect me.

Like I said, Proctor was the first one who stuck a mic in my face and started asking me how I felt and what's the first thing I wanted to do. I told him that I wanted to go to church and say some prayers of thanks. Then I'd like to visit my dad's grave.

> *I was so happy. I was just smiling and talking to anyone who wanted to listen. It was such a great feeling.*
>
> *After the reporters started to break up, I started walking towards Greg's car. I was surprised to see Proctor come up to me. He said, "You doing okay, Kenny?"*
>
> *I said, "Bill, I'm just happy as hell."*
>
> *He took out his card and said, "If you need any help, give me a call."*
>
> *That's how our friendship started.*

Kathy Swedlow described the euphoria she felt at Kenny's release.

> *When we got the news that Ken was exonerated, it was like nothing I had ever felt before in my capital cases. Here's this person who will actually leave prison and become a free man. It was absolutely thrilling.*
>
> *The best part was when I sat with Ken in court and we knew he was going to be released. We knew the DNA tests had eliminated him and we had just completed the second test. There was this total elation in court with Ken and all his friends. After his release, I believe we went to the home of some friends of Ken's. Things died down and it came time to go home after this emotionally charged day. It was so rewarding to know that I was instrumental in Ken's freedom.*

I arrived at work the next day about 9:00 am or 10:00 am. My students had been there for a couple hours. They were so excited! It was great.

As a teacher, it was a thrill to see my students realize an experience that would never be taken away. My students learned what it was like to help somebody with their legal

> work, and how powerful it could be. Their work affected change, positive change. That was really wonderful.
>
> It is a lot of hard work. And, in the end, it all comes down to a DNA test that either matches or it doesn't. I think about the capital cases I have worked on. There were so many days, weeks, and months and, sometimes, years, of being in court, of hearings that lasted weeks. It's the fruit of a lot of hard labor to realize a DNA exoneration. But, in the end, it still comes down to that little test. It's interesting that way.

Marty Hacias, a childhood friend of Kenny's, was there from the beginning of his incarceration and was present at his release. He visited Kenny many times, even bringing Kenny, Jr. a few times. He recalled those trips to Ryan Correctional Facility and the day of Kenny's release.

> He kept telling me, "It's happening. It's gonna happen." The lawyers were quite sure that it was going to go his way. Then, one day, it did. I was in the courtroom. Marlinga was there. He apologized to Kenny and told him a great wrong had been done. He applauded Kenny's efforts for not giving up. Then he declared the motion to dismiss and it was granted by the judge.
>
> I don't remember any great cheering or anything. But everyone was real happy. A lot of hugs. A lot of smiling.
>
> I remember going to someone's house after. It was pretty laid back. I guess it was so surreal for Kenny after those years in jail. When the day of his release finally came, it was a huge load off. I was just so happy for him. It had to have been such a horrible experience, especially for an innocent man.

The mystery as to why Kenny was locked up and his freedom delayed for close to two hours was that Kenny's ex-wife had filed a claim for back child support for the time he spent in prison. How dreadful that must have been when, just as he was set free, he was unceremoniously led away **back to jail**! The police waited until his release to arrest him.

Kenny bristled as he recalled the event.

Gail did not want me to cause a scene at the jail. She didn't tell me why I was detained until we got to Greg and Terry's house.

As a matter of fact, Gail took me in a bedroom to tell me about it. Away from everybody. Just her and I in the room. I told her the charge was all bullshit. When we were first divorced, one of the stipulations of the custody and child support agreement was that neither of us can take our son out of Michigan without both of us agreeing to it. Well, Denise did that. It was in around 1984. I couldn't find Kenny for months. So, I went to court and the judge rescinded my child support. Denise never refiled. They saw I was getting out of jail and they just wanted a paycheck.

Later, we were on the back patio of Greg and Terry's home when I asked everyone to gather around. I raised my glass and said, "If I can, I'd like to propose a toast to good friends and the truth. I just thank God for giving me the strength and the help of these friends to get through this situation. It's been a nightmare."

There were satellite dishes parked in front of Greg's house. Greg looked out the window and said, "Look at this shit. I can't believe this."

I looked out the bedroom window and I see these trucks out there. All their neighbors were coming out thinking, "What the fuck was going on?"

I think I was talking to Marty and Kathy when the doorbell rang. I looked up and saw a couple of cops on the porch. They came in and asked Greg if everything was okay. Greg said, "Actually, everything is real good."

Oddly, they were Clinton Township cops. Someone must have called them.

It was a great party. Gail was there. Kim was there. Some of the students that worked on my case were there. Many other friends, too.

It was also the first time I ever saw my grandkids! Kenny and his wife, Jamie, brought them. Adam, my youngest grandson, was only five weeks old. I got to hold him. I got pictures of that.

Later, Kim Shine came up to me and asked what time the cemetery closed. There was so much going on that I lost track of time. Terry called Resurrection Cemetery and she was told it closed at 6:00. It was just after 5:00. Kim said we'd better go right now. We put together this caravan and we sped off to the cemetery. We pulled in and stopped outside the office. I didn't know where my dad's grave was.

We walk up to the office and the hours were posted on the doors — 8:30-4:30. It was 5:15 pm. I pulled on the door and it was locked. I started knocking and, thankfully, a guy comes out of the back office wearing a shirt and tie. He opened the door and told me, "I'm sorry. You see we are closed? The office closes at 4:30."

I said, "Look."

And I pointed to all the people behind me, including the television cameras.

I told him, "I am going to tell you a story. You may not believe it. But if you watch the 6:00 news, you'll know it's true."

I proceeded to tell him.

He said, "I don't think you can make that up."

He let us in and gave me a map showing where my dad's grave was. We were walking back to our cars when he said, "I'm sorry, we don't allow cameras in the cemetery."

I just stared at him.

Then he said, "Go ahead."

We found my dad's grave. Kim was by my side. I knelt and brushed off some dirt that was on the headstone. I said a couple prayers then tapped his headstone and said, "Dad, I made it home."

And you could feel a little drizzle come down on me. Kim and I felt it. I looked up. Not a cloud in the sky. I looked at Kim and she looked at me.

She said, "Kenny, I don't believe this."

I told Kim, "You know, Kim, my Dad's crying right now because he knows that I am home."

I thought about my mom. She wanted to be there. The first time I saw her was on her birthday, ten days after my release. Everyone was real pissed that my brothers were keeping her from me.

Terry said, "We'll throw her a birthday party on the 28th. I'll get her here somehow."

My good pal, Jimmy Sardelli, was furious with my brothers, especially Tommy. We both knew we couldn't reason with him. So, Sardelli called Jimmy, my other brother, and convinced him to bring my mom to a birthday party at Greg and Terry's home.

My mom was crying because she was so happy. It was a special moment for the both of us. A long time coming. Yup, a very special moment.

My brother, Tommy, just refused to believe I was innocent. He refused to let my mom see me. I could never forget that. We never got back together. He passed on May 31, 2004.

> *After Tommy died, Jimmy played a telephone message recording from some time after I was released where Tommy seemed to be coming around. On it, Tommy asked how I was doing and that he hoped I was getting my act together. But I never spoke with him before he died from liver disease.*

On June 18, 2003, the day after Kenny's release, a television show titled *Legally Speaking – Innocence Project* was recorded. It was hosted by investigative news reporter Charlie Langton and it aired on the Sterling Heights cable television station from July 14, 2003, to July 28, 2003. Mr. Langton sat down with Mr. Marlinga, the prosecuting attorney, and Gail Pamukov, the defense attorney, to explore Kenny's case.

Mr. Marlinga was very forthcoming in his assessment of what happened at Kenny's trial. Both he and Ms. Pamukov were especially critical of the victim identification process.

> CARL MARLINGA: *The part that concerns me the most is, at the lineup, this should not have happened, where she left the room where the lineup was, conferred with either a police officer or an assistant prosecutor or the both of them, and there's no record of what those people said. But, when she came back in, she was able to make a positive identification. Once you make a positive identification as an eyewitness, then it's done.*
>
> *Now, of course, knowing that the guy is completely innocent, I mean there is an obvious flaw in what happened.*
>
> *Looking at the transcripts and looking at what we have left over, I got to say that the eyewitness identification is highly suspect. And it bothers me a great deal.*

Mr. Marlinga had a real hard time with the fact that the defense attorney had only two days to prepare.

CHARLIE LANGTON: *Does it also bother you that Ken Wyniemko's attorney had only two days?*

CARL MARLINGA: *That was terrible. That's an outrage. . . . I do think it's a failure in the system that the defense attorney didn't have more time to prepare.*

What seemed to bother Mr. Marlinga the most was the time Kenny had to remain incarcerated while the second DNA test of the buccal swab was being conducted.

After I analyzed what the DNA evidence meant with the police crime lab, I realized that this not only puts a hole in the evidence, this conclusively proves the opposite. This was an innocent man. Every minute he spent in jail from the time I made my decision last Wednesday night, until he was freed yesterday, I was in agony. I wanted him out immediately.

I was relieved when he was finally set free, obviously not as much as Gail and Mr. Wyniemko. There was a real emotional release when he was released.

The lack of DNA testing in 1994 came up. It was the Michigan State Crime Lab forensic scientist David Woodford's contention, when he testified in his 2004 civil suit deposition, that the DNA samples were probably too small to test. At that time, the Michigan State Crime Lab used the older DNA testing technique, Restriction Fragment Length Polymorphism (RFLP). Ms. Pamukov emphatically stated that Polymerase Chain Reaction (PCR) was available at the time of Ken's trial. PCR is a much improved method over RFLP, and it is possible to conduct successful DNA tests with much smaller samples. DNA, RFLP, and PCR were never mentioned in any of the trial transcripts in 1994.

GAIL PAMUKOV: There was PCR testing available at that time. It came online about the late 1980s. And it became widely accepted in the scientific community, probably in the early 1990s. So, it was on board. And there's a case in Michigan called People vs. Lee that really starts to lay out the foundation of PCR DNA testing.

CHARLIE LANGTON: So, then why wasn't DNA testing done back then?

GAIL PAMUKOV: That's a very, very good question. The technology was out there. Whether the Michigan State Crime Lab used the technology may be another issue. But the technology was definitely in place.

Mr. Langton asked Ms. Pamukov if Kenny was bitter.

Mr. Wyniemko is really quite an amazing individual. He's a man of great faith. I would say that he has responded to this with tremendous composure and humility. I don't detect bitterness. He has been pretty confident throughout the years that at some time he would be vindicated. And he, right now, is just enjoying the smell of cooking bacon.

Mr. Marlinga recalled the events leading up to Kenny's release.

CARL MARLINGA: It was emotionally significant for me. I had always understood that with all of the convictions that we obtain in the system, because we are human beings, some percentage must be flawed. Inevitably, some innocent people would be convicted. But when I had a clear example of something that happened on my watch, it was an emotional punch in my gut. This travesty actually happened *in spite of all the safeguards, all of my cautionary instructions to my assistant prosecutors. With all of my personal beliefs, I could not stop it from happening, even with me in charge. And it told me how prevalent the problem must be because I prided myself in an office that would do everything we could to make sure that we did not get a wrongful conviction. Yet, in a very significant case, it happened. That was the first part of the emotional experience.*

The second part of the emotional experience was actually seeing Ken when I went to court the day I moved to have him released immediately. Ken said something to me that I will never forget. He said, "Mr. Marlinga, I have been praying for you. I knew that if there was some prosecutor, somewhere, who would be willing to look into this to correct a mistake, it would be you."

It brought tears to my eyes then. It still brings that emotional rush even now. When I think about it, here's a man who had been wrongfully convicted and spent years in prison for a crime he did not commit. And his father died while he was in prison. He had been written off as a brutal rapist, whose entire life had been ruined by people who worked with me and under me, and therefore, to some extent me, myself. And, instead of being bitter, vindictive, arrogant, and haughty, he said what he said. I will never forget that day for the rest of my life.

Mr. Marlinga revealed a conversation he had immediately after Kenny's release.

When news stories were coming out that I had moved for a dismissal of Mr. Wyniemko's case, I came back up to the office and had a call from a juror who had been on the case.

She said, "Mr. Marlinga, I respect you. But I have to tell you I think you're doing the wrong thing here."

I said, "Why do you say that?"

She said, "I was one of the jurors who looked at all of the evidence. I'm convinced that this man is guilty. Are you absolutely sure he's innocent?"

I said, "I assure you I am absolutely sure."

Then we talked for about 45 minutes. She went over all of evidence. I had to explain to her that these were witnesses she heard. And those witnesses had to be incorrect. I talked to her about the DNA evidence. We talked awhile about how sure we are that the lab could not have made a mistake.

I said, "Well, all I know is that the judge has echoed what you just said. He wanted one more DNA test before we actually release him on bond or grant him the final release. So, we are running the one additional test just to make sure. But, remember, there are three items of biological evidence. It's the semen remaining on the panty hose, it's the saliva on the cigarette, and it's the skin scrapings under the fingernails. You have all three whose DNA is the same and it's not Mr. Wyniemko's. It's not just one piece of biological evidence."

I told her, "You were at the trial. You were a juror. You know what happened and you know the significance of the pantyhose that was used. You know the significance of the cigarette that was found and you know the significance of the scrapings under the fingernails. If these tests came back to three different people, you'd still have an exoneration. But it would be more of a puzzle. But here you've got confirmation that the same unknown perpetrator left all of this biological evidence. And it's definitely not from Ken Wyniemko. That's what makes me absolutely sure. And as far as everything else that you heard, realize that we are human beings, we're capable of making mistakes."

At the time, I was convinced that all of these were innocent mistakes. We found out later that was not completely true.

But it was the only way to talk to her because she was awfully, completely sincere. You don't want to argue with somebody who is so crestfallen that perhaps a guilty person is being freed or perhaps they got it wrong. I emphasized to her that human beings are capable of making mistakes. That has to be something we recognize. And that the best thing that we can do when a mistake is made is admit it, bring it to everybody's attention, apologize for it, and start trying to readdress the wrong that was done.

But, yes, I told her I am absolutely sure that, with this new evidence, Ken Wyniemko is an innocent man. And still, at the end, it was one of these. "Well, I'll trust your judgment. But I want you to know that I am still not sure."

I said, "I understand."

That's all you could do at the time. The entire gist of the conversation was her belief in his guilt. I was very much in tune to the emotions in her voice. It wasn't as much guilt on her part. She found it so hard to believe that all of the evidence, which was so convincing, was just flawed.

You have to remember that this was a terribly moving time for me because this was on the same day that Ken told me what he said about praying for me.

It had been 14 years since Bill Proctor, the Channel 7 television investigative reporter, waited outside the Macomb County Courthouse. His assignment was to interview a stranger by the name of Ken Wyniemko who had just been released from prison after being incarcerated for a crime he did not commit.

Here is his recollection of that day.

It started as just another assignment. However, Kenny's was one of the cases that set my mind and interest and heart in motion.

With Kenny, with this white guy, and I'm going to say that nice and loud, a lot of people don't understand that this is not something that essentially only minorities suffer. Minorities suffer at a greater rate mainly because they don't have the ties to good lawyers or good money to pay for all the various elements that might help them get better treatment on the appellate side of the process. I guess the bottom line with Kenny was how some guy who was a bowling alley manager gets jammed up by a police department in the suburbs.

I was there among the reporters just on assignment that day. And, yes, Kenny and I developed an affinity after I met him. But the real bottom line was that all of these white people are in a circle — the school, the prosecutor, Gail, the reporter, all the cops. You line all them up and it's all white folks. Now, I'm not one of those people on the planet who always runs to race when it comes to any point or issue, because I just don't. People are people.

All of these things hit me in the face. You have to understand that, at this point in our history, we didn't, as a nation, start to talk about wrongful convictions.

I listened to Kenny's empathy, Kenny's belief that it was his faith in God that essentially saved him. I remember him saying those kinds of things that he wouldn't have survived without his faith. Not that I'm any heavyweight religious person, but the fact of that the matter is, you don't have to have an understanding or an affinity for the victims of wrongful conviction to know that to have someone take away your freedom for something you didn't do, it's kind of the ultimate stealing of your life. I looked at this guy who spent almost nine years in prison. He's walking out today and it's a reporter's story line that helped get him there,

> *along with college students. It was that kind of stuff and the things I heard from Kenny that made me say, "Hey, he survived some pretty heavy stuff and here he is saying the things he is saying."*

It is amazing how Kenny has had such a profound influence on two bigger than life personalities like Bill Proctor and Carl Marlinga.

Mr. Proctor has become as determined as Kenny in his involvement in wrongful convictions. He has founded Proving Innocence, an organization like the Innocence Project that works with wrongful convictions, that is based in Detroit.

Shortly after Kenny's release in 2003, Carl Marlinga left the Prosecutor's office and became a defense attorney and an ardent supporter of the wrongly convicted. Working with the University of Michigan's Innocence Clinic, he was the primary counsel in a wrongful conviction case in which a young lady by the name of Julie Baumer was exonerated.

A few days after his release, Kenny returned to Ryan to pick up the rest of his personal belongings.

> *Scott Nobles, the deputy warden at Ryan, was always there for me. I remember the day I went back to Ryan to pick up my locker. The locker contained all my legal stuff and other items I wanted to keep. Scott had it sitting in his office.*
>
> *There were two corrections officers standing outside his office. They both shook my hand and congratulated me. It was great.*
>
> *Dave Payton, my work supervisor in the Rec. Department, was in his office. In fact, he helped me carry the locker out to the car that Terry and Greg let me use. We loaded it in the back of the SUV. I shook Payton's hand and drove off. My last visit to Ryan.*

At the time, Kenny did not know that if it were not for Scott Nobles, he would have had a very difficult time even entering the facility to retrieve his locker.

Mr. Nobles recalled the event.

> *After his release, Ken still had some personal property at Ryan. We had an administrator who wasn't going to let him come back into the facility to pick up his property.*
>
> *It was the administrative correctional mindset that you're a prisoner and now we're letting you come back after getting off on a technicality. So, I intervened and made sure Kenny could get his stuff. He's not a parolee. He's not a prisoner. He's exonerated and he didn't do it!*

First Halloween with Ken's grandchildren and son, Kenny, Jr.

Chapter 8 — Acclimation to Society

"*I needed to know what I could do to help Kenny get back in society. He had no money and nowhere to live. I had to buy him a suit, glasses, and other stuff for his court appearance.*"
— Gail Pamukov

After years of the most regimented life imaginable and in constant fear for one's safety, an exoneree re-enters society a broken, confused, and frightened individual. He or she has to start over in life. No job. No money. No place to call one's own. Their self-worth is zero.

Getting acclimated into society can be very difficult and often overwhelming. Support of friends and family helps. But the process is extremely challenging.

When Kenny was released in 2003, the State of Michigan did not have programs that provided any form of assistance for exonerees. For prisoners released after serving time for a crime they did commit, there were government provisions and programs that aided in their adjustment to being a free man or woman. Convicted rapists, child molesters, and murderers were given state-funded job counseling, medical coverage, psychiatric and mental healthcare, and other benefits. Guys like Kenny got nothing.

Years of wrongful imprisonment have long-lasting effects. Kenny has always insisted that mental health care is a necessity for all exonerees immediately after their release if they are to have a smooth transition.

During his civil suit in 2003, Thomas Howlett, one of Kenny's attorneys, convinced him to see a psychologist who Tom highly recommended.

> *Tom told me he thought it would be beneficial to me to see a psychologist by the name of Dr. Ralph Schillace. Dr. Schillace came along when I needed him most. I still see him when I need to talk to someone.*
>
> *It's another example of the good people I met since I was released. Every exoneree needs mental health assistance. Dr. Schillace, to this day, offers his services free to all exonerees. That is the only way I could have afforded him.*

Kenny was paranoid in public places. Women made him uncomfortable. Cops scared the hell out of him. He couldn't land a job. He had to rely on the charity of his friends for expenses and a place to stay. He struggled to fit back into society.

In a television telecast a few months after his release, Kenny said something very poignant.

> *It's been about four months now and I still don't feel free. It was nine years of living hell. My faith in God kept me going then and it keeps me going now.*

Kenny was asked what the best thing was about being a free man. He didn't hesitate to talk about the simple things in life.

> *Just being able to take a shower for 10 to 15 minutes if I want to. Going to a restaurant and being able to choose what I want to eat. To play a round of golf or to just drive around the country.*

Family was great comfort. He loved spending time with his mother and his son's family, specifically the three grandchildren who were born while he was in prison. Two months after he was released he got a German Shepherd puppy that a friend had rescued from the side of a freeway. The German Shepherd, named C, was a constant companion and became Kenny's best friend.

> *Right after I was released, Gail would come by almost every day after she worked in the office. And Kim stopped by a couple of times to take me out to lunch. Sometimes Gail and Kim and I would meet in downtown Mt. Clemens. It was real nice.*
>
> *I was having a difficult time and their friendship helped me along. There were so many people there for me. I was very blessed.*
>
> *I remember going to see Frankie Valli at Freedom Hill Amphitheater in Sterling Heights. I took Gail as my date. Freedom Hill Management popped for the whole night. We got a limo and everything. After the concert, we went back stage to meet Mr. Valli. It was a great evening.*

Simple tasks that we take for granted can be a severe strain on a newly released exoneree's psyche.

> *Jimmy Sardelli gave me $1,000 and Greg took me to buy some clothes. I didn't have much of anything.*
>
> *We went to Lakeside Mall in Sterling Heights. I don't think we were there ten minutes when I told him that I had to leave. I got real nervous. I was still looking over my shoulder like I did when I was in prison. I told Greg, "We gotta get out of here. I'm too paranoid."*
>
> *Then Greg's wife called and told Greg that a friend of theirs, Phil Karanja, left a check for $500. Phil felt bad and wanted to help me out. So, I went to pick the check up and open a checking account.*
>
> *The check was drawn on Comerica Bank. That was the first time I met Krystal Stokes. She was a teller at the time.*

I knew that the rules were that you had to have some form of ID to open up an account. I didn't have a license or any other ID. I had nothing to prove who I was with the exception of the front page of the Free Press from the day before with my picture on it.

So, I went up to the teller window with "Krystal Stokes" on the name plate. I told her I don't have a license or a Social Security card or any form of ID, but I knew my social security number. I gave it to her.

She said, "I don't know if that's going to work."

That's when I put the Free Press on the counter in front of her. She looked at the paper and she looked at me. She said, "I saw you on TV yesterday. You were the guy who was in prison for nine years, right?"

I said, "That's me."

She looked at me and almost started crying. She asked me to wait a minute and went to the back to get her manager, Keith Starling. He came out and listened to my story. He shook my hand and he told Krystal that it was good enough for him.

After everything was filled out and we're getting ready to go, Krystal said, "Kenny, can I give you a hug?"

I said, "Sure."

So, she came around from behind the counter and she gave me a hug and a kiss and she was crying. She said, "Kenny, God bless you!"

I said, "Thank you."

That's how we met. And, to this day, she is one of my dearest friends. Another good person who the Lord sent my way.

It took me a year and half to two years, believe it or not, to get somewhat adjusted. It's a hard thing to go through. Remembering Linda Davis, the prosecutor, was on TV and calling me a menace to society, a sexual pervert. That's not an easy thing to get over either.

Kenny related a story about the time he was stopped by the Michigan State Police on the freeway, a few years after his exoneration.

This happened in, maybe, 2007. I golfed on Fridays with some friends. At the time, we were golfing at Cherry Creek at 24 Mile and Van Dyke. So, I'm in my car, in my Jeep Grand Cherokee, with the license plate that says "INNOCENT."

I was driving on the Van Dyke e-way and I was running a little late to get to the course. I looked in my left side mirror and I saw a State Police car coming up to my bumper, slowing down, pulling back, and pulling up. To this day, I still get nervous when there's a police car behind me. Then this cop turned on his flashers. I think, "Fuck! Now, what's going on?"

I pulled over and the cop came up to my window. I asked him, "What's the matter, officer?"

He said, "Are you Ken Wyniemko?"

I said, "Yes, I am officer. And how did you know?"

He said he noticed my license plate and he ran it through his computer in his car.

I said, "What did I do wrong?"

He told me, "I didn't say you did anything wrong."

I said, "Then why did you pull me over?"

He said, "Because I wanted to know if it really was Ken Wyniemko driving this car."

I said, "Why is that?"

Then the officer said, "Do you know Sergeant Artis White from the Lansing State Police?"

I said, "Yes I do. Artis and I are good friends."

And this trooper said that he was friends with Artis, too. Artis had told him what happened to me. He knew Artis did a couple of interviews with me and was working on a documentary about my case.

I'm looking at this cop and wondering what he was driving at. He then said that he just wanted to take the time to shake my hand and apologize.

It proves this point. When I'm speaking, a lot of people will ask me if I despise cops and I tell them that I don't. I still believe most cops are good. There are times, however, when there are bad cops and it's been proven they did something wrong. They get what they deserve if they are crooked or dishonest. But this trooper, here, is an example where I have been saying all along. I still believe most cops are good. I will always believe that.

The horrors of jail remain with exonerees for the rest of their lives.

An exoneree is never totally free from what happened to them. There is that occasional reminder of what they went through for the rest of their lives.

A lot of exonerees, who I know personally from around the country, have been home ten years and they still aren't over it.

In reality, no exoneree gets over his ordeal. There will always be a case where something will pop up that will remind them of what happened. Just like that. You get flashbacks. And there are almost always bad memories. It's a form of post-traumatic stress syndrome, PTSD, just like soldiers.

There came a time during the writing of this book when recalling memories of what happened in jail took a toll on Kenny. For four months, he was unable to talk about his experiences and we rarely met for interview sessions. Whenever something was planned, Kenny would make an excuse, not answer the phone, or just refuse to answer the door. Reliving these experiences bothered him to the point where he could not function. And this was 13 years after he was set free!

> *It's just hard for me talking about these memories. You have to understand. I have to try to recall stuff that I've been trying to forget for a long time.*

Eventually, Kenny was back in the swing of things. But the problems he had even after so many years of freedom displayed the mental anguish an exoneree suffers. And Kenny is a streetwise, tough-minded, determined individual.

In late 2014, Kenny returned to Jackson State Prison to film a documentary on his case. The prison had been closed for over a decade.

> *On my way home after the taping, I had to pull to the side of the road I was shaking so hard. I had nightmares for a month. You never get over the memories, especially when you spend time in a place like Jackson.*

Kenny was asked if any prison habits carried over after he was released. Did he continue to do things like making his bed every morning?

> *Ha! Fuck, no! Making my bed was the last thing on my mind. When someone tells you for nine years what time to get up, what time to go to sleep, what time your bed has to*

be made, and then you're free! You don't worry about that stuff.

I still say the Rosary every day. Not three times each day like I did in prison. And I still say my prayers from the same prayer books that I had when I was imprisoned. In fact, the Rosary and the prayer books are still sitting by my bedside.

In Kenny's bedroom, the Rosary and several severely worn softcover prayer books lay on the night table next to the head of his bed. The prayer books looked more like they were a century old instead of a couple decades old.

Chapter 9 — Lawsuit and Settlement

"In either event, a fact finder could determine that Ernst conspired with Ostin and Marlatt to deprive Plaintiff of his constitutional rights. . . . For these reasons, in a light most favorable to Plaintiff, the Court concludes that there is evidence that each of Marlatt, Ostin and Ernst did conspire with one or more other persons to engage in the continued prosecution of Plaintiff." — Judge Lawrence P. Zatkoff's Decision of March 3, 2005

"I needed to get on with my life and to start doing the things I was meant to do. If you look at some of these federal lawsuits, they are rarely successful and they can last years, even a decade. In my case, it took less than two years. The real reason it was settled so fast is because we proved exactly how bad they treated me, that they actually committed crimes against me." — Kenny Wyniemko

In July of 2003, Gail Pamukov introduced Kenny to civil attorneys George A. Googasian and Thomas H. Howlett from The Googasian Firm, P. C., of Bloomfield Hills, Michigan.

Mr. Howlett recalls meeting Kenny and making the decision to take on his case.

> *Gail called and said that she had this client we needed to speak with. She reached out to us, as I recall, just before the hearing where the judge released Ken. We knew that the exoneration was in the offing.*
>
> *I think within a week or two after we talked, Ken was in our office being introduced to us by Gail. We were not able to make him any promises about whether he had a civil case to pursue. But he certainly had a compelling story. One*

of the things I remember in that first meeting was Ken saying how he essentially felt like he was punished by the trial judge for being truthful — that he wouldn't apologize for something he hadn't done. It was a very poignant thing to tell us.

We began the laborious process of gathering facts. We spent a considerable amount of time doing fact-finding before we filed the suit. Because of Ken's long legal battle for his freedom, there was a fair amount of evidence that was out there for us to review. But, in terms of doing the work of the depositions and getting people under oath, we couldn't do that until we were in a court case.

Kenny provided an abundance of legal documents related to his case. After a thorough review, The Googasian Firm, P. C., decided to represent Kenny in a civil lawsuit against members of the Clinton Township Police Department and the Charter Township of Clinton, with the possibility of including his attorney Albert Markowski, Assistant Prosecutor Linda Davis, and the Honorable Michael D. Schwartz as defendants.

There were several reasons to not pursue the civil case against Mr. Markowski, Ms. Davis, and Judge Schwartz. Most importantly, the Clinton Township Police Department was the most culpable. It was easier to prove members of the police department were guilty of acts of malfeasance and that they engaged in a conspiracy to convict Kenny. And, since the Clinton Township Police Department officers were city employees, the Township of Clinton would be part of the civil lawsuit.

The rate of success of suing a lawyer, a judge, or a prosecutor was not high. By concentrating the civil suit against one entity, defendants were not able to engage in back and forth finger pointing as to each other's culpability.

Normally, police officers are protected from being subjected to lawsuits. Convicting the wrong individual is not grounds for a civil suit. Negligence and carelessness on the part of law enforcement officials are not grounds either. The Googasian Firm, P. C., had to show that the investigating officers violated Kenny's civil rights and that they conspired to convict an innocent man.

On November 25, 2003, The Googasian Firm, P. C., filed a *Complaint and Demand for Trial by Jury* in the U. S. District Court for the Eastern District of Michigan. Civil Action No. 03-74749 named Thomas J. Ostin, Bart M. Marlatt, Alexander C. Ernst, and the Township of Clinton as Defendants. The 12-point, 137-paragraph complaint made allegations and claims that pertained to Kenny's arrest, conviction, and subsequent incarceration.

After the civil suit was filed, both parties deposed witnesses during the discovery period. Witnesses can be called through subpoenas or with written requests through an individual's attorney. Clinton Township Police Department personnel were notified through written requests. Depositions started in February of 2004 and lasted through September, 2004. Mr. Googasian and Mr. Howlett conducted the depositions for the plaintiff. Attorney Roger A. Smith of the Garan Lucow Miller, P.C., Law Firm, conducted the depositions on behalf of the defendants.

There were over 20 depositions taken during the investigation of Kenny's case. It was disheartening to discover that individuals sworn to uphold and protect America's judicial system would engage in such illegal actions to convict an American citizen.

On March 3, 2005, the Honorable Lawrence P. Zatkoff published his *Opinion and Order*, a 51-page, scathing indictment of the actions of the Clinton Township Police Department and the Macomb County Prosecuting Attorney's Office. All of the Defense Motions were denied. Judge Zatkoff severely criticized the investigation and the witness identification lineup process. Furthermore, Judge Zatkoff wrote that the investigating officers routinely failed to disclose impeachable and exculpatory evidence that greatly hindered the plaintiff's ability to cross-examine and discredit the prosecution witnesses, acted with a reckless disregard for the truth, and violated the plaintiff's constitutional rights.

Judge Zatkoff's Opinion prompted an out-of-court settlement. In September of 2005, both parties came to an agreement. Kenny received a lump payment of $1.8 million and lifelong, monthly payments of $6,409 that increased 3% a year. The payments covered a minimum of 20 years, with Kenny's beneficiaries receiving any undistributed payments in the event Kenny passed away during the 20-year period. The settlement amounted to a minimum of $3.8 million.

Defense Motions
The Defense filed several motions in an attempt to halt Kenny's civil suit.

Motion for Summary Judgment
The Defendants maintained the Clinton Township Police Department and the Township of Clinton should be entitled to *Summary Judgment* and the case should be dismissed. The *Motion for Summary Judgment* claimed there was no case because there were no triable issues in Kenny's civil suit. Judge Zatkoff denied the motion and held the Clinton Township Police Department and the Township of Clinton culpable.

> *The Court finds that, for purposes of summary judgment, there is sufficient evidence on the record that the (mis)conduct [sic] of Defendants was instrumental to the continued confinement, prosecution and conviction of Plaintiff and that such conduct tainted the legal process such that Plaintiff was denied a fair trial . . . .*

> *The Court finds there is sufficient evidence on the record to create a genuine issue of material fact as to the Township's liability.*
>
> *There is evidence that no one in the Department supervised either of them (Ostin and Marlatt) with the investigation. Further, Sergeant Waldoch stated that such a lack of supervision was the policy and custom of the Department. In a light most favorable to the Plaintiff, the Court concludes that such a policy and custom could be found by a fact finder to be "deliberately indifferent" to the rights of the Township inhabitants. Accordingly, the Court finds that the Township is not entitled to summary judgment in this action.*

In addition, Ernst, the acting supervisor in the Clinton Township Police Department, was also found culpable.

> *Ernst's actions or inactions supported the arrest, continued investigation, and prosecution of Plaintiff, including the withholding of exculpatory evidence. Accordingly, the Court concludes that Ernst is not entitled to summary judgment in this action.*

Motion for Doctrine of Collateral Estoppel
The *Doctrine of Collateral Estoppel* prevents a party from litigating issues covered in previous proceedings. The Defendants claimed that the issues raised in Kenny's suit had already been argued in Kenny's appeals. Judge Zatkoff ruled against the motion, stating the plaintiff was never given the opportunity to litigate these issues since the true facts were unknown due to the inappropriate actions of the Defendants.

> *In the instant case, the Court finds that Plaintiff did not have a full and fair opportunity to litigate the issues regarding his*

> *continued prosecution in the criminal proceeding. . . . This is particularly true with respect to the failure of the Defendants to provide Plaintiff with exculpatory evidence after the preliminary examination. . . . As such, the Court concludes that Plaintiff did not have a <u>full and fair</u> opportunity to litigate these issues at trial, on appeal or in his habeas corpus petition. For the reasons stated, the Court finds that neither collateral estoppel nor res judicata operates to bar Plaintiff's claims that Defendants' [sic] maliciously prosecuted Plaintiff following his arrest.*

Motion that claimed the investigating officers were entitled to Qualified Immunity and cannot be sued.
Police officials are normally immune from being prosecuted for wrongful convictions. Judge Zatkoff ruled the actions of the officers resulted in their loss of that immunity.

> *The Court finds the Defendants are not entitled to qualified immunity with respect to their conduct in seeking an arrest warrant against Plaintiff.*

> *The Court also finds that the failure to disclose exculpatory and impeaching evidence was material and there is a reasonable probability that the result of the proceeding would have been different had such evidence been produced. Accordingly, the Defendants are not entitled to qualified immunity with respect to Plaintiff's post-arrest malicious prosecution claims.*

Motion to Strike the Declaration and Preclude the Testimony of Glenn McCormick

The Defendants claimed Mr. McCormick should not be allowed to testify at trial because his Declaration conflicts with previous sworn testimony and that there is evidence Mr. McCormick believes he could receive a large payday for his testimony. Judge Zatkoff denied the Defendants' motion. He acknowledged that Mr. McCormick's statements have been inconsistent but his Declaration and statements are consistent enough to be allowed at trial. This was a major blow because Mr. McCormick's testimony implicated Detective Thomas Ostin in the Suborning of Perjury to obtain Mr. McCormick's testimony.

> *Defendants maintain that Mr. McCormick's testimony is (i) "inherently incredible because it materially conflicts with numerous prior and contemporaneous statements he has made regarding (Plaintiff's) admissions while they shared a jail cell in 1994," and (ii) "incredible and fundamentally untrustworthy because new-acquired evidence suggests that McCormick anticipates that he will receive a substantial amount of money for his assistance in this case."*

> *The Court declines to adopt Defendants argument. Without question, Mr. McCormick has made some inconsistent statements with respect to this case over the last 11 years. There are several statements set forth in the Declaration that contradict the testimony Mr. McCormick gave under oath in 1994. Contrary to Defendants' assertions, however, the answers supplied by Mr. McCormick in the December, 6, 2004, interview is replete with instances where Mr. McCormick's statements on key issues appear to be consistent with the statements made in his Declaration and not his testimony under oath 1994. . . .*

Defendants' Motion to Strike the Declaration and Preclude the Testimony of Glenn McCormick is DENIED.

The 1994 Investigation
One of Judge Zatkoff's major concerns was the lack of an investigation.

Plaintiff's brief and the record are littered with examples where Ostin and Marlatt did not disclose (or follow up on) evidence that would have been exculpatory to Plaintiff.

During the deposition of Detective Marlatt, Mr. Howlett thoroughly questioned the detective on the lack of follow-up on over 30 numerous tips and leads. These included a two-month delay in investigating the anonymous tip on Kenny. A neighborhood canvas uncovered multiple leads from neighbors who spotted individuals who looked like the composite walking next to or near the victim's home the night of the attack. The canvas also revealed two occasions where a similar Chevy Caprice was occupied and parked across from the victim's home, once on the day of the attack. Several phone tips originated from law enforcement officials from other police departments where a possible suspect matched the composite and, on one occasion, described a just-released convict where the modus operandi of his crime matched that of the April 30th attack. In another instance, three separate phone tips mentioned the same person as the possible perpetrator. One of these tips originated from a fellow law enforcement official. None of the tips were pursued.

There were four bars located in the immediate area of Clinton Township and near Detroit's Metropolitan Airport that were frequented by the victim. No one was interviewed at any of the establishments.

The victim asserted that she had won $2,500 in cash at a bowling alley and the money was stolen the night of the attack. This claim always bothered Kenny on two fronts.

Her testimony on the bowling winnings always bugged me. She claimed they paid her with cash. First of all, winning that amount of money was rare for a male pro bowler back then, let alone a female who is not a pro. Secondly, when you work at a bowling alley, everyone is bonded. If there were someone winning that kind of money, it would have been paid out in a check. No way would she have been given that amount of cash.

In his 2004 deposition, Detective Marlatt testified that no one contacted the bowling alley to verify that the victim had won the money. They never followed up on the affair partner to verify the infamous panties were part of an earlier consensual sexual liaison. They simply took the victim's word that the affair occurred, just like they did her claim about the bowling alley winnings.

The investigating officers wanted to speak with the anonymous caller who phoned in the tip on Kenny. Yet, no one ever thought of contacting Joseph Whitcher, the ex-husband of Cathy Whitcher, Kenny's ex-girlfriend who testified at his trial.

At the time of Kenny's arrest, there was no love lost between Mr. Whitcher and Kenny. Kenny was constantly caught in the middle of arguments concerning Cathy's son. In addition, Cathy slept with Mr. Whitcher, her ex-husband, on at least a couple occasions while living with Kenny. Mr. Whitcher left numerous contentious messages on Kenny's answering machine. Detectives Ostin and Marlatt knew this yet both of them testified they never entertained the thought the anonymous caller could be Mr. Whitcher.

Here is a question posed to Detective Ostin in his 2004 deposition.

Q. Did you ever consider whether he was the anonymous caller, Joseph Whitcher?
A. I don't believe it ever crossed my mind.

Here is that same question asked Detective Marlatt in his 2004 deposition.

> *Q. Okay. Did you ever — did you ever, in the course of your work, talk to Ms. Whitcher's ex-husband, Joseph Whitcher, in person?*
> *A. No, sir.*
>
> *Q. Did you ever undertake any efforts to determine whether Joseph Whitcher might have called in this anonymous tip?*
> *A. No, sir.*

Judge Zatkoff criticized the victim identification.

> *The record includes substantial evidence (of which Defendants were aware when seeking the arrest warrant) that Defendants had reason to believe that Ms. Klug was mistaken in her identification of Plaintiff at the line-up.*

Judge Zatkoff believed the police misled the court and prosecution and that the evidence did not warrant an arrest.

> *The Court finds that (a) the volume, strength and materiality of omissions in this case provide evidence of a reckless disregard for the truth and an intent to mislead the prosecutor and magistrate into believing that the case against the Plaintiff was much stronger that it was, (b) the omitted material would negate probable cause for Plaintiff's arrest if taken into considerations, and (c) that without such omissions, an arrest warrant would not have been issued.*

Withholding Exculpatory Evidence

Judge Zatkoff's Opinion identified several instances where the Clinton Township Police Department routinely withheld exculpatory evidence that resulted in the malicious prosecution of Kenny.

> *In the instant case, the Court finds that Plaintiff did not have a full and fair opportunity to litigate the issues regarding his continued prosecution in the criminal proceeding. . . . there are several instances on the record where the Defendants failed to provide Plaintiff with impeaching or exculpatory evidence. . . . Plaintiff's brief and the record are littered with examples where Ostin and Marlatt did not disclose (or follow up on) evidence that would have been exculpatory to Plaintiff. . . . In other words, a fact finder could determine that Defendants were engaged in a malicious prosecution of Plaintiff.*

In a Case Investigation Work Report from Detective Ostin dated September 1, 1994, Michelle Wright, Mr. McCormick's girlfriend, stated that McCormick "has a drug problem – stealing her checks and property." She was in constant fear he was going to beat her. Detective Ostin wrote that he contacted Mr. McCormick and "advised (him) part of deal was to remain squeaky clean to continue to be a credible witness."

On September 20, 1994, less than three weeks later, Ms. Wright contacted Detective Ostin again, this time to advise him that she had "kicked out Glenn McCormick last night — using crack and alcohol — stole their bikes and sold for crack." She also stated that, "Glenn filed a false stolen report" regarding the "stolen" bike. Detective Ostin documented the conversation in his notes.

None of these conversations between Detective Ostin and Michelle Wright were ever turned over to the prosecutor or to the defense attorney.

DELIBERATE INJUSTICE | 197

> **Davis**
> EXHIBIT NO. 6
> 6-11-04
> S.M. CHAMPA

CLINTON TOWNSHIP POLICE DEPARTMENT

CASE INVESTIGATION WORK REPORT

INCIDENT NO.

9-1-94

Came in to see Eakenrode about unrelated comp. — Filing eviction papers

Michelle Wright
- Hm 307-8951
- Wk 313-966-5146

Girlfriend of Glen McCormick states thinks has drug problem — stealing her checks & property — afraid he's going to beat her.

— Advised Linda Davis — Per her request — I phoned Glen — Advised part of deal was to remain squeeky clean to continue to be a credible witness. If he assaults Michelle or is charged with anything — No longer credible & deal is off — He denies all — Warned & also advised to contact me with new address if evicted.

Police Report regarding Mr. McCormick's girlfriend complaining about his illegal activity that was never turned over to the defense

The most egregious act of withholding evidence concerned the answering machine tapes confiscated during the execution of a search warrant of Kenny's home.

In a typed *CTPD CONTINUATION AND* SUPPLEMENTARY *REPORT* dated July 14, 1994, Detective Ostin indicated that Kenny asked Detective Ostin if he knew the whereabouts of the tapes. Here is an excerpt from that document as written by Detective Ostin.

> *He (Kenny) asked me to take the phone cassette tape to verify his story. Two phone cassette (micro) tapes were found near the phone and were taken by writer and held with my files for review. These were not taken relative to the search warrant. And Wyniemko later asked if I had the tapes and stated that he wanted me to have them to verify what he said.*

The report ends there. There is no indication as to what Detective Ostin told Kenny regarding the answering machine tapes.

The *CTPD PROPERTY REPORT for Incident No. 94-17059* dated Thursday, July 14, 1994, 9:00 pm, lists the items taken from Kenny's home. There is no mention of the tapes.

In his 2004 deposition, Detective Ostin admitted he took the tapes during the search of Kenny's home, and that he never submitted a report acknowledging the tapes to the defense or to the prosecution. Detective Ostin seized the tapes during the search and hid them in the stalking file. The prosecutor and the defense were never aware of them.

This question begs for an answer: If the tapes were not taken as part of a search warrant, then how could they have been taken at all?

Taking the tapes was proper. Not documenting their removal was wrong. A property report should have been prepared in both the stalking and rape files with each cross-referencing the other.

That is why Judge Zatkoff was so critical of Detective Ostin's actions. It was exculpatory evidence withheld from the defense and the prosecution.

In her 2004 deposition, Ms. Davis confirmed this evidence was never disclosed to the prosecution. She had never seen the reports of the conversations with the girlfriend nor had she listened to the answering machine tapes.

In his 2004 deposition, Public Defender Attorney Albert Markowski acknowledged these evidentiary items were never disclosed to the defense. He had no knowledge of the missing phone message tapes that contained threats from Cathy Whitcher. He had no knowledge of the notes from the phone conversations between Detective Ostin and Michelle Wright, Mr. McCormick's girlfriend. In his deposition, Mr. Markowski also could not recall Kenny ever mentioning the existence of the tapes during the 1994 trial.

Mr. Markowski was prevented from using several crucial pieces of evidence that would have enabled him to vigorously cross-examine Ms. Whitcher and Mr. McCormick. And the prosecution was saved the embarrassment of having two of its three prosecution witnesses discredited.

The threats on the tape and the fact that Ms. Whitcher had filed a stalking charge against Kenny could have been used to picture her as most hostile and vindictive towards Kenny. Judge Zatkoff agreed.

> *Plaintiff's ability to impeach Ms. Whitcher without the tapes was minimal, especially when Prosecutor Davis challenged him to produce the tapes being held by the man sitting next to her at counsel table (Ostin).*

Judge Zatkoff ruled Detectives Ostin, Marlatt, and Ernst engaged in a conspiracy to prosecute Kenny.

> *The Court concludes that there is evidence that each of Marlatt, Ostin and Ernst did conspire with one or more*

other persons to engage in the continued prosecution of Plaintiff.

The Jailhouse Snitch

Kenny knew that Glenn McCormick had lied at the 1994 trial. In 2004, The Googasian Firm, P. C., needed proof, especially as to how Mr. McCormick knew so much information related to the crime.

When Kenny and his legal team began their investigation, Mr. McCormick was on the lam after jumping bond for charges pending against him. Help in locating him came in the strangest way.

Kenny related the story.

I got in the habit of reading the obituaries when I was in prison and I continued to do so after I was released. I was reading the obits on June 14, 2004, the day before my birthday. I noticed a man by the name McCormick had died. He was in his mid-seventies and the name of one of his children was Glenn. Even if he was on the run, I figured he'd make it back for his dad's funeral. I called Tom (Howlett) and told him that this might be a shot in the dark, but it's worth a look. Tom read the siblings in the obituary. Sure enough. It had to be the Glenn McCormick we were looking for.

Tom sent a couple private detectives to the funeral home in Garden City. When Glenn went out for a smoke, they nabbed him. They interrogated him long enough to find out what they needed before they turned him over to the cops.

I remember getting a call from Tom the next day, June 15th, the day of my birthday. Tom started the conversation by telling me that they got a birthday present for me. I told him I didn't need anything from them. He laughed and told me the present was that they nabbed McCormick and his

> *statement would be very damaging for the prosecutor and Ostin.*
>
> TOM HOWLETT: *Dealing with Glenn McCormick was a very important part of the case and, also, very, very poignant. I mean this guy had a very rough life, a lot of mistakes, and a lot of problems. I think he had been bearing the burden of the guilt for what he had done to Ken for a long time.*

Mr. McCormick, overcome with guilt from contributing to Kenny's conviction, was very forthcoming. He told Kenny's legal team that he had found God and wanted to make amends. He wanted Kenny to know that he was very sorry for lying and for being part of what sent him to jail.

Mr. McCormick submitted a 17-point Declaration detailing his involvement with the police department and the prosecution's office.

His complete Declaration can be found in "Appendix *B – Glenn McCormick's Declaration.*"

In his Declaration, Mr. McCormick stated that he was initially contacted by Prosecutor Linda Davis asking to speak with him about Mr. Wyniemko. Mr. McCormick claimed that he was offered a deal to avoid prison if he testified that Kenny had admitted he had committed the rape. He accepted.

Mr. McCormick indicated that he learned details of the crime from police reports given to him by Detective Ostin. He also indicated that Detective Ostin and Ms. Davis coached him on what exactly to say on his taped statement.

Here are a couple excerpts from Mr. McCormick's 2004 Declaration.

> *Mr. Wyniemko never told me at any time that he had committed any crime. He never told me that he had any involvement in the rape and robbery of Diane Klug.*

I am making these statements to get the weight off of my shoulders from my involvement in Mr. Wyniemko's preliminary examination and trial. I feel badly about what I said he did.

It was a coup for Kenny and his legal team. They now had solid evidence that the police had acted with complete disregard for the truth, engaged in a conspiracy, and suborned perjury.

An analysis was performed on the tape containing McCormick's 1994 recorded statement. Steve Cain, the president of Forensic Tape Analysis, Inc., in Lake Geneva, Wisconsin, found several anomalies on the tape that indicated it was stopped, paused, and rewound. These findings corroborated the declarations made by McCormick that he was interrupted on several occasions when he was coaxed and directed as to what to say.

Judge Zatkoff ruled that Detective Ostin knew Mr. McCormick lied on the stand and that Mr. McCormick was given a police report by Detective Ostin and/or Prosecutor Davis. It was this belief that allowed him to decide that Mr. McCormick's Declaration was admissible and that Mr. McCormick would be allowed to testify.

While imprisoned for his parole violation in 2004, Mr. McCormick was frequently in contact with Michelle Wright, his girlfriend in 1994. His phone conversations were recorded and his letters to Michelle Wright were examined. Copies of these conversations and letters were made available to The Googasian Firm, P. C.

Mr. McCormick's letters professed his sadness of what he had put Ms. Wright through during the time they were together. He vowed to make things right.

Mr. McCormick's Declaration had been admitted as evidence and it was a distinct possibility that he would have to testify at the impending civil suit. Mr. McCormick also indicated in several letters that he thought he might be in line for a large payout in exchange for his testimony.

A letter from McCormick to Ms. Wright was examined. Here is an excerpt of that letter dated December 7, 2004.

> *I want you to be aware that 2 police officers from the Clinton Twp. Internal Affairs department came up here to talk to me.*
>
> *(Before I continue let me just inform you that at no time during this interview did I say you were involved in this case. I told these two officers you had nothing to do with this in any shape or form. I also told them that I did not want them to involve you in this in any way for the simple reason you had nothing to do with this. I also mentioned to these two officers that I was extremely afraid for you, Angela, as well as for myself. So, I just want you to know this. And if anything happens to me, Michele, while I'm incarcerated, I want you, my family, Thomas Howlett, and anyone else who cares that if I'm injured or killed, and or a suicide, that I truly believe that the Clinton Twp. Police Department, Linda Davis, Det. Ostin and anyone else involved with law enforcement including the Michigan Department of Corrections had something to do with my injuries and or my death. And let it be known,*

I would not and could not commit suicide for any reason what-so-ever.)

Michele, I just want you to know that Det. Ostin and Linda Davis did do something wrong and even though it wasn't <u>all me</u> who got Kenneth Wyniemko convicted, I honestly feel bad for everything that happened to him. So, it's time for me to do the right thing that should have been done almost 10 years ago. At <u>no time</u> did Kenneth Wyniemko tell me he committed this crime. Det. Ostin & Linda Davis had me "word my words" in a way that said he (Wyniemko) did say to me he did it. When, in fact, he never told me this. As you know, Michele, Linda Davis was using that pending charge against me as a "threatening tool" to convince me to say something different against Kenneth Wyniemko....

Mr. McCormick never testified and he never received any compensation.

On November 11, 2004, Mr. McCormick was charged with Welfare Fraud. The charge stemmed from statements he made in phone conversations and letters to Ms. Wright.

The Forensic Evidence

One of the most puzzling facts of Kenny's case is how he could have been convicted when every shred of forensic evidence excluded his presence at the crime scene. In the 1994 trial transcripts, DNA was never mentioned and there was never a thought of someone else committing the rape.

The 2004 depositions uncovered the fact that the victim had an affair earlier during the day of the 1994 attack. The prosecution and the defense had an agreement that this affair would not be brought up in trial. The defense never disclosed this arrangement with Kenny.

There seemed to be two reasons for not testing the DNA.
- DNA testing would have uncovered the victim's sexual liaison, something the prosecution and the police took great measures in keeping out of the court record.
- The prosecution and the police were focused on Kenny as the perpetrator and they did not want to do anything to jeopardize a conviction, like the presence of an unknown donor at the crime scene.

In his 2004 deposition, Mr. Markowski deemed it "foolish" to have insisted on any additional forensic testing, despite the fact the blood type analysis had eliminated Kenny from being a donor. Here is an excerpt of his 2004 deposition.

Q. And would you have considered potential DNA analysis to fall into the, quote, foolish, end quote, category as far as further forensic testing in this case?
A. Since there was nothing linking Mr. Wyniemko, there would be no reason to submit anything further to see whether or not it was his.

Identifying the presence of an unknown donor should have been the number one priority. Mr. Markowski's logic for not subjecting the forensic evidence to DNA testing makes absolutely no sense since the blood test excluded Kenny from being a donor on any of the forensic evidence.

Mr. Howlett's counter to Mr. Markowski's claim that DNA testing would have been impractical was a classic.

Here is an excerpt of his deposition.

Q. Do you know how—why Mr. Wyniemko is sitting with me here today rather than locked up in the Michigan Department of Corrections serving a 40- to 60-year prison sentence?
A. Yeah.

Q. Why?
A. He was cleared based on DNA.

Q. So, evidence, as you understand it, collected from the crime scene conclusively established that he was not the perpetrator, is that right?
A. Yes.

During his 2004 deposition, Laurence H. Peppler, Kenny's original defense counsel, stated that it was his intent to send the forensic evidence to an independent facility for additional testing. He also testified that he had told Mr. Markowski that the forensic evidence needed to be tested for DNA by an outside agency. This statement is credible based on Mr. Peppler's brief *Demand for Preservation of Tangible Evidence/Test Samples* dated September 22, 1994. In it, Mr. Peppler demanded all DNA evidence to be preserved and all test results made available to the defense. This is the only 1994 document uncovered in the research for this book that contains the term "DNA."

No one can answer definitively as to whether DNA testing could yield any conclusive results in 1994. RFLP (restriction fragment length polymorphism) was the method of DNA testing widely used. PCR (polymerase chain reaction) is an advanced method that was developed in the late 1980s. PCR allowed the extraction and examination of DNA material from a much smaller sample of forensic evidence.

At the time of Kenny's trial, the Michigan State Crime Lab used RFLP. In the opinion of David Woodford, the forensic scientist responsible for evidence testing, the amount of material in the forensic samples available in the forensic evidence could have been insufficient to obtain a DNA profile using RFLP.

Whether Mr. Peppler would have obtained a DNA test using PCR is unknown.

But there is absolutely no mistake that the pursuit of DNA testing was tempered by the fact that the blood analysis of the samples did not match Kenny's blood type and that any DNA tests would not yield any advantage to the prosecution's case. This opinion was reiterated throughout the discovery period in depositions given by the prosecution, law enforcement, and Mr. Woodford himself. In other words, if it couldn't be linked to Kenny, then what use was there for further testing?

In his 2004 statement, Mr. Woodford indicated that he was told to not test any of the forensic evidence for DNA. Here is an excerpt of Mr. Woodford's deposition.

> *Q. Did anyone at the Clinton Township Police Department request that you do DNA testing on any of the evidence with respect to the Klug case?*
> *A. The question came up whether it—whether we had sufficient sample to do DNA testing, and it was my decision that, no, we did not have enough to do DNA testing. And I can tell you one other further thing on that.*
>
> *Q. Yes.*
> *A. Being that we basically ruled him out as a donor of those semen samples through blood typing, there would have been no need to do DNA testing at that time.*

> Q. Because you already knew that Mr. Wyniemko—there was no physical evidence linking Mr. Wyniemko to the case, correct?
> A. Correct.

This was supposed to be an investigation to find a violent and sadistic rapist. Mr. Woodford's statements are more proof that the sole purpose was to convict Kenny. There would be no DNA tests conducted on any forensic evidence if it did not further Kenny's conviction.

The Victim's Affair

According to Lieutenant Ostin's 2004 deposition, the panties contained evidence of an affair the victim engaged in earlier in the day before the night of the attack. Under a rape shield agreement between the prosecution and the defense attorney, the presence of the panties was not to be brought up in any legal proceedings pertaining to Kenny's trial. This agreement was put into place to save the victim's public embarrassment of the affair and to avoid putting any additional burden on the victim's marriage already reeling from the rape.

In his 2004 deposition, Mr. Markowski freely admitted avoiding any reference to the panties.

Here is the problem: Kenny was **never** notified of this agreement by Mr. Markowski.

Gail Pamukov had a very strong opinion on the lack of a court record regarding the victim's affair.

> *That whole issue of the affair partner, that should have been brought out and that should have been on the record. There should have been motions filed and that should have all been addressed as to whether or not that evidence should have come in under the rape shield.*

> *Now, from what I could tell from reviewing the file, I could not find any evidence that had been addressed. Ever!*
>
> *But the issue is if there was a stipulation from the defense attorney and the prosecutor to keep that out, that should have been on the record. I never saw anything related to this backroom agreement.*

Recall Kenny's conversation with Mr. Markowski during the trial.

> *I'm sitting there thinking and said to Markowski, "Is somebody picking these numbers out of the fuckin' air? How can it go from 5 to 17 to 19 and now back down to 15?"*
>
> *He told me, "Well, Kenny, every time you stuck your finger in her..."*
>
> *I said, "Let me stop you right there. I didn't stick my finger in anybody. Don't you understand? I'm not the guy that did this, you know."*
>
> *He then said, "Okay. Let's move on, Kenny. Let's move on."*

Was it Mr. Markowski's belief in his client's guilt the reason he never mentioned the deal he made regarding the affair to Kenny? Was it more important to him to protect the victim's rights than those of his client?

Here are excerpts from Mr. Peppler's 2004 deposition regarding his knowledge of the victim's affair the evening before the attack.

> *Q. Okay. Do you know if Mr. Wyniemko knew before the trial that Ms. Klug had had an affair shortly before the alleged attack?*
> *A. Not with certainty.*

Q. Okay. When you say not with certainty, what do you mean?
A. This is something I would have discussed with Mr. Wyniemko. Whether I had gotten around to it at that point in time, I can't say with certainty.

Q. And what you're saying is because of the fact you were discharged, you don't know if you had—
A. That's correct.

Q. actually consulted with him on this issue?
A. That's correct.

Q. But it was your intent to do so?
A. Oh, yeah.

Kenny had this to say about Mr. Markowski's knowledge of the affair.

Never did Markowski tell me anything about the affair and never anything about that secret deal he made with the prosecutor. He knew about it and decided it was more important to protect the victim's reputation than to defend me? (Shaking his head in disgust) My own defense attorney!

It should be noted that the Clinton Township Police Department continued to withhold information about the affair after the trial. The *CTPD Continuation and Supplementary Report* dated July 18, 1994, contained Detective Ostin's notes of Ms. Klug admitting the affair. It was never included in any documents received by Kenny while he was in jail. This prevented Kenny and his attorneys from addressing the undisclosed affair in their numerous appeals.

Conclusion

The 2004 depositions shed light on so many questions related to the events of 1994.

Whether the prosecutor or the police believed that Kenny was the perpetrator of the 1994 attack on Diane Klug was not the issue. The problem was that Kenny was presumed guilty.

With that thought in mind, numerous leads from the public and law enforcement sectors were ignored, forensic evidence testing was halted since it did not further a conviction of Kenny, evidence crucial to the defense was withheld, a court appointed attorney was ordered to go to trial in a capital case with just two days to prepare, the subornation of perjury of a jailhouse snitch was justified, and the rape shield rights of the victim superseded Kenny's rights.

In the American court system, the accused are to be presumed innocent. The purpose of an investigation is to cover all bases until the investigators are positive they have the right man.

The Clinton Township Police Department readily admits that this was an unusually violent and publicly visible case for them. Every possible lead and every possible angle should have been exhausted. The incarceration of the **actual** perpetrator of this horrific crime should have been priority one. That is why their indifference throughout the investigation to the voluminous number of tips is bewildering. The audacity with which they bent the rules, even broke the law, is perplexing.

If an eyewitness incorrectly identifies a suspect in a crime and if that crime is investigated honestly, the subsequent prosecution and incarceration of an innocent person is an unfortunate mistake. Kenny's conviction and subsequent incarceration was not an innocent error. Kenny's rights were violated when the Clinton Township Police Department engaged in a conspiracy to convict an innocent man.

Kenny related a story about an incident that showed the brashness with which the police operated even in the wake of Kenny's exoneration.

> *We had our first meeting in Federal Court after I filed my lawsuit. My lawyers, George and Tom, were there. And the attorneys from Clinton Township and Ostin and the other two detectives were scheduled to meet. George and Tom asked me if I could take someone with me to the courthouse because they were anticipating that there would be a moment where they would leave to meet with the defense attorneys in a conference room. They didn't want me sitting in the courtroom alone by myself because they weren't sure if Ostin or the other two cops would be there, too. They didn't want the cops to harass me or try to egg me on.*
>
> *I took my friend, Roxanne, and Paul, my golfing buddy. We walked into an empty courtroom to just sit and talk. The only person in the courtroom was Judge Zatkoff's court assistant. She was getting all the cases lined up for him to look at.*
>
> *Roxanne, Paul, and I were sitting there in the last row of seats, right hand side of the courtroom. I heard some guys laughing and I looked over to the double door that was leading into Zatkoff's courtroom and I could see the detectives standing outside in the hallway looking in. One of them was Ostin. He saw me and walked into the courtroom. He sat in the bench right in front of Roxanne, Paul, and me. He put his hands on the back of his pew, spread out, and turned back and winked at Roxanne. He then smiled at me and got up and walked out.*
>
> *I was so pissed off I was shaking.*
>
> *Paul asked me, "Why didn't you just fucking knock his ass out?"*
>
> *I calmed down and told him, "Because I'm gonna knock him out in a legal way. Do it right."*

And I did.

That goes to show you how arrogant that prick was. I was proved innocent and he still fucked with me like that. He had no remorse for what he did and no sympathy for what he put me through.

I never regretted settling out of court. I needed to get on with my life and to start doing the things I was meant to do. If you look at some of these federal lawsuits, they are rarely successful and they can last years, even a decade. In my case, it took less than two years.

The real reason it was settled so fast is because we proved exactly how bad they treated me, that they actually committed crimes against me. They went out of their way to convict me. But I was fortunate because it was one of the quickest settlements in cases like these.

After Zatkoff wrote his Opinion, they knew they were fucked. I can remember this newspaper article by Peter Henning. He was the Law Professor at Wayne State University. After the Opinion was made public, Professor Henning was quoted in the paper as saying, "The question now is not will he win, but how much will he receive?"

Tom and Gail knew what I wanted. I wanted to settle the case as soon as possible. And my long-range goal was to do what I am doing right now, helping the other exonerees in any way I can.

TOM HOWLETT: *Every case that goes forward contains risk and reward. I think Ken made a very wise decision to resolve the case when he did. I think one of things that weighed on Ken the most was his dad passing and his dad never knowing that Ken would be proven innocent.*

Ken's case was the most deeply satisfying case of my career — a career I have spent trying to right many wrongs.

Chapter 10 — System Failure

"*Kenny's case, when taken as a whole, is one of the most egregious miscarriages of justice I have ever seen. The whole system failed Kenneth Wyniemko.*" — Patrick T. Cahill, Former Michigan District Court Judge

This chapter examines the roles played by the defense attorney, the prosecuting attorney, and the presiding judge in the conviction of Kenny.

Defense Counsel Albert Markowski

"*The basic duty defense counsel owes to the administration of justice and as an officer of the court is to serve as the accused's counselor and advocate with courage and devotion and to render effective, quality representation.*" — American Bar Association (ABA) on the responsibilities of the defense counsel.

Mr. Markowski did not come close to rendering "*effective, quality representation.*" His 2004 deposition uncovered a great deal about his perception of his contribution to Kenny's wrongful conviction. He described himself as a troubleshooter of the Macomb County Circuit Court for court appointed attorneys, someone who stepped in when other attorneys failed, someone assigned to the A-list cases or major cases.

Mr. Markowski had no second thoughts about suppressing the information about the victim's affair from Kenny. He claimed he was fully prepared and that Kenny was completely comfortable with him proceeding. He was unyielding in his belief that DNA testing was not warranted. He was unwilling to admit Kenny's conviction had anything to do with the defense he provided, adamant he did the best job possible.

In defense attorney Kenneth Karam's appeal to the Michigan Court of Appeals in 1996, Mr. Karam claimed Kenny's conviction was a direct result of ineffective counsel.
Here is an excerpt from that appeal.

Defendant (Ken Wyniemko) believes an evidentiary hearing is needed to flesh out various facts and reasons for defense attorney's actions during the case. These reasons include but are not necessarily limited to failure to file a motion for continuance, request an independent forensic expert, interview any witnesses, adequately prepare for cross-examination, et cetera.

Laurence Peppler, Kenny's initial court-appointed attorney, believed that Judge Schwartz was bullying Mr. Markowski into going to trial without sufficient time to prepare a proper defense. He was also critical of Mr. Markowski not insisting on DNA testing. Here is an excerpt of Mr. Peppler's deposition.

Q. What had you done to obtain the assistance of an expert?
A. I believe I was in the process of trying to get some funds authorized, because Mr. Wyniemko was indigent, so that I could hire a forensic expert, and about that time, you know, it was necessary for — I became in a conflict situation with him because of the grievance.

Q. Do you know if you shared your feelings in that regard with Mr. Markowski?
A. Yeah, I did.

Q. What did you tell him?
A. I told him that I was very upset because I felt that Judge Schwartz was hammering him to go to trial and he didn't — he needed more time to prepare and he needed to really consult, from my point of view, with an independent forensic expert and get some money for that purpose and — but he was — he's being manhandled, that's what I — I told him that, and that was my feeling then and it's still my feeling now.

Here is an excerpt of Mr. Markowski's 2004 deposition. Attorney Roger A. Smith, acting counsel for the defense), questioned Mr. Markowski.

Q. As I understand it, you were appointed in this case approximately one week before the actual trial date?
A. From an independent recollection, I don't know the specific date, but I would not disagree. It was a short time before.

Q. And regardless of what the time frame is before the trial, my question to you is: Did you in your own mind feel that you had sufficient time and expertise to prepare to effectively defend the case against Mr. Wyniemko?
A. Well, let me answer it this way: When I first got the call and was appointed, I was informed of the situation, the fact that there was an attorney on it who had gotten off the case. At that point I was only told what the charges were. I didn't know the extent of them.

So, I mean, naturally before I could make up my mind whether I'm ready to go in a couple of days, I have to talk with the attorney, review the file, talk with prosecutors, what have you, review all the police reports and records, have a chance to talk with my client, and in this particular case, that's what I did.

Q. And after doing that, were you comfortable with your ability to effectively defend the claims made against Mr. Wyniemko?
A. Yes.

Q. If, for example, Mr. Markowski, you felt that you weren't — strike that. Or that you didn't have the time to become prepared, did you have options back then?
A. Well, the only option would have been to petition the Court for an adjournment or a delay in the trial proceedings.

Q. Do you remember doing that in the case?
A. No, I didn't.

Q. Okay. And is there a reason why you didn't?
A. Because, again, after going over the entire case, having a chance to speak with Mr. Wyniemko, kind of laying it out for him. I was in the position that I was ready to go and it was a question of whether or not Mr. Wyniemko was comfortable with me proceeding, and I believe we discussed that at the Macomb County Jail.

Q. And what was the result of that discussion?
A. We were ready to go.

Q. Mr. Wyniemko conveyed to you that he was comfortable with you and ready to go?
A. As I recall, yes.

Q. Had Mr. Wyniemko suggested that he was not comfortable with you and/or did not feel you were ready to go, what would you have done?

A. I would have made a motion before Judge Schwartz or made attempts to approach him in chambers and I just — I've never been placed in that position. I guess when you said what would have been my recourse, I guess my last recourse would have been to just flatly refuse.

Kenny vehemently objected to Mr. Markowski's statements.

I never thought he could have provided a good enough effort with the time he had to prep for my case. I never told him I was comfortable with him. Never. And, in my opinion, he did not do a good job.

Thomas Howlett's deposition examination of Mr. Markowski reveals that same reluctance to accept the fact that DNA testing was warranted in 1994.

Q. Do you know how — why Mr. Wyniemko is sitting with me here today rather than locked up in the Michigan Department of Corrections serving a 40- to 60-year prison sentence?
A. Yeah.

Q. Why?
A. He was cleared based on DNA.

Q. So, evidence, as you understand it, collected from the crime scene conclusively established that he was not the perpetrator, is that right?
A. Yes.

Mr. Markowski's refusal to recognize any culpability in Kenny's wrongful conviction was both puzzling and sad. The reality is his efforts were nothing more than a supreme act of ineffectiveness of counsel.

Assistant Prosecutor Linda Davis

"The duty of the prosecution is to seek justice, not merely convict." — American Bar Association (ABA) Criminal Justice Section on the responsibilities of the prosecution.

"(He) is the representative not of an ordinary party to a controversy, but of a sovereignty whose obligation to govern impartially is as compelling as its obligation to govern at all; and whose interest, therefore, in a criminal prosecution is not that it shall win a case, but that justice shall be done. As such, he is in a peculiar and very definite sense the servant of the law, the twofold aim of which is that guilt shall not escape or innocence suffer. He may prosecute with earnestness and vigor—indeed he should do so. But while he may strike hard blows, he is not at liberty to strike foul ones. It is as much his duty to refrain from improper methods calculated to produce a wrongful conviction as it is to use every legitimate means to bring about a just one." — U. S. Supreme Court Justice Alexander George Sutherland, Berger v. United States, 295 U.S. 78 (1935)

A bothersome theme resonated throughout the trial. How could the prosecutor, an officer of the court sworn to seek justice, stand by and allow so many obvious unasked questions and dubious actions and decisions go unchallenged?

These are not the actions of a prosecutor whose primary objective is to seek truth and justice.
- The prosecutor allowed the acting defense attorney to be duped at the lineup when he was informed the victim never

saw her attacker's face. With four stand-ins with mustaches, the victim identified the defendant by recognizing his face.
- The prosecution endorsed a questionable lineup identification. The prosecution went along with the victim's identification of her attacker even though none of her previous descriptions remotely matched the defendant and even though the victim consistently claimed to never have seen her attacker's face.
- The prosecution did not object to or voice an opinion with respect to the judicial decision to force the defense attorney to go to trial with two days to prepare. In fact, she did just the opposite when she implored the court for a speedy trial for the sake of the victim. It was a travesty of justice and it prevented Kenny from having an adequate defense.
- The prosecution promoted theories during trial that she knew were not accurate.
- The prosecution agreed to the 'deal of the century' to obtain the self-serving testimony of a lifetime criminal and liar.
- The prosecution never questioned the lack of investigation into the source of the footprints found at the scene.
- The prosecution never questioned the lack of DNA testing with the voluminous amount of forensic evidence.
- The prosecution never questioned the veracity of Kenny's claim that the Clinton Township Police Department detectives removed exculpatory evidence from his home.

The prosecuting attorney's actions and inactions came under strong scrutiny on several occasions in post-trial appeals, judicial opinions, and interviews.

Here is an excerpt from Attorney Kenneth Karam's appeal of Kenny's conviction to the Michigan Court of Appeals in 1996 where Mr. Karam addressed the actions of the prosecution in connection to the inadequate defense.

> *As an officer of the court and a law enforcement official, the prosecutor must act not only as the sword of justice but also as the shield of justice.*

> *In this case, Mr. Wyniemko's newly-appointed attorney should have demanded a continuance so that he could adequately prepare for trial. Instead, it appears that this case was steamrolled into a trial at an incredibly breakneck speed, which made a mockery of fair play and fair justice. This writer believes that the prosecutor in this case had a duty to advise the court of the complexity of the case and request an adjournment of this matter so Mr. Wyniemko's attorney could familiarize himself with the file and adequately prepare.*

Judge Zatkoff's Opinion addressed the issue of the jailhouse snitch testimony in the 1994 trial.

> *As to the Defendants' contention that if Plaintiff knew Mr. McCormick was lying, Defendants did not disclose (and Plaintiff therefore would have no way of knowing) that McCormick had received a police report from Ostin and/or Ms. Davis, if that in fact happened. . . .*

> *In the light most favorable to Plaintiff, there is also evidence that demonstrates Ostin engaged in some misconduct, or was aware that Ms. Davis engaged in misconduct (of which misconduct Marlatt was aware), which enabled Mr. McCormick to put together a believable story that Plaintiff had confessed to Mr. McCormick that Plaintiff had committed the crime.*

Ms. Davis and Detective Ostin have never been officially charged or questioned regarding Mr. McCormick's deposition claims and Judge Zatkoff's Opinion regarding their possible misconduct related to Mr. McCormick's perjury.

Former Prosecuting Attorney and current Circuit Court Judge, Carl Marlinga, had quite a few problems with Kenny's conviction. He strongly criticized the lineup. He was appalled at the thought of an attorney having only two days to prepare for a capital case such as Kenny's. He was also critical of the investigation and prosecution.

> *I won't point fingers because I don't think it has any value. Some of the people who were connected with that case, whether it was Assistant Prosecutors or Police Officers, or whatever, people fall back on this secondary way of saying, "Well, he might not have done it, but he can't be totally innocent because of such and such."*
>
> *They still try to justify that which cannot be justified because their unwillingness to admit their own negligence or their own mistakes or their own jumping to conclusions. They will come up with absurd theories in order to avoid the reality of their own wrongdoing.*
>
> *I mean there were people who made more than simple mistakes, people who avoided the truth or glossed over the truth, or didn't care to do their jobs the right way.*

The false testimony of a jailhouse snitch is one of the major causes of wrongful convictions.

Glenn McCormick perjured himself by testifying that Kenny admitted to the 1994 rape of Diane Klug. His knowledge of the details of the crime is the premise on which Assistant Prosecuting Attorney Linda Davis sold his testimony to the jury.

In his 2004 Declaration, Mr. McCormick was very clear as to how he obtained details of the crime. He was given the details by Detective Thomas Ostin and Assistant Prosecutor Linda Davis. He was coached. He was told to lie.

In 1994, Ms. Davis insisted everyone believe Mr. McCormick that Kenny confessed to raping Ms. Klug. She insisted he be believed despite one obvious flaw in that reasoning — that Mr. McCormick's primary reason for testimony was to avoid decades of incarceration.

In 2004, Ms. Davis insisted no one believe Mr. McCormick's claims that Detective Ostin and Ms. Davis suborned perjury in obtaining Mr. McCormick's testimony despite the fact the Mr. McCormick had nothing to gain. She claimed no knowledge of Mr. McCormick receiving any police reports. She also testified she had no knowledge Mr. McCormick was anything but truthful, basing this theory on Mr. McCormick's knowledge of details of the crime.

How and when do you believe Glenn McCormick, lifetime criminal and liar?

What is certain is that Mr. McCormick never learned specifics of the crime from Kenny since Kenny was never there. His explanation that he received the details from Detective Ostin and/or Ms. Davis is certainly plausible, if not certain.

Judge Michael D. Schwartz

"A judge should uphold the integrity and independence of the judiciary. An independent and honorable judiciary is indispensable to justice in our society. A judge should participate in establishing, maintaining, and enforcing, and should personally observe high standards of conduct so that the integrity and independence of the judiciary may be preserved. A judge should always be aware that the judicial system is for the benefit of the litigant and the public, not the judiciary." — Michigan Trial Court Administration Guide, in Section 1-02 – Judicial Power and Conduct.

In the 1994 trial, Judge Schwartz did not act as an impartial officer of the court whose primary goal was to seek truth and justice when he demanded Kenny's attorney go to trial with only the weekend to prepare. Did his belief in Kenny's guilt cloud his impartiality from the outset? Did it continue to affect his trial decisions when he blatantly ignored evidentiary issues and prosecutorial misconduct? How does someone as distinguished and as well versed in court proceedings not demand an answer regarding the missing tapes? How can one not be worried about a mistrial when a defendant accuses a police department of withholding exculpatory evidence taken from the defendant's home?

It was an abuse of power for Judge Schwartz when he ordered the defense attorney to go to trial to defend an individual with 17 felony charges with only a weekend to prepare. As an experienced judge, he knew this order would probably result in a guilty sentence for Kenny. Carl Marlinga, the Macomb County prosecutor during Kenny's trial, was adamant in his belief that what Judge Schwartz did was wrong.

> *That was terrible. That's an outrage. . . . I do think it's a failure in the system that the defense attorney didn't have more time to prepare.*

One of the major reasons Kenny was convicted is that he did not receive anything close to adequate defense representation. Judge Schwartz's actions contributed mightily to that.

Chapter 11 — Vindication

"*Some people might think that I got out on a technicality, which is something that I never wanted to happen. I wanted the truth to come out. And thank God that it did.*"
— Kenny Wyniemko

Kenny envisioned the day when the actual perpetrator of the 1994 rape would be identified and brought to justice. He could then look even the staunchest disbeliever in the eye and declare his innocence. It would be a day of total vindication.

Kenny and the Innocence Project had fought successfully for a statute in Michigan that made it mandatory for all convicted felons to have their DNA tested and recorded in CODIS (Combined DNA Index System), the national DNA database, before their release from prison.

Craig Hamilton Gonser was serving a 15-month sentence in Cheboygan County Jail in Cheboygan, Michigan. The sentence began on May 6, 2008, and was scheduled to end on August 13, 2009. During his incarceration, a buccal swab of Mr. Gonser's DNA was obtained and entered into CODIS. The DNA test results revealed Mr. Gonser to be the source of the unknown donor's DNA at the scene of the 1994 rape of Diane Klug. DNA evidence from a cigarette butt and from under one of the victim's fingernails matched conclusively. DNA recovered from one of the stockings could not exclude him. Under the statute of limitations of rape at the time, Mr. Gonser could not be charged for the 1994 incident.

In 2008, Tina Jewell filed child abuse charges in Macomb District Court (Macomb, MI) against her former husband, Craig Gonser. He was transported from Cheboygan County Jail to Macomb District Court and bound over for trial. He was charged with distribution of obscene matter to children, aggravated indecent exposure, and indecent exposure, all stemming from an incident that occurred in 2004. Bond was set at $500,000. The high bond assured that Mr. Gonser would not be released from Cheboygan as scheduled in August, 2009.

Macomb County Case 2008-54833-FH was convened on October 10, 2008. Judge David F. Viviano presided. Assistant Prosecuting Attorney Michael E. Servitto represented the prosecution. The defense attorney was James M. Simasko.

Details of the 2004 offense were repulsive. Craig Gonser sat naked from the waist down in front of his computer. He was masturbating while viewing porn sites with his infant daughter standing next to him and watching. The incident was witnessed by his wife, who had arrived home unexpectedly. Mr. Gonser's wife reported the incident in 2008. She claimed that she was not aware that Mr. Gonser had violated any laws at the time of the incident.

It was the intent of Mr. Servitto to have the court designate Mr. Gonser as a sexually delinquent person. This would allow the judge to consider the 1994 rape in sentencing, even though Mr. Gonser had not been convicted or even charged for the crime.

Mr. Gonser's case history was referred to Leo Niffeler, a Macomb County court examiner from the Eastwood Clinic in Eastpointe, Michigan. Mr. Niffeler ruled Mr. Gonser to be a sexually delinquent person. Here is an excerpt from his findings.

> *This examiner believes that the conduct of Mr. Gonser was a pattern of repetitive assaults that grew in, in intensity over time. The rights of the victims were disregarded and forced. Physical contact was perpetrated upon them. The most blatant being the alleged rape scenario, followed by additional descriptions of stalking and grooming of future victims. It is this, this examiner's belief that Mr. Gonser fits the criteria of a sexually delinquent person.*

During the jury trial, Mr. Gonser agreed to a plea of "no contest" to two counts related to the 2004 incident at his home. At the Plea Hearing held on March 5, 2010, Mr. Servitto cited previous sexually related convictions and the fact Mr. Gonser had been declared a sexually delinquent person. He stated that he believed these facts should be considered at Mr. Gonser's sentencing. Mr. Servitto also recommended that sentencing considerations should include the fact that Mr. Gonser was the perpetrator in the 1994 rape of Diane Klug.

Mr. Gonser and the Court entered into a Cobbs Agreement in which Mr. Gonser's sentence would not exceed 10 years.

This is the definition of a Cobbs Agreement.

> *A Cobbs Plea is a legal mechanism that allows a person to plead guilty to a criminal offense with some certainty as to what their sentence from the judge will be. . . .*
>
> *If the Defendant likes the Cobbs agreement he can plead guilty and come back for sentencing. If the Defendant does not like the offer the judge makes then the person can reject the offer and proceed to trial.*
>
> *If the judge entered into a Cobbs agreement with the Defendant and then reneges the Defendant is legally entitled to withdraw their plea and proceed to trial.*

Here is an excerpt of the trial transcript where Judge Viviano addresses the defendant's decision to enter a plea under the Cobb's Agreement.

> THE COURT: *You understand that the Court is not bound by the Cobbs Agreement to, to cap your sentence at the ten years that we have discussed, but if I choose at the*

sentencing date to go above that cap, the ten-year cap, I'll then give you an opportunity to withdraw your plea; do you understand that?

DEFENDANT: Yes, I do, sir.

THE COURT: Then to the charge of attempt gross indecency as a sexually delinquent person, how to you plead?

DEFENDANT: No contest.

THE COURT: And to the charge of indecent exposure as a sexually delinquent person, how to do you plead?

DEFENDANT: No contest.

THE COURT: And again, Mr. Simasko, why did the, why do you believe a, a no contest plea is appropriate in this case?

MR. SIMASKO: Potential civil liability, Your Honor.

Mr. Simasko disagreed with the examiner's report that designated Mr. Gonser as a sexually delinquent person and notified the Court that the defense would argue for a sentence below the ten-year designation.

The hearing was concluded at 11:08 am. Sentencing was scheduled for April 15, 2010.

Sentencing

Sentencing commenced at 11:33 am on April 15, 2010. Judge David F. Viviano presided. Assistant Prosecuting Attorney Michael E. Servitto represented the prosecution. Attorneys James M. Simasko and Sandra A. Harrison appeared for the defense.

Victim Impact Statements
Victim Impact Statements are statements from victims at the sentencing hearing. They can be oral or written.

Tina Jewell, Mr. Gonser's ex-wife, testified on behalf of her daughter.

> *I would like to tell the Court that, with everything that has gone on, Mr. Gonser is, has no respect for a court. He has no respect for the law. He thinks he's superior and thinks he can get away with whatever he wants and he's hurt God knows how many people and I just want you and the Court to be able to put him away so that he wouldn't be able to hurt anybody else, because nobody needs to go through that.*

Kenny requested and was granted permission by Judge Viviano to give a Witness Impact Statement at Mr. Gonser's sentencing. It was an unusual request for an unusual situation.

Mr. Simasko strongly objected. He claimed that, while Mr. Wyniemko was certainly a victim in his wrongful conviction, the fault lies with the Clinton Township Police Department. He further claimed that Mr. Gonser was not responsible for what happened to Mr. Wyniemko.

Judge Viviano ruled that Mr. Wyniemko deserved to give a statement, that he was as much a victim of Mr. Gonser's actions as anyone.

Kenny's profound speech at Gonser's arraignment was a moving account of the pain that his wrongful conviction caused Kenny and his family. His statement was directed at Mr. Gonser. Kenny blamed him for ruining his life, his family's lives, and the life of the victim. He called him a coward.

> *I've been waiting and praying for nearly 16 long years for this day to happen. I truly believe that only through the grace of God that this day has finally arrived so that I can address you, face-to-face, like a man.*
>
> *It pleases me that every citizen will know that you are the person that raped Ms. Klug, not I. You were aware I was falsely arrested and convicted and sentenced to prison. I'm certain that during my court proceedings, as well as the nearly ten years I spent in prison and the years that my family suffered the pain and anguish along with me, you were laughing to yourself, knowing an innocent man paid for your crimes. You don't seem to be laughing right now. It pleases me to know that you'll be going to prison, hopefully for a long time.*
>
> *I want you to think of my father each and every day that you are in prison. My wrongful conviction and imprisonment for crimes that you committed took a very heavy toll on him. I truly believe that the stress that he suffered caused his death. He was a good man, a loving husband to my mother, and a good father to my brothers and me. He proudly and honorably served his country in the Navy in World War II. You should think about what your actions did to him.*

Judge Viviano commended Kenny for his work with the Innocence Project and with the wrongfully convicted.

Prosecution Argument

Mr. Servitto listed the numerous sexually related offenses committed by Mr. Gonser since the early 1990s.

This is what he specifically said about the Criminal Sexual Charges from 1992.

> *And again, the evidence from those two cases exhibit the same modus operandi that he had exhibited in the two counts that he plead guilty to, mainly that he would masturbate in parking lots in front of grocery stores. He would wait for unsuspecting women to pass him by and when they would pass him by he would grab their buttocks.*

Mr. Servitto again reminded the court that Mr. Gonser had been designated a sexually delinquent person. For that reason, Mr. Gonser's involvement in the 1994 rape should be considered at time of sentencing. Mr. Servitto cited Mr. Wyniemko as another victim who Mr. Gonser must answer for.

> *For this Defendant to spend one day less than what Mr. Wyniemko has already served in the Michigan Department of Corrections would offend the sensibilities of justice.*

Mr. Servitto requested the maximum sentenced allowed.

> *Under these circumstances, Your Honor, I think there's more than enough evidence and more than enough reason as far as substantial and compelling reasons go for this Court to substantially deviate from the guidelines and I would ask that the Court set a maximum upwards of 35 years.*

Defense Argument

Mr. Simasko objected to Mr. Servitto's comments on several points. He claimed that Mr. Gonser was masturbating in the privacy of his bedroom when his daughter unfortunately walked in.

> *And the underlying offense was that he was convicted of, was that he was attempting to masturbate in his own bedroom when his one-and-a-half-year-old daughter came in and he was convicted of attempted gross indecency and also indecent exposure. Again, this was in his own house.*

Mr. Simasko claimed that Mr. Gonser regrets his prior bad acts in the 1990s and that his client has found religion after the suicide of a close friend in 1999.

> *But he's also here to tell you that he changed his life. In 2000 and in 1999, he's had some revelations. He turned to God. He's stopped using alcohol and drugs. He became active in his church. He became baptized and joined a church in Detroit and he turned into a very good person.*

Mr. Simasko further argued that the crimes of 2004 do not warrant excessive sentence since the incident had no long-lasting effects on his daughter.

> *The little girl had no memory of this whatsoever. She is not a victim of this crime. She doesn't remember it. Nothing bad happened. There was testimony that she never went to counseling, she never had any future problems, she had no recollection of this whatsoever.*

Mr. Simasko did not agree with the court examiner's findings that labelled Mr. Gonser a sexually delinquent person. He further indicated that Mr. Gonser should not be punished for the 1994 crime because the statute of limitations had run out and Mr. Gonser had never been charged nor convicted of this crime. Mr. Simasko claimed Mr. Gonser did not commit the 1994 rape and the only explanation for the DNA match is that the evidence had become tainted.

Sentencing

Judge Viviano said he weighed justice for the victims, including Kenny and the victim in the 1994 rape, and found "ample reason" to depart from the guidelines.

> *The next question of course is what is justice in this case for Mr. Wyniemko? He is of course not a crime victim under the Crime Victims Act and not a victim in the traditional sense, but this is not a traditional situation.*
>
> *It is my hope as to Mr. Wyniemko that this case gives him some closure.*
>
> *As for justice for and arriving at an appropriate sentence for Mr. Gonser, sir, although you cannot be charged and convicted for something that happened in 1994, it is appropriate under the sexual, sexually delinquent persons' statute for the Court to consider that in deciding what is an appropriate sentence for you. As I mentioned, I do recognize that you have made some strides in your life. But I also believe that you need to be punished for some of the mistakes that you have made and some of the terrible things that you have done and the impact that they have had on people's lives. . . .*
>
> *Unfortunately your criminal activity did not stop when you had this change of heart in 1999, leading up to of course what was the underlying crime in this case, the incident involving your young daughter. But also later the domestic violence conviction involving Miss Jewell and interfering*

with electronic communications. When I read the allegations surrounding that incident it is clear to me that you continued to act aggressively towards women and in a dangerous way. The Court has to take all of these things into consideration and I also have to consider of course the 1994 rape. I can't ignore the forensic evidence that points to you as being the person who committed that horrible, horrible offense.

As I mentioned before, I don't believe that I need to assert or state substantial and compelling reasons to depart from the guidelines in this case, but to the extent that I do I believe, as Mr. Servitto has suggested, that there are ample reasons for departure in this case. Taking into account all of the charged and uncharged and of course dismissed sexual offenses, the ones dismissed as part of your plea agreements in these various cases, including the 1994 rape, after carefully considering all of those factors, the Court is going to sentence you to ten to 25 years in the Department of Corrections. On the count three, which is the indecent exposure count I will give you credit of course for the 359 days that you served so far. You are going to be required to register under the Michigan Sex Offender's Registration Act and comply with all of the requirements of that act. You will pay a $68 State cost on that charge and a crime victim rights assessment in the amount of $60.

On count two I will sentence you to one year in the Macomb County Jail and again I'll give you credit for the 359 days that you have served. You will pay a $68 State cost on that count as well.

Craig Hamilton Gonser, 42, was sentenced to 10-25 years in jail. His history of sexual offenses had finally caught up with him in 2010.

The defense did not object to the sentence.

The hearing was concluded at 1:12 pm.

After the sentencing, Kenny had plenty to say in interviews outside the courtroom. He felt a huge weight lifted from his shoulders. And he was quite adamant in his admonishment of Mr. Gonser.

> *Gonser's cowardice cost me 10 years of my life. When I got out of prison, when they finally believed I didn't rape the woman, I couldn't get a job. That still bothers me.*
>
> *I feel 10 pounds lighter already. It's been a long time coming. This finally closes the door for me. I'll sleep better knowing he's in jail, and a lot of women and children will feel safer.*
>
> *I can never get those years back. I can never get my dad back. The only thing I can do is move forward.*

The fact remained that there were individuals who believed that Kenny got off on a technicality. The public perception is that the scales of justice are being constantly tipped in the direction of the criminal. To many, Kenny's case was just another example. That is why April 15, 2010, is so important to Kenny. For it was on this day that Kenny could declare himself to be innocent beyond any reasonable doubt.

Macomb County Prosecuting Attorney, Eric Smith, emphatically declared that the DNA match of Mr. Gonser completely clears Kenny Wyniemko of any involvement in the 1994 rape.

In an interview, former Macomb Prosecutor Carl Marlinga called the situation a "prosecutor's worst nightmare, especially if the actual rapist committed other crimes between the 1994 rape and his recent identification."

"It means that, because of this wrongful conviction, [there's] not only the injustice for Ken Wyniemko, but some other person has been victimized," said Mr. Marlinga, who, at the time of Mr. Gonser's conviction, was in private practice as a defense attorney.

"Until the actual perpetrator is caught, there are always skeptics and doubters who continue to secretly harbor suspicions against the person who has been exonerated," Mr. Marlinga said. "This is as close as we can get to absolute proof."

Mr. Gonser appealed his sentence in 2012 and was denied. The following excerpt from the State of Michigan Court of Appeals' decision describes Tina Jewell's testimony as to her recollection of the events of 2004. It demonstrates the true nature of the crime and dismissive attitude of Mr. Gonser.

> *Defendant's ex-wife testified that she came home from work early to discover Defendant sitting at the computer with their twenty-month old daughter standing next to him and looking directly at him. She testified that the computer screen displayed a picture of a fully nude woman.*
>
> *Upon hearing her gasp, Defendant stood up and turned around, allowing her to observe that he was naked from the waist down. Defendant said, "I'm playing with it, do you mind?" A bottle of personal lubricant was on the desk. She testified that Defendant had previously used this brand of lubricant to masturbate.*

Mr. Gonser's arrest record was obtained from the Sterling Heights Police Department, located in Macomb County, Michigan. It revealed some interesting facts, especially when compared to the timeline of the events leading up to Kenny's arrest and trial.

April 9, 1994 — The Sterling Heights Police Department responded to a call from Sterling Heights Fire Station #4 at 12850 15 Mile Road. A woman escaped from her abusive boyfriend's car after suffering a physical assault and entered the fire station as a safe haven from her attacker. The boyfriend had "left, threatening to kill (victim) if she pressed charges." The assailant was Craig Hamilton Gonser.

Mid-April, 1994 — Assault and Battery (A&B) charges were filed against Mr. Gonser.

April 28, 1994 — Mr. Gonser is arrested on the Assault and Battery charges and makes bond.

April 29, 1994 — On the day after Mr. Gonser's A&B arrest, Diane Klug is brutally raped for a period of three hours.

August 4, 1994 — Mr. Gonser was summoned to Macomb County Court for a bond hearing on the A&B charge. It was noted that he had previously been charged with two separate stalking charges in two separate cities. His bond is raised to $50,000 cash/surety only. Mr. Gonser is incarcerated until trial.

August 11, 1994 — Kenny's preliminary exam for the 1994 rape.

August 22, 1994 (10:30 am) — Mr. Gonser is convicted of A&B during a bench trial before visiting Judge Matthew Rumora. Mr. Gonser was in the middle of a three-year probation period after serving six months in jail stemming from several counts of Criminal Sexual Conduct (CSC) in the Fourth Degree in 1992. Despite his probation status and the two counts of stalking the victim, Mr. Gonser is sentenced to 40 days in jail, with 19 days served, and is fined $300.

August 23, 1994 (10:30 am) — Just 24 hours after Mr. Gonser's A&B conviction, Kenny is arraigned in Macomb County Court on 17 felony charges, including 15 counts of CSC-1. Trial is set for November 1, 1994.

In 2010, Assistant Prosecutor Servitto was campaigning for Circuit Court Judge when he recalled the Gonser case in an interview.

> *The most interesting trial was People vs. Craig Hamilton Gonser. I tried the case in November of 2009. Judge David Viviano presided over the case, and James Simasko was the Defendant's attorney. In 1994, the Defendant broke into a woman's home, held her hostage, and brutally raped her. A man named Kenneth Wyniemko was wrongfully arrested and convicted of the crime. DNA comparisons exculpated Mr. Wyniemko in 2003, but the Defendant's comparison DNA sample was not available until he committed another felony in 2008. By then, the statute of limitations precluded prosecution of the 1994 case. After further investigation, we discovered the Defendant masturbated in front of his 20 month-old daughter in 2004. Consequently, my office charged Defendant with Gross Indecency, Indecent Exposure and the sentence enhancement Sexually Delinquent Person. I conducted the jury trial and convicted him of Attempted Gross Indecency and Indecent Exposure.*

> Under Michigan law, the enhancement of Sexually Delinquent Person is the only sentence enhancement that requires a second trial. Although the Defendant's prior criminal history was inadmissible in the first trial, the second enhancement trial would allow me to present evidence of the 1994 rape and his incidents of indecent exposure. Faced with that overwhelming evidence, Defendant chose to plead guilty in early 2010.

Kenny discussed how he found out that Mr. Gonser had been identified as the perpetrator in the 1994 rape for which Kenny was convicted.

> *I first found out about the DNA match from Gail (Pamukov). I was with Tina, the girl I was dating at the time. We were at Macy's at Lakeside Mall picking up a gift for my mom when my cell phone rang. It was Gail. Her voice was kind of shaky and I was a little apprehensive.*
>
> *She said, "How you doing Kenny?"*
> *I told her, "I'm okay. How are you?"*
> *She said, "Are you at home?"*
> *I said "No, I'm at Lakeside shopping for a gift for my mom. What's up?"*
> *She said, "You better find a place to sit down."*
> *I said, "Gail, what's going on?"*
> *"Just find a place to sit down."*
> *Tina saw the look on my faced and asked me, "Kenny, what's the matter?"*
> *I told her, "I don't know. Just hang on for a second."*
> *I couldn't find a chair but there was a display table full of jeans. I pushed the jeans over and sat down right there.*
> *I again asked, "What's going on?"*
> *She said, "I just got a phone call from Ostin."*
> *I said, "What the fuck does he want?"*

She said, "Well," and she started to cry now.

I was getting a little scared. "What's the matter with you? What's the matter? What does that mother fucker want?"

"They caught the guy, the actual rapist."

I froze. I don't know for how long, but I must have just sat there in shock for several seconds.

"You there, Kenny?"

I said, "Kind of. How'd this happen?"

So, she told the story about how the guy that did the rape had been identified from DNA. They couldn't release the name yet because no one was charged.

Gonser was in prison in Northern Michigan. It was mandatory that his DNA be tested. This was one of those new laws that I had fought for right after I got out. People were bitching that someone would get out of prison and they would go right back in. It made sense to me. If someone was in jail there for a crime they committed, get a DNA sample before they are released. Because you never know how many other crimes could be solved.

They got the DNA swab and ran it through the system. He was taken from prison where he was at and brought down to Macomb County Jail to be charged for the incident with his daughter.

The prosecutor was Assistant Prosecutor Mike Servitto who just happened to be the son of Judge Edward Servitto, the same judge who freed me in 2003.

When Gonser was convicted, I requested to give my own Victim's Impact Statement. It was never done before by someone like me. I approached Servitto and asked him to speak with Judge Viviano and see if I could give the statement. He said he had never heard of anything like that and that if he does that, Gonser's attorney will undoubtedly quash it.

I said, "What the hell do I care about him? Just give it a shot."

So, Mike went into chambers with Gonser's attorney to talk about it with Judge Viviano.

Judge Viviano said, "Mr. Wyniemko is just as much a victim as the girl and he paid his dues. He's a free man. There are no wants or warrants on him. He can say what he wants to say."

That's how I was able to give my speech at his sentencing.

Craig Gonser is on the left. Ken is on the right. Mr. Gonser was six-foot-six and 260 pounds, while Ken was five-foot-eleven and about 180 pounds. Yet, Ken was identified as the rapist.

Chapter 12 — A Juror's Regret

In the spring of 2017, Mr. Gerald Innes, a juror from Kenny's trial, was contacted. Using a mutual Facebook friend as a temporary go-between, Mr. Innes was asked if he was willing to relate his thoughts regarding Kenny's trial. At first, Mr. Innes was very leery. He feared Kenny held a lot of animosity toward the jury for his conviction and that he blamed them for his incarceration. Once Mr. Innes was assured that Kenny felt no bitterness towards the jury, he agreed to an interview. His thoughts were quite revealing.

> *I had never been involved in jury duty before the trial so I didn't know what was in store for me. The fact that this was a capital case with felony charges was surprising. I did my best to judge impartially and to come to a logical conclusion for the verdict.*
>
> *I remember there was no link to Kenny as far as evidence. The prosecutor mentioned the shoe prints at the crime scene but never connected them to him. I thought it odd the prints were even brought up. And, they couldn't tie any of the forensics to him either. The prosecutor explained that the defendant was methodical in his approach to the crime and had a great deal of preparation to make sure he didn't leave any evidence. The absence of evidence still didn't prove the absence of a crime or that Kenny didn't do the crime. It's just that there was nothing tying him to the scene.*
>
> *I had to make a determination based mostly on the witness testimony.*
>
> *The jailhouse snitch was not believable. No one on the jury gave him the time of day. He just seemed like a lowlife looking for a break.*

The victim and the girlfriend were very impactful for me. You felt so sorry for the victim and the hell she went though.

And the girlfriend was believable. That she had been in a bad relationship.

Detective Marlatt didn't seem like he wanted to be there. He wasn't sincere and it was like he just mailed in his testimony.

Detective Ostin came across as very effective as he described his efforts to resolve the case and make us think Kenny was the guy. He was believable.

I remember thinking the victim identification was sketchy. I felt sorry for her and I know she picked him out in court. But she was blindfolded throughout the attack. I just didn't consider her identification as an absolute.

When we started deliberations, we went around the table for an initial vote. Everyone was leaning towards a guilty verdict. One guy had made up his mind that Kenny was guilty and no one was going to change his mind. A few of the women made comments like "He must be guilty or they wouldn't have arrested him if he didn't do it." And "They wouldn't have prosecuted him if he didn't do it."

I felt it was our duty to go through all the evidence. There was one guy and one woman who agreed with me. And, that's what we did. We had questions about a lot of stuff. We made a T-graph and went over the evidence. But, in the end, we all voted guilty.

The crime was so shocking back then without the Internet and social media we have today. I kept wondering what kind of guy could even consider doing such a horrific thing. I asked myself, "How could anyone to this? How sick did they have to be?"

I can't speak for others but I think the reason I voted guilty was as much the attacks on Kenny's character as anything else. In the end, it seemed like he was a guy who could have committed the crime.

The prosecution played up the drug use, the video tapes the cops took from his home, and his sexual preferences with his girlfriend. His ex-girlfriend went a long way in my mind of making me think Kenny was capable of this. Also, Ostin did a good job of his claim that Kenny was the kind of guy who could have committed this rape. It was all these people pointing at Kenny as a guy who had it in him to do this terrible thing.

Like I said, it wasn't the actual evidence that convinced me of his guilt, but the way he was portrayed throughout the trial.

Mr. Innes was asked if the defense had produced phone message tapes where the ex-girlfriend had threatened Kenny on numerous occasions that she is going to kill him, that she is going to ruin his life, could that have made a difference?

Oh, I'm sure it would have. I am not sure if I would have held out for an innocent verdict, but it would have made a real difference in how I felt about his guilt. I never thought of the girlfriend as vindictive during her testimony. Just a woman Kenny took advantage of.

After we gave our verdict, Detective Ostin and Judge Schwartz met with us. I think it was to set our mind at ease. Judge Schwartz was actually shocked we didn't return a guilty verdict in 20-30 minutes. He gave us reasons for his sentencing decision. He also said there was a lot more evidence that they couldn't get in and that we did the right thing. I left that courtroom thinking that Kenny was guilty.

Mr. Innes was assured that he made the best decision based on the evidence he was presented. He still could not get over the fact he sent an innocent man to jail.

> *Clearly we could only work with what knowledge was presented to us. If we didn't get the real story, then it's hard to come to the right conclusion. But, there's still no getting around the thought that I was part of sending an innocent man to prison.*

> *I have thought about that trial thousands of times. I am at the age where I have felt that it was time for me to make amends for some of the things I have done in my life, that there is a lot of stuff that I have screwed up. And, now, with what I have learned about Kenny's case, my actions as a juror is just another failure of mine.*

Mr. Innes was shocked to hear about a lot of things that have come to light since Kenny's release.

> *I remember reading in 2003 that Kenny was released. I remember thinking then that here was just another guy who got off based on a technicality. I really didn't follow his story much after that.*
>
> *As I am finding out today about what really happened, it just makes me sick. One of the things that bothers me is how his attorney could have kept the victim's affair from earlier the day of the crime from Kenny. Who does that?*
>
> *The more I read about Kenny's case, the more I feel that I was part of one big scam to put an innocent man in jail. Like I said, it really bothers me to this day.*

The interview revealed some amazing facts about the state of mind of one of the jurors. It wasn't the witness identification that convinced Mr. Innes of Kenny's guilt. It wasn't the evidence either. It was the constant hammering at Kenny's reputation with the repetitive mention of cocaine use that didn't exist and should have been quashed by the defense. And it was the vindictive testimony of a former girlfriend, a testimony that could have been easily discredited with the missing answering machine tapes. In the end, despite the fact Mr. Innes believed there was no clear evidence that linked Kenny to the crime, there weren't enough reasons to convince him to stand alone against his eleven fellow jurors.

Chapter 13 — Spokesperson

"*He is a perfect cross between a bulldog and a saint. Ken is so well motivated. His ability to forgive is unsurpassed. But his ability to seek justice for other people is unparalleled. He will not give up.*" — Circuit Court Judge Carl Marlinga

After all the hoopla around his exoneration, there came a time when Kenny asked himself, "Now what?" He wanted his exoneration to mean something. He wanted to be worthy of all the efforts that won his freedom.

Shortly after his release, Kenny was invited to speak on the Mitch Albom Show, a popular radio show in the Detroit area. Before long, there were numerous requests for his time. He spoke at law schools like those at the University of Michigan and Harvard. He appeared on the radio frequently, including appearances with Richard Bernstein (a well-known attorney in Michigan) in the *Fighting for Justice* series on the late Angelo Henderson radio show. Mr. Bernstein, legally blind since birth, was later elected to the Michigan Supreme Court. Kenny spoke at church halls and libraries. There wasn't a venue he refused.

Kenny found his passion. He dedicated his life to the release and support of every wrongfully convicted prisoner.

In 2003, Kenny was appointed to Cooley Law School Innocence Project's Board of Commissioners. In November, 2003, the Kenneth Wyniemko Foundation was established in honor of his dad. The foundation's sole purpose is to promote the work of the Innocence Project and other similar organizations, and to support newly released exonerees.

In 2005, Kenny was named an honorary member of The Criminal Defense Attorneys of Michigan for his work on behalf of assisting new exonerees' efforts to get their lives back in order. In 2006, *The Price of Innocence*, a documentary film about Ken's wrongful conviction, won an Emmy award. In 2008, he was given the *Allene and Martin Doctorff Liberty Bell Award* from the Oakland County Bar Association for his continued efforts to educate the public about the serious problems in the American justice system. He now serves on the board of Project Innocence and advises the Michigan Innocence Clinic at the University of Michigan.

> *I think it was maybe a month after I was released when I decided that there are a lot more people like me who were still locked up in prison and who might not be as lucky as I was. They never had an opportunity to meet people like Gail or Kim. I was going to use my connections and do what I could to get the innocent out of prison.*
>
> *Mitch Albom was the first person who contacted me to speak on his radio show. About two weeks after I was released, he called Gail. On the show, Mitch wanted to hear from me. Gail insisted on being there the first three or four times I spoke. She was always worried about what I'd say.*
>
> *Then we got a call to do a show called "Due Process." It was hosted by Henry Baskin. He was on Channel 4 back then. Outside of the day I was released, that was the first TV show I did. I met Gail and Donna McKneelen at the Channel 4 Studio in downtown Detroit. Donna was a lawyer for the Innocence Project who worked on my case.*
>
> *I was really nervous. Gail told me, "Kenny, let Donna and I do the talking, okay?" Henry Baskin, who was a well-known attorney, told Gail, "I want to hear from Kenny. People want to hear from Kenny." Gail said, "Right now, Kenny is not saying a word."*
>
> *I told Gail, "You know this is totally new to me. I've never done this before and I don't want to get nervous and*

Emmy Awards - Pictured Gail Pamukov, Senator Steve Bieda, Producer Charlie Langton, Ken, Professor Donna McKneelen, Producer Matt Phillips, Macomb Bar Assoc. Exec. Dir. Rick Troy, Professor Marla Mitchell

Ken with Emmy Awards for *The Price of Innocence* (2006)

say the wrong thing. We can tell this guy that we can come back next month when I am ready to speak on his show."

We were getting so many calls and we had to work around Gail's schedule. She wouldn't let me go anywhere without her by my side. Scheduling was real tough.

Then it got to the point where the more I spoke, the more comfortable I felt. I knew what I could and what I couldn't say. I had to be real careful because the lawsuit against Clinton Township was pending. It was probably after the fourth or fifth appearance when Gail told me, "Kenny, you're a smart guy, you know how to play the game."

I think the first time I did an interview on my own was for the Flint station. Then I did a few in Lansing and a few more in Flint. I was ready to be on my own. But I was grateful Gail was there at the beginning.

The Innocence Project was getting a lot of PR and they came up with this idea to get me involved. That is when they put me on the Board of Commissioners. Norm Fell, Jim Samuels, Kathy Swedlow, and a couple of other board members contacted me. Norm is the founder of the Innocence Project in Michigan.

When I went up to speak at the celebration, everybody was standing up and clapping. I got to the microphone and I froze. I broke down and started crying. I was thinking, "I just can't believe this. I'm the only non-attorney here and I get named to the Board of Commissioners for the Innocence Project."

It was overwhelming. I decided that this is what I wanted to do right after that dinner.

On the Angelo Henderson Radio Show with
Michigan Supreme Court Justice Richard Bernstein and Angelo

In Lansing, MI, with Donya Davis, Julie Baumer, Bishop Thomas Gumbleton,
Tommy Highers, Ray Highers, and Ken

Ken Brown, Ken, Rachel Nevado, and Mitch Albom on the Mitch Albom Radio Show

Ken with Senator Tonya Schuitmaker and Governor Jennifer Granholm at signing of first DNA testing extension (2005)

Barry Scheck, the original founder of the Innocence Project, arranged for me to speak at Harvard University.

I stayed at the Boston Marriott. I can remember walking around campus and looking at the name plates on the dorms. The buildings are just so old. There is so much history. I felt like I was walking on air.

I remember the auditorium where I spoke. I think it sat about 1,100 people. The original wood end floors were still squeaking. It was hard to believe that I was at Harvard and that strangers were coming there to hear me speak.

I appeared at the University of Michigan for the first time right after Harvard. I was speaking at Wayne State with Gail and Norm Fell. Richard Bernstein, who is currently a Michigan Supreme Court Judge, came to hear me. At the time, Richard was still an adjunct Professor at Michigan. After he heard me speak, he said, "Kenny, I want you speak at U of M."

I went there on a regular basis. Tom Howlett, who was a graduate of Harvard and Michigan, brought me to U of M a couple times, too.

The National Executive Council for Wrongfully Convicted got started around this time. There were fellow exonerees like Dave Shepard and Herman Atkins, seven in all. They picked us because we all were doing similar work – going around the country and speaking. Our motto was, "Each One. Reach One. Teach One." When someone was exonerated in our area, there would be somebody there to help them when they were released.

This is what I have dedicated my life to. I won't stop until every wrongfully convicted prisoner is released.

Kenny related a story about an event that was held at a local church. What started as an simple gathering turned into a memorable moment.

> There was this one time I was at the hall at St. Michael's Church on Hayes Road in Sterling Heights. It was through the Macomb County Bar Association. James Maceroni was there. He was an attorney at the time. He's a Circuit Judge now. He contacted Gail and asked me and Stephanie Chang, a member of the State of Michigan House of Representatives, to come there and speak.
>
> I was speaking in the same room where we later had the luncheon for my mom's funeral in 2016. Maceroni spoke first. I spoke after him. We showed a video about different wrongful convictions and opened it up to questions. One of the questions had to do with the death penalty. I named two people who always proclaimed their innocence and who were executed. Later, DNA testing proved they were telling the truth. There were people shaking their heads in disbelief. I asked, "How many people here can honestly believe that no innocent person has ever been executed?"
>
> One guy puts his hand up. One guy!
>
> I thought, "What the hell? Haven't you been listening?"
>
> So, I am thinking to myself, "How can I make an example of this guy without getting him pissed off or embarrass him?" And I get up and approach him.
>
> I said that I can't understand how you can honestly believe one innocent person has never been executed in our country, or anywhere in the world. How can you believe that?
>
> He said that if someone was found guilty, they must have committed a crime.
>
> I'm thinking, "Lord, just tell me what to say."
>
> Then I looked down at the cross I was wearing — the same one that I wear to this day.

I said to him, "I assume you, like the other people here, are a member of St. Michael's, correct?"

"Yes, I am."

"That's good. My mom and dad belonged here. Been Catholic all your life?"

"Yes."

"Tell you what. I am going to ask you one question, and if you give me an honest answer and you still think there has never been an innocent person executed, I will pack up my briefcase right now and go away and never make a public appearance anywhere."

"Okay."

"Do you see this cross here? See this man on the cross?"

"Yes."

"Here's my question. You tell me what crime this man committed that caused him to be executed. You tell me one crime he committed and I will shut my mouth and leave right now."

He put his head down and started crying. He was probably 70 years old and I embarrassed him. I tapped him shoulder and asked him to stand up. He stood up and I gave him a hug and told him, "I still love you."

He said, "You're right, Kenny. You're right."

Everybody started clapping.

Stephanie got up in front of the microphone. She was crying and she said, "Ladies and gentleman, we have appeared in so many places together for many years. This man is a very special person and I am proud to be with him today."

I remember this other occasion when I was wearing my Proving Innocence jacket at Meijer's Food Center. An older couple walked by and this guy was staring at my jacket. He asked me, "What's that Proving Innocence? What's that all about?"

So, I told them.

He said, "I'm glad to hear some attorneys are doing good work like that."

I told him, "I'm gonna stop you right there. I'm not an attorney."

"You're not? How are you taking this on?"

"I was in prison for nine years for a crime I didn't commit."

Both of their jaws dropped. "You gotta be kidding me!"

"I wish I was. But I'm not."

We went over to the sub shop in Meijer's and had coffee and talked for 45 minutes. I gave him a couple of my cards and told him if he wanted my information, just Google my name or go to the Innocent Project or Proving Innocence websites. I told him he'd be there all week just learning. Moments like that are precious.

That is why I have "Innocence Project" on the side of my car. That is why it's on my jackets, sweatshirts, and t-shirts. I want to be a walking billboard. A lot of people stop me and ask me what it's all about.

In 2007, Davontae Sanford was convicted in Wayne County, Michigan, of a quadruple homicide at the age of 14 years of age. Two weeks after his conviction, a hit man confessed to seven drug related hits in the Detroit area, including the murders of which Mr. Sanford was imprisoned. The police believed the hit man in every instance but the one in which Mr. Sanford was convicted. The hit man led police to the gun used in the killings. Ballistic tests confirmed his claim. Yet, Mr. Sanford remained in jail for over eight years.

In 2014, the University of Michigan's Innocence Clinic and Northwestern University's Center on Wrongful Convictions for Youth starting examining Mr. Sanford's case. On June 8, 2016, Mr. Sanford was released. He was 23 years of age.

A celebration of his release was held the next day at the Matrix Center at McNichols Avenue and Gratiot on Detroit's east side. Kenny attended.

> *As I approached the Center, I was surprised to see about sixteen DPD officers standing outside the church in full riot gear. I approached one of them and asked if he was expecting trouble. He replied that they were there to show support of Davontae.*
>
> *After the festivities were done, a couple of the officers came up to me and said, "I heard your story about being convicted and released. Tell me, how do you feel about police officers?"*
>
> *I told them, "I am glad you asked that question. I get asked that a lot. I can tell you that I am speaking for just about all the exonerees that I have met, and I have met just about all of them. Beat cops, the cops that patrol the streets, have our utmost respect. You have a job that I know I cannot do. You guys go to work every day without knowing you will be able to come home. I have problems with dishonest detectives and prosecutors that bend and break rules to get a conviction and another feather in their cap."*
>
> *They couldn't thank me enough. A couple of them were surprised, but extremely pleased. We shook hands and I left. That felt good. Cops protect us each and every day.*

Perhaps Kenny's crowning achievement as an advocate for the wrongfully convicted was the passage of the Michigan Wrongful Conviction Compensation Act in 2016. Kenny made the bill his top priority for close to a decade.

> *I was so frustrated. It passed the Senate unanimously five months prior. I couldn't understand why the House was sitting on the bill for so long.*

> *It was December 7, 2016. Pearl Harbor Day. On every Pearl Harbor Day, I pray for the fallen soldiers. For some reason, I turned to the soldiers and asked for their help with the Compensation Bill.*
>
> *This is the honest God's truth. Not 15 minutes later, Michigan State Representative Stephanie Chang called and told me that the bill had just been introduced on the House floor and it was ready to be voted on. It wasn't long before she called me back and told me it passed.*

On June 6, 2016, Michigan Senate Bill 0291 (SB0291) passed unanimously in the Michigan Senate. On December 8, 2016, Michigan House Bill 4536 (HB4536) passed by a 104-2 vote in the House of Representatives. The bill was approved by Governor Rick Snyder and signed into law on December 21, 2016. Michigan became the 32nd state to offer compensation and assistance to the wrongfully convicted. SB0291 and HB4536 provide Michigan exonerees with $50,000 per year of incarceration and the same state-sponsored reentry services offered to parolees.

State Senator Stephen Bieda and State Representative Stephanie Chang were the primary forces behind the bill's passage in the Michigan State Legislature.

> STEPHEN BIEDA: *The lives and reputations of these individuals have been devastated as a result of being in prison for a crime they did not commit. It's a very important statement to make as a state, and it's just the fair thing to do.*
>
> *Kenny was extremely affective in the Committee and in the public and media. I don't think this Legislation could have happened unless we had somebody like him. He was the perfect poster boy for the cause because he's soft spoken and he's direct. There was no man more dedicated to having this bill passed than he.*

STEPHANIE CHANG: *People worked so hard on this bill for a long time. I am especially happy for Senator Bieda and Kenny.*

This was my first term and it was so satisfying being part of this much needed legislation.

For exonerees like brothers Tommy and Ray Highers, the bill provides some piece of mind for lives ruined by a wrongful conviction. Tommy and Ray are brothers who were wrongfully convicted for the murder of a drug kingpin. They spent 25 years in jail until they were exonerated in 2012.

TOMMY HIGHERS: *The bill will change all of our lives. It's been a struggle since we've been home, trying to rebuild after two and a half decades in jail. It's going to do wonders for everyone in our immediate family, to be financially secure enough to not worry every day about how we'll get by now and what might happen in the future. I am very grateful.*

RAY HIGHERS: *For me, the compensation bill means two things. First of all, the state has finally recognized what they did to us. And, secondly, it provides a future for our family. I'll be 51 and I won't be able to continue my hard work. I've bought a house and cars and without this bill there is always a danger to lose everything. We live check by check and any serious injury would put us in deep trouble. We don't have a pension or any social security to speak of. We're on our own like we have been since our release. And, it's also an opportunity for us to give back to some of those who lent their support when we needed it most.*

Julie Baumer, released in 2010 after serving six years for a wrongful conviction, had her own view of what the bill meant to her.

> JULIE BAUMER: *Maybe the bill can help healing some emotional wounds because the state has finally acknowledged I was wrongfully convicted and imprisoned. I have never received an apology.*
>
> *I've been home for over six years now. Certainly, if I would have received this when I first got home, it would have made a much larger impact. I had to work two full time jobs, one to live on and one to fix my credit that was ruined during the time I spent in jail. For those first two years, I don't know how I survived. With this bill, others won't have to go through what I did.*
>
> *I have spoken to an investment consultant and I would like to use some of the earnings to help others, perhaps in the form of a transitional house for people who are exonerated and for those who qualify.*

While Kenny was ecstatic at the passage of the bill, he wondered why it took so long for Michigan lawmakers to pass the bill.

> *Well, I look at it as the lawmakers finally waking up. Or, it might be they got fed up with me constantly complaining in sessions or to the media. Maybe a little of both. The main thing is it's passed and it's going to help a lot of deserving people, innocent people at that. I couldn't be happier.*

At Polish Yacht Club with Professor Donna McKneelen, Bill Proctor, Senator Mike Kowall, Julie Baumer, Senator Steve Bieda, and Ken

At the signing of the Michigan Wrongful Conviction Compensation Bill in Lansing, MI

With Senator Bieda, Professor Marla Mitchell-Director Innocence Project at Cooley Law School, and Ken

At Lansing State Capital with Rep. Martin Howrylak, Rep. Stephanie Chang, Sen. Steve Bieda, Sen. Rick Jones, Ken, Sen. Tonya Schuitmaker, and Rep. Pete Lucido

Senator Stephen M. Bieda

Michigan State Senator Stephen M. Bieda has been in the forefront of the battle for the wrongfully convicted in the Michigan Legislature from the very beginning.

He sponsored the extensions to the DNA testing statute and was instrumental in the removal of the sunset date from the bill in 2015.

Senator Bieda was the initial driving force behind the Wrongful Convicted Compensation Act that was enacted in early 2017. He introduced the bill while a State Representative and continued to sponsor the statute while in the State Senate.

No one in the Michigan Legislature has meant more to the plight of the wrongfully convicted than Senator Bieda.

I started working on it (Compensation Bill) about 12 years ago and the inspiration was Kenny's case. His case brought to light, frankly, the mistreatment, call it the plight of people, who were wrongfully convicted and incarcerated.

The Comp Bill became so personal because I got to know the exonerees and their stories. It hurt to see a system that I love, my country, fail. I am an attorney and I love the system of justice. You want the best out of the system you can get. Then you see such a glaring injustice, something so un-American, and you just have to do something about it.

The bill went to a vote during each of my terms in the House, but failed. As I neared my term limit in the Senate, it still hadn't passed. About a year ago, with the Governor's (Governor Snyder) support, we were able to get it out of the Senate and move it to the House.

I have to tell you that at the end of each session when it would die, the hardest calls I had to make was to some of the people, particularly the exonerees, and to Kenny. It was very emotional for me because it was a closure for government recognizing something was wrong and something should be done and it was a hard call every time.

The Compensation Bill is the most significant piece of legislative action I have had the privilege to work on. And it is the one I am most proud of.

There were many people willing to come forward and share their admiration for Kenny and how he has carried himself since his exoneration.

Circuit Court Judge Carl Marlinga, Former Macomb County Prosecutor

He is a perfect cross between a bulldog and a saint. Ken is so well motivated. His ability to forgive is unsurpassed. But his ability to seek justice for other people is unparalleled. He will not give up. And I think, possibly, it's the thing that makes the most sense. It's like you've lost so much of your life, in order to make your life meaningful, you've got to take that experience and not just let it twist in your gut. You've got to make something positive about it. You've got to turn it around and free other people. That's what he's done. Psychologically, it's the healthiest thing he could do. But, even with all of that, his efforts still can't be explained. It's super human strength. It really is.

Bill Proctor, Investigative Reporter

I can say this for the book, for my friend, for everybody who reads this to know: Kenny Wyniemko had every reason to be vengeful, hateful, disrespectful, and very upset about the people who were responsible for his wrongful conviction and the nine years he lost and not being able to go to his father's funeral. But this country, if not the world, should be very proud of the person Kenny Wyniemko decided to become. He is a person who has committed time, money, and dedication to do something for people like him, people who suffered the loss of their freedom for something they didn't do. And it's not a flash in a pan thing for Kenny Wyniemko. He's dedicated to it. He has spent the last eight years trying to get the Wrongful Conviction Compensation Bill passed. And he has been at the release of other wrongfully convicted people ready to give them money, ready to give them support. He has been to national conventions to show a strong example of what a person who suffered like he did can become. Kenny has become that. People should know that and be proud of Kenny Wyniemko.

Judge Patrick T. Cahill

As a District Court Judge for almost 11 years, I watched as many litigants got swept up into the criminal justice system and ground down by it. They were frequently represented by overworked and underpaid public defenders who were usually more interested in a quick plea than a protracted trial. The presumption of innocence seemed to be turned upside down, especially if you were naive and too trusting. Ken Wyniemko experienced these systemic failures first hand and has now become a beacon, working tirelessly to shed light on inequities in the justice system. He is a role model, a proud exoneree, and an eloquent advocate for change.

Michigan State Senator Stephen Bieda

Kenny was extremely effective in the Michigan Senate and House and in the public and the media, all of these things. I don't think this Legislation could have happened unless we had somebody like Kenny. Kenny was my inspiration for this bill and the perfect poster boy for the cause because he's soft-spoken and he's direct. There was no man more dedicated to having this bill passed.

Stephanie Chang, Michigan State House Representative
Kenny is truly an inspiration.

Thomas Howlett, Defense Attorney
So, even after what Ken went through, he has become an upstanding citizen, preaching the gospel with regard to exonerations so well now.

Norm Fell, Director of Cooley Law School Innocence Project
Ken was invaluable and he still is. What Ken did so well in the beginning, particularly at the speaking engagements, was to get the word out and to influence so many people. Students would tell their parents. Parents would then contact me, asking me about the Innocence Project. Some of these parents from U of M are very influential. Ken, by what he is doing, is putting himself out there, facilitating this spread of knowledge that legitimizes our work.

Scott Nobles, Deputy Warden—Ryan Correctional Facility
Kenny was imprisoned for nine years, especially in a prison like Ryan, for something that he didn't do. He maintained his faith the entire time he was incarcerated. To me, that says a lot about him and it just radiates. In my mind, Kenny is the poster boy for exonerees. He's what people should strive for. He did not let bitterness overtake him. He maintains his faith and he's moving forward with a purpose and a direction.

Kathy Swedlow, Attorney—Cooley Law School Innocence Project
He's a wonderful ambassador. And, quite honestly, he or any other exoneree doesn't have to be. I think about the folks who have been wrongfully convicted and what they have been through. I can't even begin to imagine. They don't have to become a spokesperson. Everyone would understand if they said I am done with this and they went off and tried to live a normal life. I admire Ken for choosing to speak on these issues in the years since he's been exonerated.

Marty Hacias, Childhood Friend of Kenny
I think it is wonderful that he didn't take his good fortune and ride off into the sunset. I admire him and I am totally behind him. I am proud to call him friend.

At University of Michigan with Michigan Supreme Court Justice Bridget Mary McCormack

DELIBERATE INJUSTICE | 269

In San Jose (2008) Barry Scheck, Donna McKneelen, Ken, and Peter Neufeld. Barry and Peter are co-founders of the first Innocence Project in New York

In San Jose (2008) Ken with Bill Proctor, founder of both Proving Innocence and Seeking Justice, with Alcatraz Prison in the background

Pictured left to right:

Bobby McGlaughlin, 17 yrs., Brandon Moon, 17 yrs., Barry Gibbs, 19 yrs., Gloria Killian 17.5 yrs., Ken Wyniemko, 9.5 yrs., John Restivo, 17 yrs., Jimmy Ray Bromgard, 15.5 yrs., Mike Piaskowski, 17 yrs., Marvin Anderson, 15 yrs., Calvin Johnson, 16 yrs., Anthony Hicks, 7 yrs., David Shephard, 10 yrs., George Hernandez 17 yrs., Michael Williams. 24 yrs.

**TOTAL YEARS OF WRONGFUL IMPRISONMENT:
220.5**

Part II – Quality Time

Chapter 14 — The Prosecutor and the Warden

"*But it makes you feel good to see Kenny succeed. Doing something silly has never entered his mind. He's focused and he didn't let the bitterness of his incarceration and all of the things that happened to him change his mind-set about people in general. And I think that it would be very easy for quite the opposite to happen.*" — Scott Nobles, former Deputy Warden at the Ryan Correctional Facility

As part of the research of this book, I accompanied Kenny to many events over the past several years. It was through these events I realized the impact Kenny has made on so many lives and the inspiration he has given so many individuals from all walks of life.

Among the more unusual aspects of Kenny's story is how he has remained friends with former Prosecuting Attorney Carl Marlinga and former Deputy Warden Scott Nobles. It was under Mr. Marlinga's leadership that the Macomb County Prosecutor's Office convicted Kenny. And it was under Mr. Nobles' supervision at the Ryan Correctional Facility where Kenny was incarcerated the last five years of his prison term. Kenny became friends with the person who essentially put him in jail and the person who kept him there.

That's a funny way of putting it. But it's true. I consider Carl and Scott very good friends.

The first time Carl and I got together after my release was at Focus Hope headquarters in Highland Park. Gail called me and told me that she, Carl, and I are to speak. My case was

still really fresh. It was only a week after I got out. Ever since that day we've hit it off.

At first, Gail and Tom (Howlett) didn't want me to say anything wrong in front of Carl. We didn't know how deep things got during my arrest and trial.

I remember this time Gail, Carl, and I went to lunch at Andiamo's on M-59, Hall Road. Carl became emotional.

He said, "Kenny, I can't apologize enough. I can't tell you how sorry I am."

I told him, "You didn't have anything to do with it. Please. You don't need to say anything. You apologized once. This isn't necessary."

He did that quite a few times when we were together.

Right after that, he got indicted for an illegal campaign funds thing. It was a bogus charge.

I had this prayer written for me when I was still in Jackson. It's wrapped in plastic. It was given to me by Father Kettleberger, who used to come to Jackson to say Mass once a week. One of his parishioners by the name of Rose actually wrote it. I still have the letters she sent me when I was in prison.

I went to see Carl and I told him that I believed he was innocent. I gave him this prayer and I told him it worked for me and I know it will work for him. He thanked me for everything, for forgiving him for my conviction, for my support now when he needed it most. Well, he was acquitted and we've been extremely close ever since.

In Scott's case, he was at that dinner for my foundation at the Polish Century Club right after my release. Dave Payton and Doug Walters were there, too. Doug was the rec director at Ryan. And Payton was my supervisor there.

After I bought my house here in Rochester Hills, Scott and his wife were two of the first people to come by. They *brought a house warming gift. We just continued to see each other over the years.*

Scott was always there for me at Ryan. I remember the day I went back there to pick up my locker. The locker contained all my legal stuff and other items I wanted to keep. Scott had it waiting in his office for me.

On Thursday, May 5, 2016, I accompanied Kenny, and Tommy Highers, a fellow exoneree, to the Bath City Bistro Restaurant in downtown Mt. Clemens to meet with Judge Carl J. Marlinga and Scott Nobles. The repartee throughout the evening was most enjoyable.

First Mr. Nobles joined us, then Mr. Marlinga.

Mr. Marlinga was about 20 minutes late. As he approached our table, he apologized.

"Well, here comes the late Carl Marlinga."

I quipped, "At our age, it gives me an uneasy feeling when someone uses the word 'late' in front of our name."

The table had a good laugh.

The conversation inevitably turned to the wrongfully convicted.

Tommy Highers related how hard it was to convince strangers that he and his brother, Ray, are actually innocent. He then told us a story about a time when he was still in jail.

"I was sitting in the Chow Hall next to another prisoner. He was adamant that he was innocent. I thought to myself, 'Yeah, right. No one is guilty.' Then I thought to myself, 'If I don't believe this guy, and I'm an innocent prisoner myself, how do I expect complete strangers to believe in my innocence?'"

That brought another laugh at the table.

A short time later, Mr. Marlinga and I left to conduct an interview in the back room. As we were returning to the table to rejoin the others, I told Kenny, "I thought you said Carl was your friend."

Kenny smiled and shook his head.

Mr. Marlinga told Kenny he had only one favor to ask.

"I'd like Harrison Ford to play me in the movie."

I told him, "That would require Mr. Ford spending a lot of time in makeup to get him to look a lot younger than he does."

"Did I tell you I like this guy?" Mr. Marlinga said with a smile.

It was a great evening.

SCOTT NOBLES: *Our friendship is extremely unusual. I do run into ex-prisoners. But, other than Kenny, I never had any communication with them.*

I think it was shortly after Kenny got out when he contacted me to go to a release party. My wife and I went there to support him.

And we've been friends ever since. We socialize together. We've been out to dinner. We've been out to lunch. He's been to my home and I've been to his.

I appreciate the fact that we are friends. And, I think, for a career Corrections employee, it's difficult to make the transition to be friends with someone, especially an exoneree, and to not do a disservice to all of their comrades within Corrections. I never tried to hide the fact Kenny and I are friends. Anyone who knows me knows that.

CARL MARLINGA: *I think it would have been harder for him to meet me and to talk to me if he really thought I was part of that decision-making process during his trial. I suppose that's what Ken said is part of the reason for the friendship.*

He realized that I was the head of the Prosecutor's Office. But he was right. Of all the prosecutors in Michigan, I think I was probably the one who was most wary of the possibility of wrongfully convicting somebody, the person most tuned to the reality of it happening. I think it is some of the reason why we could have this friendship is that there wasn't any personal malevolent act I did. It's just that I was a part of the process.

Ken is a special person. You just can't imagine the human spirit being that good as to allow for that type of forgiveness.

Chapter 15 — One More Time

As the creation of *Deliberate Injustice* came to a close, Kenny and I sat down and talked about his life and how he was able to overcome terrible odds to become the man he is today. He recalled the many individuals who came along just when he needed them most. He was very fortunate in his journey from convicted rapist to respected advocate for righting wrongful convictions.

> *How lucky have I been? It all started in Jackson when I hooked up with guys like Ernie and Augie and with HASTA. Who knows if I'd have survived that place without them?*
>
> *I've met good people like Jimmy Jones, Tommy Rastall, and Bill Ramsey. I got a cushy job with Jimmy, protection from Tommy and Big Jack, and, with Bill's friendship, I was able to learn the law. A free education that I use to this day.*
>
> *Then Kim and Gail come along. My two angels. They saved my life.*
>
> *And, I can't say enough about the Innocence Project. They put me under their wing and gave me a purpose in life — an ability to work with and for the wrongfully convicted.*

> *But, you know, I never lost faith. In all the years I was in jail and after all the appeals we lost, I always believed I would see the day when I was released and the truth would come out. My faith in God kept me going. I never thought that I would serve the rest of my sentence. Never.*

We talked about the difficulties he had during the writing of this book when he had to recall some of the nightmares that he experienced. There were times when he had become visibly upset.

Yeah. Some of those memories just messed me up for a bit. But I wanted everyone to know everything that happened to me, what really happened. I wanted them to realize what the cops, the witnesses, the DA, and my own lawyer did for me to get convicted. It seemed like I was the only honest person in the courtroom and I was convicted of 17 felony counts and sentenced to 40 years in jail.

Kenny has always had a unique way of looking at things.

On Thursday, November 13, 2014, I had the opportunity to join Kenny and Bill Proctor and attended a welcome party for exoneree Jamie Lee Peterson at the Innocence Clinic at the University of Michigan Law School. Jamie served 17 years for the murder and sexual assault of a 68-year-old woman in Kalkaska, Michigan. His release was achieved through the efforts of the Innocence Clinic and Northwestern University of Law School's Center on Wrongful Convictions in Chicago.

During the evening, Kenny introduced me to the newly elected Supreme Court Judge Richard Bernstein. We congratulated him on his recent victory. He paused for a second and said, "You know, Kenny, that you are the person who inspired me to run for Supreme Court? Yes, it was you that taught me that we could change the world and that the world needs changing."

I could see Kenny's eyes start to well up. It was a nice moment and another example of the profound effect Kenny's work has had on so many people.

> *How amazing is it for a Supreme Court Justice to say that to me?*
>
> *And that's what I have been saying all along. So many people have helped me in so many ways. I am so grateful that I have this opportunity to give back.*
>
> *I have been blessed in so many ways. Life is good.*

Our conversation turned to Kenny's work with Michigan's legislature. The statute for the mandatory DNA testing of felons prior to their release resulted in the identification of Craig Gonser as the perpetrator of the 1994 crime for which Kenny was convicted. And the recent passage of the Wrongful Conviction Compensation Act Bill went a long way to repair the lives of exonerees.

In addition, Kenny was extremely proud of his efforts in the removal of the sunset date for the Michigan's DNA testing statute (MCLA 770-16) that was first passed in 2001. After multiple extensions, it became permanent law in 2015. This was the same law that enabled Kenny to apply for the DNA testing that led to his release from prison. Without it, many wrongfully convicted prisoners would have never had the opportunity to appeal their conviction using DNA testing.

> *It took 13 years for the sunset date to be removed on the DNA testing law. That just blows my mind. Right after I was released, that was the first thing I wanted done. There should never be a time limit on anyone proving their innocence.*
>
> *There is one reason I am proud of this, Bob. It would have initially expired on January 1st of 2006 after it took effect on January 1st of 2001. The inmates were given a five-year window to apply for DNA testing. Only five years! If we wouldn't have been given that first extension, inmates would have been barred from applying for DNA testing. The police could continue to use DNA to convict. But it couldn't be used to exonerate, which was totally senseless. If we didn't have those two extensions, some of the exonerees would still be sitting in prison. And, now, it is permanent law. Still. 13 years!*

I asked Kenny if he would cut back in his efforts in Lansing now that the Wrongful Conviction Compensation Act Bill has been passed. He bristled at the thought.

> *If the people in Lansing think I am going away now that the bill has been passed, then they are badly mistaken. I'll take a month or so off to recharge my batteries. I'm coming back louder than before. There's still a lot to do.*

Ken with Bob Henige, author of *Deliberate Injustice*

Bill Proctor and Ken

Celebration at Ken's home with Hamtramck St. Ladislaus High School classmates

Chapter 16 — Final Thoughts from the Author

"*What do you want the reader to get from* Deliberate Injustice*? What do you want to accomplish with its publication?*"

These are questions that I have contemplated greatly.

Certainly, goal number one has always been to tell Kenny's story. Recounting how an innocent person's life can be destroyed because of a wrongful conviction and how that person can triumph in the face of such extreme adversity is an uplifting experience. Kenny, with the help and generosity of countless friends, and a driving desire and determination, is a shining example of an exoneree who has overcome enormous obstacles to build a life where he is making a real difference in the world.

But there must be more to *Deliberate Injustice*. I want the reader to realize that wrongful convictions exist in this great country of ours more often than we want to admit. This issue does not discriminate. Wrongful convictions transcend race, religion, gender, and class.

Writing *Deliberate Injustice* introduced me to the Innocence Network, a large and growing assemblage of legislatures, attorneys, and individuals from all walks of life who work tirelessly to free innocent men and women. You can fill a book with all the lawyer jokes in the world. But you can't ignore the fact that a great deal of members of the legal profession contribute countless hours of pro bono work in their endless effort to right the most severe wrongful act imaginable, the conviction of an innocent person. They are an integral part of the Innocence Network's effort.

When 34% of exonerations involve false confessions, perhaps interrogating techniques need to be changed. When over 70% of wrongful convictions involve incorrect witness identification, we may need to rethink the value of someone being picked out of a lineup and using that identification as a sole reason to convict. If American society truly wants to end the wrongful conviction epidemic, then we most assuredly need to re-examine the way things are done in areas like law enforcement, the prosecutor's office, and within the judicial system.

The public is becoming aware of wrongful convictions as a result of programs like *Dateline*, *The Making of a Murderer*, and *Legally Speaking*. As the education of the American public continues, perhaps disturbing stories of discrimination towards exonerees can become less frequent. The sooner we accept the fact that wrongful convictions occur, the more readily wrongfully convicted individuals will be treated with compassion for what they went through instead of with the preconceptions associated with former convicts. Exonerees need to be considered victims. They deserve our sympathy, not our disdain and mistrust.

If *Deliberate Injustice* can accomplish the abovementioned, then it will be a success.

Thank you,

Bob Henige

Acknowledgements

There were so many individuals who dedicated their time and expertise to *Deliberate Injustice*. I would like to thank them for their extraordinary efforts.

Thank you to Judge Pat Cahill for your legal consultation and all your support.

Thank you to everyone who enriched the book with their candid and insightful interviews: Bill Proctor, Carl Marlinga, Gail Pamukov, Jerry Innes, Kathy Swedlow, Marty Hacias, Norm Fell, Scott Nobles, Stephanie Chang, Stephen Bieda, and Tom Howlett.

Thank you to the reviewers: Arthur Woodford, Bill Proctor, Ken Nutt, Mary Woodford, Paul Garcia, Sally Pregitzer, and Steve Munoz.

A special thank you to the following individuals who worked so long and hard on the editing and proofreading: Becky Morabito, Joyce Bannister, and Nancy Ruppman.

To my son, Scot, for his terrific artwork on the book covers.

To my wife, Laura, who transcribed the interviews, constantly reviewed and edited the text, and was my rock of support throughout this effort.

Bob Henige

Appendix A — 2003 DNA Test Results

The 2003 DNA test results of the forensic evidence samples matched the DNA profiles of the victim, the victim's husband, John Doe (the victim's affair partner from earlier that day), and an unknown donor. Kenny was excluded in all instances.

Here are the details of the results of the forensic testing.

> *State of Michigan Department of State Police Forensic Science Division*
> *(Laboratory No. 21831-94 SUPP, Record No. 0300397)*
>
> *LABORATORY REPORT*

Here are summarized results from the *Conclusions* section of the Laboratory Report.

1. DNA Samples 397.03A1B3 (Semen A), 397.03A1B3 (Semen A), 397.03A1B3 (Semen A) (from fitted sheet samples) matches the DNA profile of the victim's husband. Kenny and John Doe are excluded as donors.
2. DNA Sample 397.03A1B1 (panty) revealed the major donor to be that of John Doe. The victim's husband was listed as a possible minor donor. Kenny is excluded.
3. DNA Sample 429.03A1A (Cigarette Butt) revealed the DNA source is **unknown donor**. The victim, victim's husband, John Doe, and Kenny are excluded as donors.
4. DNA Sample 429.03A15I1 (left middle finger under nail) revealed a match with the DNA profile of the **unknown donor**. The victim was listed as a minor donor. The victim's husband, Kenny, and John Doe are excluded.

5. DNA Sample 429.03A9D1 (Nylons, hip area) revealed matches with the DNA profile of the victim and the DNA profile of the **unknown donor**. The victim's husband, Kenny, and John Doe are excluded.
6. DNA Sample 429.03A9B1 (Nylons, ankle area) matches the DNA profile of the victim only. All others, including Kenny, were excluded.
7. DNA Sample 429.03A14D1 (Nylons, area near knot) matches the DNA profile of the victim only. All others, including Kenny, were excluded.

Excerpts found in the *Remarks* section of the Laboratory Report.

1. Upon submission of additional reference samples further comparisons can be made in order to determine the possible source of DNA types identified in samples 429.03A1A (Cigarette Butt), major donor to sample 429.03A15I1 (left middle finger under nail), and the minor donor to the non-sperm fraction of sample 429.03A9D1 (Nylons, hip area).
2. The DNA types identified from sample 429.03A1A have been entered into the casework database of the Combined DNA Index System (CODIS). You will be notified if a search of the database reveals an association.

Appendix B — Glenn McCormick's Declaration

This is Glenn McCormick's complete Declaration. Although his name in all other documents, legal or otherwise, is spelled Glenn, this transcript uses the alternative spelling of Glen.

Case Number 03-74779
KENNETH WYNIEMKO
vs.
THOMAS J. OSTIN, BART M. MARLATT,
ALEXANDER C. ERNST, and TOWNSHIP OF CLINTON,
Defendants.

DECLARATION OF GLEN MCCORMICK

Glen McCormick, pursuant to 28 U. S. C. 1746, states as follows:

1. My name is Glen McCormick. I currently reside in the State of Michigan.
2. Kenneth Wyniemko and I shared a cell in the Macomb County jail for about two weeks starting in mid-July 1994. I have not spoken to Mr. Wyniemko since we shared a jail cell in July, 1994.
3. Mr. Wyniemko never told me at any time that he had committed any crime. He never told me that he had any involvement in the rape and robbery of Diane Klug.
4. A few days after I was released from jail in July 1994, I received a telephone call from a woman who identified herself as Linda Davis. Ms. Davis said she was an Assistant Macomb County Prosecutor. Ms. Davis said that she wanted to talk to me about Mr. Wyniemko.

5. Shortly after receiving the call from Ms. Davis, I received a telephone call from a Clinton Township police officer named Thomas Ostin. Mr. Ostin made arrangements for me to meet the next day with Ms. Davis and him at the Clinton Township Police Department.

6. On the next day, I met with Ms. Davis and Mr. Ostin at the Clinton Township Police Department. Ms. Davis and Mr. Ostin told me that if I could provide information helpful to them in their case against Mr. Wyniemko, they could help me avoid a possible life sentence as a habitual offender as a result of the charge that I had pending against me. They told me this before asking me whether I had any useful information against Mr. Wyniemko. They also told me that they had already three or four witnesses who were going to testify that Mr. Wyniemko had committed the crimes, but they would like my help as well. I was really concerned about the possibility of a life sentence if I did not help. I agreed to be a witness even though Mr. Wyniemko had not told me in any way that he had committed any crime.

7. After I indicated that I would be a witness, I was left alone in the room that we were meeting in. Before leaving the room, Mr. Ostin placed a police report regarding Mr. Wyniemko and the crimes against Ms. Klug directly in front of me on the table that we were sitting at. Mr. Ostin said he was going to leave me alone for a little while, or words similar to that. After Mr. Ostin put the police report in front of me and said he was going to leave me alone, I assumed that I was supposed to review the police report. By reading the police report, I learned details about the crime against Ms. Klug. I later used these details in the testimony I gave at the preliminary examination and trial. I would not have been able to talk or testify about the crimes against Ms. Klug without the police report that I reviewed in the room.

8. After I had been left alone in the room with the police report for a while, Mr. Ostin and Ms. Davis returned to the room and

asked me what Mr. Wyniemko had told me about the crime against Ms. Klug. I proceeded to tell them things that I had just read in the police report.

9. During this meeting with Mr. Ostin and Ms. Davis, I received suggestions regarding statements that I should make. One of the statements that was suggested to me was that I say that Mr. Wyniemko had told me that "they ain't got shit against me" or words like that. It was also suggested to me that I say that Mr. Wyniemko had told me that he had gotten rid of the evidence. Mr. Wyniemko had not told me these things.

10. During this meeting with Mr. Ostin and Ms. Davis, they made a tape recording of an interview with me. During the interview, the tape was stopped on numerous occasions. When the tape was stopped, I received suggestions on the way I should say certain things.

11. After the meeting with Mr. Ostin and Ms. Davis was over, Mr. Ostin gave me a ride home in the front seat of a police car.

12. During Mr. Wyniemko's preliminary examination and trial, I gave testimony based upon the police report that I had reviewed at the time of this meeting and the suggestions made to me during this meeting.

13. I have not spoken with Mr. Ostin or Ms. Davis since Mr. Wyniemko's trial in 1994.

14. The statements made in the declaration are being made voluntarily and freely on my part without any threats or duress or offers of any kind.

15. I am making these statements to get the weight off of my shoulders from my involvement in Mr. Wyniemko's preliminary examination and trial. I feel badly about what I said he did.

16. Because I am making these disclosures, I am fearful for the safety of my family and myself. I do not want any harm to come to them or to me because I have come forward and made these disclosures.

17. I declare under penalty of perjury that the foregoing is true and correct.

Glenn McCormick signed the Declaration, dated October 5, 2004.

Appendix C — The Innocence Network

"The Innocence Network is an affiliation of organizations dedicated to providing pro bono legal and investigative services to individuals seeking to prove innocence of crimes for which they have been convicted, working to redress the causes of wrongful convictions, and supporting the exonerated after they are freed."
— www.innocencenetwork.org

"Without the Innocence Project, I would not be a free man."
— Kenny Wyniemko

The Innocence Project's importance in changing the landscape of our legal system cannot be understated. This organization was the start of a legal movement that has become known as the Innocence Network.

In the late 1980s, Deoxyribonucleic acid (DNA) was being used to obtain convictions in an increasing number of criminal cases. Barry Scheck and Peter Neufeld, two prominent defense attorneys from New York, asked the question on which the Innocence Project would be based, "If DNA can be used to convict, could it be used to acquit the falsely accused and to exonerate the wrongfully convicted?"

In 1992, Mr. Scheck and Mr. Neufeld founded the Innocence Project at the Benjamin N. Cardozo School of Law at Yeshiva University in New York. The Innocence Project was established as a pro bono effort of law students, lawyers, legislative representatives, judges, and individuals from all walks of life to free wrongfully convicted persons, relying primarily on post-conviction DNA testing.

The Innocent Project's influence has been profound. It has transformed the criminal judicial system and obtained the freedom of hundreds of wrongfully convicted individuals. What started as a novel idea in the 1990s, the fight for the wrongfully convicted has grown exponentially.

While the Innocence Project continues to handle primarily DNA related cases, a host of other organizations have taken up the cause to free the innocent in both DNA and non-DNA related cases. Today, the Innocence Network includes dozens of organizations throughout the United States and across the world.

The National Registry of Exonerations was established in 2012 by the University of Michigan Law School's Innocence Clinic in conjunction with the Center for Wrongful Convictions at Northwestern University School of Law. As of May 21, 2017, their website has identified 2,030 exonerations. The number of exonerations has grown from 87 in 2013, to 125 (2014), 149 (2015), and 166 (2016).

In May, 2017, the Innocence Project celebrated its 25th anniversary. The Innocence Project has effected 349 exonerations. The real perpetrator has been identified in 149 of these cases, primarily through a DNA match on CODIS with the crime scene forensic evidence. The Innocence Network is not only interested in freeing the innocent, but it also desires to ensure the guilty are caught and incarcerated.

Long-standing sources of testimony and evidence have come into question, especially eyewitness testimony. According to the National Registry of Exonerations, the primary contributing factors in wrongful convictions are mistaken witness identification, perjury or false accusation, false confession, false or misleading forensic evidence, and official misconduct. Other major contributors to wrongful convictions include the use of informants and snitches and inadequate defense.

Mr. Marlinga had this to say about eyewitness identification and its application in Kenny's trial.

How could you tell the woman who was terrorized, who saw her perpetrator eye to eye, "We just don't believe you?" Remember, in those days, every channel's evening news was called Eyewitness News. Eyewitness was the gold standard. You saw it with your own eyes and it had to be true. And so the ability for people to disbelieve eyewitness testimony is very low. That's true today because they still think of it as the gold standard.

Eyewitness identification is the weakest evidence there is. We now know that. I'm past the point of having a debate in my mind. I realize that eyewitness identification is to be always taken with a grain of salt because there are so many things that influence it. And there's a high degree of unreliability. But, even with a prosecutor knowing all of the flaws of eyewitness identification, there are still those who believe, "My God, if she identified him, it has to be true."

The Innocence Network has also established support groups and counseling services to assist exonerees' efforts to become acclimated into society. It has worked within the legal system to promote government compensation and health and medical assistance for exonerees. At one time, an innocent man released from prison received nothing — no governmental assistance in any form. Convicted rapists and murderers were afforded job placement assistance, job counseling, medical coverage, and other benefits. It was a staggering inadequacy that made absolutely no sense. Today, 32 states, including Michigan, have compensation bills in place. Many of those statutes include monetary compensation.

Laws and statutes now exist to accommodate the ever-changing landscape of evidence gathering and preservation. The evidence in Kenny's case could have been legally destroyed once he exhausted his appeals in 2002. Today, that same evidence now has to be stored for the duration of a person's incarceration. It is mandatory that the DNA of individuals being released from prison or charged with specific felonies be registered in CODIS (Combined DNA Identification System), the FBI's DNA database system.

The Innocence Network continues its efforts to change the mindset of those in the legal, judicial, and law enforcement arenas, as well as making society aware of the need for change and support.

The law students' tireless efforts and countless hours of research play a significant role in the process of obtaining the freedom of a wrongfully convicted individual. The long-term effects of participating in this process are invaluable.

Envision a law student who has worked on a case where a wrongfully convicted person was released. Imagine the elation of restoring the most precious gift in a person's life: freedom. Imagine the lasting effect this experience has on the student's law career. Learning the law in the classroom is one thing. Seeing how poor execution within the legal system can contribute to the conviction of an innocent person is quite another.

The work of the Innocence Network has become a deterrent for future wrongfully convicted cases. Knowing organizations exist to fight for the rights of the accused has let the system know that the sins of the past will not be tolerated.

Law enforcement departments and agencies across the nation have made several changes regarding eyewitness testimony, interrogation techniques, and the use of jailhouse snitches.

While eyewitness testimony was once the gold standard in evidence gathering, wrongful convictions have exposed many such testimonies to be false. In many agencies, carte blanche acceptance has been replaced with the examination of an eyewitness identification based on its merits.

Policies regarding the time duration of interrogation sessions has been shortened and the mandatory recording of interrogations has been enacted. Here is an excerpt from the article *Dep't of Justice, New Department Policy Concerning Electronic Recording of Statements* that first appeared on the Harvard Law Review website on March 10, 2015.

> *Since 2003, the number of states requiring law enforcement officers to electronically record some or all interviews conducted with suspects in their custody has grown from two to at least twenty-two. Until recently, the U.S. Department of Justice (DOJ) has resisted this trend; under its previous policy, the DOJ's three chief investigative agencies — the Federal Bureau of Investigation (FBI), the Drug Enforcement Administration (DEA), and the Bureau of Alcohol, Tobacco, Firearms and Explosives (ATF) — rarely recorded custodial interviews. However, on May 22, 2014, the DOJ announced a substantial change in its policy, creating a presumption that FBI, DEA, ATF, and United States Marshals Service (USMS) agents will electronically record custodial interviews.*

Countless articles and reports have been published criticizing the use of jailhouse snitches, citing their direct contribution to numerous wrongful convictions. More and more police departments have banned this abusive and unreliable source of testimony.

In April of 2016, Norman Fell, the founder of the Innocence Project at the Cooley Law School in Lansing, Michigan, related the story behind its establishment.

> *I happened to go to the hearing before the Michigan House Judicial Committee. One of the SADO (Michigan State*

Appellate Defender Office) lawyers was testifying about the need for an Innocence Project.

The Chair said, "If we pass this bill, we will have 50,000 inmates that could use the statute. The courts would be flooded, overwhelmed. We barely have the resources to handle the criminal justice system now. How could we even think about doing this?"

The SADO lawyer said, "The Innocence Project would screen these cases thoroughly."

They asked, "What Innocence Project?"

"Cooley's Innocence Project."

The Chair asked if there was anyone from Cooley in the gallery.

They called me to testify and told me the statute was established with a 180-day rule. That meant a prisoner had only 180 days from the day the bill became law to finish the appeal process and gain their freedom before the statute was sunsetted. I knew that it took Cardozo three to four years per case to gather the evidence and to get a court hearing. They asked me what the 180-day rule would do for the proposed Innocent Project.

I said it would cut if off at the knees, not realizing that was the sound bite the media people took notice of. I remember someone from the media later asking me, "What do you mean, 'Cut it off at the knees?'"

I said, "Well, there are a lot of innocent people. At the Cardozo Law School it takes three to four years for each case. And these are people with resources."

But the reality was we hadn't started up the clinic yet. And I kept wondering about the money necessary, the legal advice. Even with voluntary help, we have to locate the evidence first. You take a 10 to 20-year-old case and you have no idea if the evidence can even be found.

But none of that mattered with the 180-day rule. We'd never gather the evidence in time.

The next day the local newspaper had this line: "The Innocence Project Cut Off at the Knees." We had a very sympathetic person who wrote that there are these innocent people who can be proven not guilty by DNA and we can't do it because the statute is so bad. It was a very positive write up.

I didn't live in Lansing so I didn't even see it. I came to work the next day and my secretary showed me the paper and told me that I got two phone calls. One was from the dean and the other was from Bill Schuette, a senator at the time and the sponsor of the bill.

I figured that I had better meet with the dean first. I entered his office and the newspaper was sitting on his desk. He was looking at the paper and he said the same thing the Judicial Chair said, "What Cooley Innocence Project?"

We were interrupted when one of the Board of Directors called and you could hear him on the other end of the phone, "What Cooley Innocence Project?"

After the phone call, the dean turned to me and said, "Well, this is the greatest thing since sliced cheese. Look at all the good publicity Cooley's got already." He had a little smile on his face and said, "I think you just sandbagged me."

I said, "Not intentionally."

Cooley stepped up to the plate and the dean was 100% behind it. This was Cooley Law School, not U of M, Michigan State, Wayne, or U of D. It was Cooley. We were the only one at that time. Cooley did not have a stellar reputation, but that changed with the Innocence Project.

The dean said, "I'll let you do the clinic. You can do that half time and the other half time you need to do criminal law classes. And the other half time you need to do the Elder Law Clinic."

I said thank you and walked away. That's what I like about lawyers. They have no idea what numbers mean.

Within a week, I had two, three hundred letters sitting on my desk. I didn't have a secretary. I didn't have anybody. I didn't even have a letter opener.

The letters were stacked in boxes. These people were asking for help, claiming their innocence. I didn't have a waste paper basket to handle all the trash from the letters, let alone a method of responding or keeping a database or having anything on record. So, I put out a general alarm to the students. I got four or five volunteers to at least help me sort through the mail. It took a year to finally get the resources. We had to develop forms, had to develop ways of keeping track of the letters, had to find out ways of identifying these people.

Cardozo made themselves available for questions and consultation. We were able to look at their structural components, their student and protocol manuals. They were also able to give us a heads up as to what to look for as well as provide their moral support. It was a new and exciting time.

One of the students who stepped up was Donna McKneelen. She came in and said, "What can I do?"

She later graduated, practiced law for about 10 minutes, and came back to Cooley. We hired her as a staff attorney. She was right there from the start.

Then Kathy Swedlow, an Adjunct Professor at the time, came on board. She was invaluable setting up the systems we needed to process the thousands of letters we had by then.

I had a friend who voluntarily set up the database. He spent hours on it. And it turned out to be really efficient.

The dilemma that was foreseen by the legislature about opening the floodgates was real. But it was Cooley that was overrun. We probably had 3,000 cases by the time Kenny's case was started. We had to go through them all. We used the students for manpower. We couldn't afford to hire lawyers. The cost would have been too prohibitive. We trained the students on what to look for. We continue to use the students today for that very reason.

They would initially screen the cases. Then they would go to their supervisors and eliminate cases further that didn't fit the statute.

There were many applicants who may very well have been innocent, but their convictions were not DNA cases or the biological evidence had been destroyed, contaminated, lost, or was just insufficient for testing.

The downside is that there were a good many inmates who applied for assistance even though they were guilty. Just to give it a shot.

But, that's what sold the project. Only the cases that have a chance to fit within the statutory scheme will be heard by the courts.

At the very beginning, we had resistance from everybody. There were few individuals willing to cooperate with the Project or with the idea of innocent people being convicted other than the criminal defense attorneys. That goes from the police to the courts to the judges to the prosecutors to the public. No support. The acceptance of the science was the turning point. Once people were aware of what the science was all about, all of a sudden the Innocence Project took on new meaning.

After Ken's exoneration, the attitude flipped. The lab people, not the administration particularly, were so excited that they found an innocent guy through their lab work that they actually came over and were affirmably helpful. Ken's exoneration caused this major turnover. It was a direct result of the first real exoneration under the new DNA statute in Michigan.

Kathy Swedlow remembers the early days at the Innocence Project.

When you think about the nuts and bolts of opening a law office, you have to set up procedures for how you're going to handle things. An Innocence Project is a law office. Most law firms start small. They start with a couple of clients and hopefully their business takes off. The Innocence Project started big. I don't know of another startup with thousands of requests asking for help in the first few weeks. It just doesn't happen.

So, a lot of what we were doing early on was trying to do some triage and some very basic screening to figure out what cases we would even begin to inquire into. I don't even want to say pursue because we weren't at that point where we even thought about going to court. We were just putting cases in piles to organize them.

As an example, you take ten letters asking for assistance. If two were from prisoners from Kansas, you can rule them out because we were focused on Michigan prisoners. If two of them are from federally convicted prisons, you can rule them out because we are dealing with state prisoners. The other six declare they are innocent and they are incarcerated in Michigan. You then delve further into those cases to figure out if they are eligible under Michigan's DNA statute. A lot of what we were doing in the early days was just trying to sort things out.

You can't always tell from a letter as to whether the case matches the criteria. We knew we weren't going to deal with cases outside the state. But what about the people who pled guilty? I didn't want to throw out the letters. I wanted to make sure I'm dealing with them responsibly in case the scope of the project changed later on. That's a really big undertaking.

> Kenny's case drifted to the top because of the materials he provided and the things he said. His was a case that we became focused on pretty early.
>
> At Cardozo, they couldn't handle the cases they received. They became involved in efforts to get other law schools in other states to establish Innocence Projects. When Cooley set up its Innocence Project, Cardozo forwarded the Michigan cases there. That's how we got Ken's case. If I remember correctly, that happened pretty quickly.

The Innocent Project's innovative thinking back in 1992 has changed the judicial landscape forever. It was the forerunner of today's global effort of the Innocence Network. This Innocence Movement continues to expand as more and more individuals hear the call for this most necessary cause.

One of the individuals who heard the calling is Carl Marlinga. Shortly after Kenny's exoneration, Mr. Marlinga became a defense attorney. It wasn't long before he became involved in the Julie Baumer case. Ms. Baumer had been convicted of first degree child abuse and had served four years in prison.

> CARL MARLINGA: *Ken Wyniemko does get partial credit for this because of the emotional impact Ken's case had on me. It not only cemented in my intellectual recognition that these things happen, but also told me that many fine people, completely innocent people, have suffered and are suffering. And the desire to work on cases that could make a difference for people like that was there. So, I would become involved in defense work. The clear majority of people who come your way have done something wrong. So, often the best you can do is lessen the blow, work out a plea bargain. But, in some cases, you go to trial and try to vindicate the person. And, occasionally, you get somebody who is stone cold innocent and the system got it wrong.*

I became involved in Julie Baumer's case in part because I had done some other work that was noteworthy for other people. Not wrongfully convicted. I got in there and defended them and got them not guilty verdicts. Also, because of my involvement in Kenny's case, the people at the University of Michigan Law School knew my emotional commitment was there.

With the Ken Wyniemko case, it is the best example of my righting a wrong as a prosecutor. And then the Julie Baumer case is the best thing I've ever done on the purely defense side in terms of taking a person who was absolutely innocent and vindicating her.

Working with Julie Baumer's case was difficult because it was without the certainty of DNA. The evidence we had to compile, all the medical evidence to show that what was once thought of as a horrific case of child abuse, was simply a tragic case of a medical event that had no human cause whatsoever.

My co-counsel was Bridget Mary McCormick, who is now a Justice on the Michigan Supreme Court. She was one of the two professors at the Innocence Clinic at the University of Michigan, along with David Moran. David is still there. But, of the two, Bridget was more active at the defense table in Julie's case.

The Innocence Clinic can take pride in the fact that one of our own has gone on to become a Supreme Court Justice. It was great working with her and with the U of M law students.

But, even with all that support, you had to scrap every inch of the way. The amount of information you have to gather is not just proof beyond a reasonable doubt, which is what you have to do as a prosecutor. But, to get somebody exonerated after a conviction, you have to have proof *beyond all doubt. The standard is so high since the rules in the State of Michigan set the bar so high. The basic attitude of the court rules is that if you get convicted and you get your appeal, you get this one shot. That's it.*

I think part of the reason for that is justified in that you don't want the families of people who have been killed, or the victims of rape who have suffered at the hands of criminals, to always worry that the case is never ending. There would always be another appeal that a person can use. And I understand that.

But the reaction can go overboard the other way. When you're talking to prosecutors, to Appellate Court Judges, to Supreme Court Judges, it's basically you're looking at people with folded arms and glazed over eyes. They've heard all this nonsense before. This person was convicted by a jury. And a jury is regarded as sacrosanct. All you're doing is raising technicalities.

In Julie's case, we had to prove that something that was misdiagnosed as a traumatic brain injury was really simply a rare, but well enough recognized, childhood stroke that happens in infants between the ages of birth and six weeks. And this child was at six weeks. But part of what makes these things difficult to overcome is the horrific nature of the crime. It makes it so politically incorrect to raise a question.

In Ken's case, you had this woman who was terrorized, raped several times, thinking she was at the point of being murdered at any moment. The horror of that night is too difficult to comprehend. This deranged person subjected her to the worse sexual degradation, plus the threat of imminent death, hour after hour after hour. The horror of that is such the human mind wants to nail somebody and put that monster away.

It's the same with Julie's case. You had an innocent, six-week-old baby. So, you think of that fragile child and somebody shaking that baby, smashing his head against the wall. The natural human reaction is to recoil so vehemently that if you can get the monster that did that, convict her, put her away, you want to do it as fast as possible. You don't want somebody to wiggle out of it with some kind of high-priced lawyer or phony excuse. It is the way that we think of things.

But when you realize that Ken wasn't the rapist. And you realize that Julie was a loving, caring, tender person who did not harm the child in the least bit. It was the doctors who misdiagnosed what was happening. Then slowly, but surely, you can reach an opposite and correct opinion, which is the injustice that Julie suffered.

If Julie had to pay for the defense afforded her in her appeal, it would have cost over a half million dollars. You take my time, and my co-counsel's time, and all the volunteer testimony from the experts that flew in from across the country. Their expenses, travel and hotel accommodations were paid for. But they received nothing for their expert testimony. Who could afford that?

I have to say that Julie's release was exhilarating. To have made such a significant difference like that, well, it's nothing like I ever experienced.*

While progress has been made, there is much more work to be done.

NORM FELL: *Today, there are a number of prosecutors who have started their own Innocence Projects throughout the country, who voluntarily put their own cases up for review. Yet there are still a significant number of prosecutors who resist even the attempt to get testing done.*

The Innocence Project has opened this awareness for everyone in the system that there are weaknesses that need to be addressed and there are ways to address them. That's what the Innocence Project has done. In my lifetime, I've seen almost a revolution. We still have a long way to go. There are a lot of innocent people incarcerated.

CARL MARLINGA: *I think that, unless you are involved personally with an exoneree, as a prosecutor and as a judge and as an Appellate Judge, you tend to try to dismiss the reality of wrongful convictions.*

I see this most commonly in the Appellate Courts. The Michigan Court of Appeals is not doing a good job with claims of wrongful convictions. But, then again, the court rules are stacked against reexamining wrongful convictions. Nobody wants to really open up the rules to allow for a decent examination of wrongful convictions. The burden, under Rule 6.508, is still so heavy on the defense side. When you have a person accused of a crime, the burden of proof beyond a reasonable doubt is on the prosecution.

Once you have a person convicted, the burden is proof is on the defendant. You are, often times, trying to prove a negative. You will get evidence, which everybody would say, "Had this been the evidence at the first trial, there is no way a jury could find this person guilty beyond a reasonable doubt." But even though there is now substantial doubt raised with regard to the prosecution case, and an Appellate Court says the evidence would not allow the conviction back then, the burden is still on the defendant. Therefore, the conviction is affirmed. That's just wrong. And the outrage at wrongful convictions is still not strong enough to move Trial Judges and Appellate Judges to do something about the rules or their applications about the rules.

Appendix D — The History of the Civil Lawsuit

November 25, 2003 — The Googasian Firm, P. C., filed a *Complaint and Demand for Trial by Jury* in the U. S. District Court for the Eastern District of Michigan. Civil Action No. 03-74749 named Clinton Township Police Department Detectives Thomas J. Ostin, Bart M. Marlatt, and Alexander C. Ernst, and the Township of Clinton as Defendants. The 12-page, 137-paragraph complaint made allegations and claims that pertained to Kenny's arrest, conviction, and subsequent incarceration. Here is the index of that complaint.

COMPLAINT AND DEMAND FOR TRIAL BY JURY
Plaintiff Kenneth Wyniemko, by and through his attorneys, The Googasian Firm, P.C, alleges as follows:

Nature of Action
1. This action arises from the wrongful conviction on rape and robbery charges of Plaintiff Kenneth Wyniemko ("Mr. Wyniemko").

The complaint alleged the following:
- Police Officer Defendants, Acting Under Color of State Law, Deprived Mr. Wyniemko of Constitutional Rights
- The Police Officer Defendants Became Involved in Securing Perjurious Testimony
- Defendants Failed to Disclose Exculpatory and Impeaching Information
- Defendant Township of Clinton's Failure to Train and Supervise Police Officer Defendants

The complaint made the following claims:
- Count I — Claim — Police Officer Defendants – Compensatory Damages
- Count II — Claim — Police Officer Defendants – Punitive Damages
- Count III — Claim — Defendant Ernst
- Count IV — Claim — Township of Clinton
- Count V — Claim — Police Officer Defendants for Conspiracy to Violate Civil Rights
- Count VI — Respondent Superior Liability — Township of Clinton
- Count VII — Violation of the Michigan Constitutional Rights — Police Officer Defendants and Township of Clinton
- Count VIII — Civil Conspiracy — Police Officer Defendants
- Count IX — Intentional Infliction of Emotional Distress — Police Officer Defendants
- Count X — Malicious Prosecution — Police Officer Defendants
- Count XI — Abuse of Process — Police Officer Defendants
- Count XII — Gross Negligence — Police Officer Defendants

Fall of 2004 — The Garan Lucow Miller, P.C., Law Firm, attorneys for the defense, submitted several motions to have the case dismissed. One of the motions was a *Motion for Summary Judgment*. The *Motion for Summary Judgment* claimed there was no case because there are no triable issues in Kenny's civil suit.

October 4, 2004 — Glenn McCormick, the jail-house informant at Kenny's trial, signed a declaration in which he claimed he had lied on the stand in 1994 and that Kenny never told him that he had committed any crime. His primary motive had been to avoid decades of incarceration. McCormick also indicated that he was given a copy of Kenny's arrest report from a member of the Clinton Township

Police Department so he could familiarize himself with details of the crime. It was most damaging for the defense.

October 27, 2004 — Kenny filed a complaint against Detectives Thomas Ostin and Bart Marlatt. The nature of the complaint was Conduct Unbecoming stemming from the two detectives' actions in 1994. Clinton Township Personal Complaint PC-04-06 was investigated by two other Clinton Township Police Department officers, Captain Gary J Franey and Lieutenant Craig Keith. In early 2005, Detectives Ostin and Marlatt were cleared of all charges.

November 1, 2004 — The Googasian Firm, P. C., submitted a *Plaintiff's Brief in Opposition to Defendants' Motion for Summary Judgment.*

March 3, 2005 — The Honorable Lawrence P. Zatkoff published his *Opinion and Order*, a scathing 51-page indictment of the actions of the Clinton Township Police Department and the Macomb Prosecuting Attorney's Office. The *Motion for Summary Judgment* was denied. The Final Pre-Trial Conference was scheduled for March 15, 2005, with the intention of establishing a trial date in early April, 2005.

Spring 2005 — Prior to the court date, the Garan Lucow Miller, P.C., Law Firm appealed Judge Zatkoff's decision to deny their *Motion for Summary Judgment.* The appeal was filed with the U. S. Court of Appeals.

September, 2005 — With the appeal still pending in the U. S. Court of Appeals, both parties came to an agreement. Kenny accepted Clinton

Township's settlement offer. The civil suit against the Clinton Township Police Department was dropped and the officers were released from all compensatory claims. The settlement terms were not released to the public.

November, 2005 — The *Detroit Free Press* filed a *Freedom of Information Act* request to obtain information of the settlement. Within a week, the terms were published. Kenny received a lump payment of $1.8 million and life-long, monthly payments of $6,409 that increase 3% a year. The payments covered a minimum of 20 years, with Kenny's beneficiaries receiving any undistributed payments in the event Kenny passed away during the 20-year period. The settlement amounted to a minimum of $3.8 million.

Judge Lawrence P. Zatkoff's Opinion and Order (March 3, 2005)
Here is a summary of Judge Zatkoff's *Opinion and Order*. It was a decisive victory for Kenny and his attorneys.
- Rejected the defendants' motion that Clinton Township Police Department Officers Ostin, Marlatt, and Ernst, and the Township of Clinton should be awarded *Summary Judgment*.
- Rejected the defendants' motion that the *Doctrine of Collateral Estoppel* applied.
- Rejected the defendants' motion to prevent Mr. McCormick's from testifying at trial.
- Rejected the defendants' motion that the Clinton Township Police Department and the Township of Clinton had Qualified Immunity and could not be sued.
- Upheld the plaintiff's claim of malicious prosecution.
- Upheld the plaintiff's claim that the Clinton Township Police Department engaged in a conspiracy to convict Kenny.

Judge Zatkoff's opinion contained some scathing comments regarding the actions of the Clinton Township Police Department.
- The defendants failed to follow up on reliable leads and other promising suspects.
- The victim identification of the plaintiff was riddled with alarming inconsistencies that, if taken on face value, should not have resulted in the plaintiff's arrest.
- The defendants routinely failed to disclose impeachable and exculpatory evidence that greatly hindered the plaintiff's ability to cross-examine and discredit the prosecution witnesses.
- The defendants acted with a reckless disregard for the truth.
- The defendants violated the plaintiff's constitutional rights.

References

From The Author

Introduction
1. *Causes of Wrongful Conviction* – Innocence Clinic of the University of Michigan website:
    a. https://www.law.umich.edu/clinical/innocenceclinic/Pages/wrongfulconvictions.aspx

Chapter 1 – The Crimes

Chapter 2 – The Arrest and Charged
1. Transcript of Oakland University ACLU-sponsored engagement – November 5, 2007.
2. Showup Identification Record regarding Kenny's lineup – July 14, 1994.
3. Case 94-2001-FH – Trial Transcript –The People of the State of Michigan vs. Kenneth Wyniemko – October 31, 1994, through November 8, 1994.
4. CTPD Incident No. 94-17059 – Trial transcripts containing Laurence Peppler resigning as Kenny's attorney – October 25, 1994.
5. CTPD Incident No. 94-17059 – Victim Statement of Diane Klug #1 – April 30, 1994 – 06:23 am.
6. CTPD Incident No. 94-17059 – Victim Statement of Diane Klug #2 – April 30, 1994 – 10:55 am.
7. Presentence Report on Kenneth Wyniemko for the Honorable Michael D. Schwartz – 1994.
8. CTPD Memo to Arduino Polisena RE: Embezzlement Charge (94-22603) – Detective Thomas J Ostin – June 10, 1994.
9. CTPD Memo to Ken Wyniemko RE: Embezzlement Charge (94-22603) – Detective Thomas J. Ostin – July 5, 1994.

10. CTPD Memo to Ken Wyniemko RE: Stalking Charge (94-21077) – Detective Bart Marlatt – June 2, 1994.
11. CTPD Work Investigation Work Report (94-21077).
12. CTPD Continuation and Supplementary Report (94-17059) – Evidence secured at crime scene – CTPD Officer T. Scherer – April 30, 1994.
13. CTPD Witness Statement (w/victim admitting never saw attacker's face – April 30, 1994.
14. CTPD Continuation and Supplementary Report (94-17059) – Investigation Reports RE: Interviews with Cathy Whitcher – Detective Thomas J. Ostin – July 15, 1994.

Chapter 3 – The Trial and Conviction

1. *Faces of Failing Public Defense Systems – Portraits of Michigan's Constitutional Crisis* – Published April, 2011, by the American Civil Liberties Union (ACLU), ACLU of Michigan, Michigan Campaign for Justice.
2. CTPD Incident 94-17059 – April 30, 1994 – Officer Scherer Supplementary – Includes description of footprint evidence taken from crime site.
3. CTPD Incident No. 94-17059 – Cathy Whitcher statement – July 16, 1994.
4. CTPD Incident No. 94-17059 – Thomas Ostin notes regarding witness Glen McCormick – August 9, 1994.
5. CTPD Incident No. 94-17059 – Glen McCormick witness statement of August 10, 1994.
6. Case No. CR-94-1595 – Preliminary Examination – August 11, 1994.
7. CTPD Incident No. 94-17059 – Thomas Ostin notes regarding statement from Michelle Wright, girlfriend of Glen McCormick – September 1, 1994.
8. CTPD Incident No. 94-17059 – Jury Verdict Form – November 9, 2004.
9. CTPD Incident No. 94-17059 – Case Investigation Work Report with anonymous tip about Kenny – May 11, 1994.

10. Composite of suspect – April 30, 1994.
11. Clinton Township Police Department Press Release of May 2, 1994.
12. CTPD Incident No. 94-17059 – Case Investigation Work Report signed by Bart Marlatt regarding update of victim dated June 27, 1994.
13. CTPD Incident No. 94-17059 – CONTINUATION AND SUPPLEMENTARY REPORT – File date July 16, 1994 – Initial interview with Cathy Whitcher – July 7, 1994.
14. Case 94-2001 – Trial Transcript – The People of the State of Michigan vs. Kenneth Wyniemko – October 31, 1994 through November 9, 1994.
    a. Day 2 – Tuesday, November 1, 1994 – Witness List – Jury Selection.
    b. Day 4 – Thursday, November 3, 1994 – Various testimony.
    c. Day 6 – Monday, November 7, 1994 – Kenny testimony, Closing Arguments.
    d. Day 7 – Wednesday, November 9, 1994 – Jury Verdict.
    e. Thursday, December 15, 1994 – Sentencing Hearing.
15. CASE 1994-002002-FC – e-Access Summary – All Information.
    a. http://courtpa.macombgov.org/eservices/home.page.14

Chapter 4 – Incarceration

Chapter 5 – Jailhouse Appeals
1. Case No. 1994-002001-FC – Michigan Court of Appeals Docket No. 183157 – January 16, 1996 – Appeal filed by Deborah Winfrey Keene, Assistant Defender, State Appellate Defender Office.
2. Case No. 94-2001 – Michigan Court of Appeals Docket No. 183157 – June 12, 1996 – Appeal filed by Kenneth H. Karam, Attorney, Peralta, Johnston, & Karam.

3. Case No. 94-2001 – Michigan Court of Appeals Docket No. 183157 – December 17, 1996 – Memo RE: ITEM NO. 22 PEOPLE OF MI V. KENNETH WYNIEMKO – Notice of oral arguments on January 15, 1997.
4. Case No. 94-2001 – Michigan Court of Appeals Docket No. 183157 – March 7, 1997 – Michigan Court of Appeals Opinion.
5. Case No. 94-2001 – Michigan Court of Appeals Docket No. 183157 – March 27, 1997 – Kenneth H. Karam – Notice of rehearing on April 15, 1997, with no oral argument.
6. Case No. 94-2001 – Michigan Court of Appeals Docket No. 183157 June 30, 1997 – Carl Marlinga, Prosecuting Attorney Macomb County, Michigan – Response to Michigan Supreme Court Appeal.
7. Case No. 94-2001 – Michigan Court of Appeals Docket No. 183157 – April 27, 1998 – Michigan Supreme Court Order to deny hearing Kenny's appeal.
8. United States. District Court – Eastern District of Michigan – Sixth District Court – Case No. 99-CV-71560-DT – April 2, 1999 – Appeal filed by James C. Horvath, attorney.
9. United States. District Court – Eastern District of Michigan – Sixth District Court – Case No. 99-CV-71560-DT – May 18, 2000 – U. S. District Court Opinion – Honorable Patrick J. Duggan.
10. United States. District Court – Eastern District of Michigan – Sixth District Court – Case No. 99-CV-71560-DT – May 18, 2000 – Order denying writ for habeas corpus – Honorable Patrick J. Duggan.
11. United States. District Court – Eastern District of Michigan – Sixth District Court – Case No. 99-CV-71560-DT – May 24, 2000 – NOTICE OF APPEAL – Filed by Kenneth Wyniemko - Inmate #240889 – In Propria Persona.
12. United States. District Court – Eastern District of Michigan – Sixth District Court – Case No. 99-CV-71560-DT – June 7, 2000 – OPINION AND ORDER GRANTING PETITIONER'S

MOTION FOR CERTIFICATE OF APPEALABILITY – Honorable Patrick J. Duggan.

13. United States Court of Appeals for the Sixth District – Case No. 00-1617 – July 31, 2000 – APPEAL OF THE ORDER DENYING PETITIONER'S MOTION FOR WRIT OF HABEUS CORPUS – Filed by Kenneth Wyniemko – Inmate #240889 – In Propria Persona.
14. Case No. 94-2001 – Michigan Court of Appeals Docket No. 183157 – May 2, 1997 – ORDER for rehearing DENIED and correspondence from Kenneth H. Karam.
15. Case No. 94-2001 – Michigan Court of Appeals Docket No. 183157 – January 15, 1997 – Affidavits of Kenneth H. Karam and Lynn M. Christoff and other correspondence relative to scheduling error regarding Michigan Court of Appeals argument of January 15, 1997.
16. Case No. 94-2001 – Michigan Court of Appeals Docket No. 183157 – January 14, 1997 – Michigan Court of Appeals ORDER granting oral argument.
17. Case No. 94-2001 – Michigan Court of Appeals Docket No. 183157 – March 7, 1997 – ORDER for immediate consideration and motion for oral argument DENIED as moot.
18. Case No. 94-2001 – Michigan Court of Appeals Docket No. 183157 March 11, 1996 – Carl Marlinga, Prosecuting Attorney Macomb County, Michigan – Response to Michigan Court of Appeals.
19. Case No. 94-2001 – Michigan Court of Appeals Docket No. 183157 – June 11, 1997 – MOTION FOR REMAND TO TRIAL COURT TO CONDUCT A HEARING PURSUANT TO PEOPLE V GINTHER, 390 MICH 436 (1973) AND TO APPOINT EXPERT TO CONDUCT SCIENTIFIC TESTS CONCERNING SEMEN SAMPLES, HAIR ANALYSIS, AND FOOTPRINT COMPARISONS, ETC. – Filed by Kenneth H. Karam.
20. Civil Docket #99-CV-71560 United States District Court – Eastern District of Michigan – Appeal dated August 28, 1999.

21. Unconscious Transference definition link: http://criminal-justice.iresearchnet.com/forensic-psychology/unconscious-transference/

Chapter 6 – Kim and Gail and the Innocence Project

1. File No. 94-2001FY – Motion for Release and Testing of Biological Evidence Pursuant to MCL 770.16, Brief in Support of Motion and Praecipe – November 21, 2002 – Filed by Gail M. Pamukov Motion to Macomb County Clerk – hard copy. Exhibits – PDF. (first copy)
2. File No. 94-2001FY – Motion for Release and Testing of Biological Evidence Pursuant to MCL 770.16, Brief in Support of Motion and Praecipe – November 21, 2002 – Filed by Gail M. Pamukov. Motion to Prosecuting Attorney – hard copy. Exhibits – PDF. (additional copy)
3. Circuit Court Case No. 94-2001-FH – Answer to Defendant's Motion for Release and Testing of Biological Evidence Pursuant to MCL 770.16 – December 6, 2002 – Filed by Macomb Prosecuting Attorney.
4. Gail M. Pamukov memo to Kenny Wyniemko on December 10, 2002 with attached Order to Release Biological Evidence for DNA Testing – December 9, 2002.
5. Gail M. Pamukov memo to Charles Barna, Forensic Science Manager – Michigan State Police – Crime Lab – regarding order requiring DNA testing – January 24, 2003.
6. Gail M. Pamukov memo to Therese Tobin regarding discovery of additional DNA evidence submitted without her knowledge – April 14, 2003.
7. Gail M. Pamukov memo to Therese Tobin regarding additional DNA evidence submitted without her knowledge – April 16, 2003.
8. File No. 94-2001FY – Motion for Release and Testing of Biological Evidence – Gail M. Pamukov – May 22, 2003.

9. Laboratory Report from the State of Michigan Department of State Police Forensic Science Division dated June 9, 2003 – Laboratory No. 21831-94 SUPP, Record No. 0300397.
10. File No. 94-2001FY – Motion to Modify and Obtain Relief from Judgment – Filed by Gail M. Pamukov – June 11, 2003. With attached DNA Report of June 9, 2003.
11. File No. 94-2001FY – Motion to Dismiss – Carl Marlinga – June 17, 2003.
12. File No. 94-2001FY – MOTION FOR RELEASE AND TESTING OF BIOLOGICAL EVIDENCE VIA EDWARD BLAKE OF FORENSIC SCIENCE ASSOCIATES, RICHMOND, CALIFORNIA – May 23 2003 – Filed by Gail M. Pamukov.
13. 94-2001-DC – Trial Transcript – Motion to allow DNA testing – Honorable Edward A. Servitto, Jr., presiding – December 9, 2002.
14. Innocence Project of Lansing, MI, correspondence regarding Kenneth Wyniemko.
15. Michigan DNA Testing Statute:
    a. http://www.legislature.mi.gov/(S(ugwwjps5ghndubvrnao4u0vg))/mileg.aspx?page=GetObject&objectname=mcl-770-16

Chapter 7 – Freedom
1. Kim Shine *Detroit Free Press* article of November 27, 2002.
2. Kim Shine *Detroit Free Press* article of December 10, 2002.
3. Kim Shine *Detroit Free Press* article of June 13, 2003.
4. File No. 94-2001FY – Motion to Dismiss – Carl Maringa – June 17, 2003.
5. Jaimie Peterson information:
    a. https://www.law.umich.edu/newsandinfo/features/Pages/jamieleepetersonexonerated090514.aspx

Chapter 8 – Acclimation to Society

Chapter 9 – Lawsuit and Settlement

1. Case No. 03-74749 – Complaint and Demand for Trial by Jury – November 25, 2003 – Civil Suit of Kenneth Wyniemko vs. Thomas J. Ostin, Bart M. Marlatt, Alexander C. Ernst, and Township of Clinton.
2. Case No. 03-74749 – Declaration of Glenn McCormick dated October 5, 2004.
3. Case No. 03-74749 – Opinion and Order of the Honorable Lawrence P. Zatkoff – March 3, 2005.
4. Case No. 94-17059 – Property Report from Search of Kenny Wyniemko Residence – July 17, 1994.
5. Affidavit of Albert Markowski w/cover letter from Gail M> Pamukov to Albert Markowski – June 20, 2003.
6. Case No. 03-74749 – United States District Court for the Eastern District of Michigan Southern District – Deposition of Kenneth Wyniemko – April 26, 2004.
7. Case No. 03-74749 –Deposition of Ryan Reynolds – April 29, 2004.
8. Case No. 03-74749 –Deposition of Honorable Linda Davis – June 11, 2004.
9. Case No. 03-74749 –Deposition of David Woodford – June 28, 2004.
10. Case No. 03-74749 –Deposition of Alexander Ernst – July 14, 2004.
11. Case No. 03-74749 –Deposition of Thomas J. Ostin – July 27, 2004.
12. Case No. 03-74749 –Deposition of Bart M. Marlatt – September 7, 2004.
13. Case No. 03-74749 –Deposition of Albert Markowski – September 10, 2004.
14. Case No. 03-74749 –Deposition of Carl J. Marlinga – September 13, 2004.
15. Case No. 03-74749 –Deposition of Laurence H. Peppler – September 14, 2004.

16. Clinton Township of Clinton Police Department – Personnel Complaint – Incident #94-17059 – August 9, 1994.
17. Glenn McCormick hand-written letter – November 11, 2004.
18. Glenn McCormick hand-written letter – December 7, 2004.
19. Charter Township of Clinton Police Department General Incident Report – Welfare Fraud – Incident Number 04-43884 – November 19, 2004.
20. Charter Township of Clinton Police Department General Incident Report – Witness Tampering – Incident Number 04-43884 – November 17, 2004.
21. Case 03-74749 – Plaintiff's Brief in Opposition to Defendants' Motion for Summary Judgment – United States District Court – Prepared by The Googasian Firm, P.C. – November 1, 2004.
22. CTPD Continuation and Supplementary Report – Incident No. 94-21077 – July 14, 1994 – RE: Phone Tapes.
23. Case No. 94-17059 – Diane Klug witness statement regarding affair. Linda Davis, Thomas Ostin, Gina Bertolini, and Diane Klug present – July 18, 1994.
24. Case 94-02001-FC – *Demand for Preservation of Tangible Evidence/Test Samples* filed by Laurence H. Peppler & Associates, P.C. – September 22, 1994.
25. CTPD PC Complaint PC-04-06 – Notes RE: Wayne Burkhardt's Declaration – October 27, 2004.

Chapter 10 – System Failure
1. American Bar Association:
    a. http://www.americanbar.org/publications/criminal_justice_section_archive/crimjust_standards_pfunc_blkold.html
2. American Bar Association:
    a. http://www.americanbar.org/publications/criminal_justice_section_archive/crimjust_standards_dfunc_blk.html
3. Michigan Trial Court Administration Guide:

a. http://courts.mi.gov/administration/scao/resources/documents/publications/manuals/carg/carg.pdf

Chapter 11 – Vindication

1. Craig Gonser Department of Corrections Biographical Information.
2. "New suspect in controversial Case" – *Metro Times* – June 25, 2008:
   a. http://www2.metrotimes.com/editorial/story.asp?id=13028
3. "Man faces charge of exposure" – Macomb Daily – October 9, 2008:
   a. http://www.macombdaily.com/article/MD/20081009/NEWS/310099982
4. "Suspect in rape sentenced to 10-25 years for being sexual delinquent – Oakland Press – April 25, 2010:
   a. http://www.theoaklandpress.com/general-news/20100415/suspect-in-rape-sentenced-to-10-25-years-for-being-sexual-delinquent
5. *DETROIT FREE PRESS CANDIDATE SURVEYS* – Publius – 2010:
   a. http://www.publius.org/ballot/Questionaire.asp?CandidateID=82718
6. CASE 2008-004833-FH – e-Access Summary – All Information:
   a. http://courtpa.macombgov.org/eservices/home.page.14
7. CASE 2008-004833-FH – State of Michigan Court of Appeals – July 21, 2009.
8. CASE 2008-004833-FH – State of Michigan Court of Appeals – May 15, 2012.
9. SHPD (Sterling Heights Police Department) Incident and Supplementary Reports RE: Gonser's Assault and Battery Charge – April 9, 1994 – August 23, 1994.
10. CASE 2008-004833-FH – Plea Hearing – March 5, 2016.
11. CASE 2008-004833-FH – Sentencing – April 15, 2016.

12. Definition of Cobbs Agreement:
    http://thelawyermichigan.com/cobbs-agreement-in-michigan.

Chapter 12 – A Juror's Regret

Chapter 13 – Spokesperson
1. Original Wrongful Imprisonment Compensation Act – Michigan House Bill No. 5509 – December 13, 2005.
2. Wrongful Imprisonment Compensation Act – Michigan House Bill 5815:
    a. http://www.legislature.mi.gov/(S(g03djytyay1ho021rsyulske))/mileg.aspx?page=getObject&objectname=2016-HB-5815
3. Wrongful Imprisonment Compensation Act – Michigan House Bill 4536:
    a. http://www.legislature.mi.gov/(S(505xo43jask5zh2tp4550ylc))/mileg.aspx?page=GetObject&objectname=2015-HB-4536
4. Wrongful Imprisonment Compensation Act – Michigan Senate Bill 0291:
    a. http://www.legislature.mi.gov/(S(g03djytyay1ho021rsyulske))/mileg.aspx?page=GetObject&objectname=2015-SB-0291

Chapter 14 – The Prosecution and the Warden

Chapter 15 – One More Time
1. Michigan DNA Testing Statute:
    a. http://www.legislature.mi.gov/(S(ugwwjps5ghndubvrnao4u0vg))/mileg.aspx?page=GetObject&objectname=mcl-770-16
    b. "**History:** Add. 2000, Act 402, Imd. Eff. Jan. 8, 2001 ;-- Am. 2005, Act 4, Imd. Eff. Apr. 1, 2005 ;-- Am. 2008, Act 410, Imd. Eff. Jan. 6, 2009 ;-- Am. 2011, Act 212,

Imd. Eff. Nov. 8, 2011 ;-- Am. 2015, Act 229, Imd. Eff. Dec. 17, 2015"
2. Wrongful Imprisonment Compensation Act – Michigan House Bill 5815:
    a. http://www.legislature.mi.gov/(S(g03djytyay1ho021rsyulske))/mileg.aspx?page=getObject&objectname=2016-HB-5815
3. Wrongful Imprisonment Compensation Act – Michigan House Bill 4536:
    a. http://www.legislature.mi.gov/(S(505xo43jask5zh2tp4550ylc))/mileg.aspx?page=GetObject&objectname=2015-HB-4536
4. Wrongful Imprisonment Compensation Act – Michigan Senate Bill 0291:
    a. http://www.legislature.mi.gov/(S(g03djytyay1ho021rsyulske))/mileg.aspx?page=GetObject&objectname=2015-SB-0291

Chapter 16 – Final Thoughts from Bob Henige
1. Statistics on the causes of wrongful convictions: https://www.innocenceproject.org/

Appendix A – 2003 DNA Test Results
1. Laboratory Report from the State of Michigan Department of State Police Forensic Science Division dated June 9, 2003 – Laboratory No. 21831-94 SUPP, Record No. 0300397.

Appendix B – Glenn McCormick Declaration
1. Case No. 03-74749 – Declaration of Glenn McCormick dated October 5, 2004.

Appendix C – The Innocence Network
1. http://harvardlawreview.org/2015/03/dept-of-justice-new-department-policy-concerning-electronic-recording-of-statements/

Appendix D – The History of the Lawsuit

1. Case No. 03-74749 – Complaint and Demand for Trial by Jury – November 25, 2003 – Civil Suit of Kenneth Wyniemko vs. Thomas J. Ostin, Bart M. Marlatt, Alexander C. Ernst, and Township of Clinton.
2. Case No. 03-74749 – Opinion and Order of the Honorable Lawrence P. Zatkoff – March 3, 2005.
   https://www.gpo.gov/fdsys/pkg/USCOURTS-mied-2_03-cv-74749/pdf/USCOURTS-mied-2_03-cv-74749-0.pdf

THE END